DT1050

THE
PROCESS
OF GROUP
COMMUNICATION

Second Edition

THE
PROCESS
OF GROUP
COMMUNICATION

Second Edition

RONALD L. APPLBAUM
California State University, Long Beach

EDWARD M. BODAKEN
University of Southern California

KENNETH K. SERENO
University of Southern California

KARL W. E. ANATOL
California State University, Long Beach

SCIENCE RESEARCH ASSOCIATES, INC.
Chicago, Palo Alto, Toronto, Henley-on-Thames, Sydney, Paris, Stuttgart
A Subsidiary of IBM

Acquisition Editor	**Alan W. Lowe**
Project Editor	**Gretchen Hargis**
Designer/Illustrator	**Barbara Ravizza**
Technical Illustrator	**Judi McCarty**
Compositor	**Typesetting Services of California**

Library of Congress Cataloging in Publication Data
Main entry under title:

The Process of group communication.

    Bibliography: p.
    Includes index.
1. **Small groups.** 2. Communication. I. Applbaum, Ronald L.
HM133.P76 1978   301.18′5   78-18501
ISBN 0-574-22710-5

We wish to thank the following for permission to reprint, abridge, or adapt material:

Fig. 2-1, Table 2-1   Adapted from *Organizational Communication* by J. Wofford, E. Gerloff, and R. Cummins. Copyright © 1977 McGraw-Hill Book Company. Used with permission of McGraw-Hill Book Company.
Fig. 3-2   From "The Watergate Drama" by Ricki Fulman as cited in *With Words Unspoken: The Nonverbal Experience* by L. Rosenfeld and J. Civikly. © Ricki Fulman. Used by permission.
Fig. 5-1   Robert Tannenbaum and Warren H. Schmidt, "How to Choose a Leadership Pattern" *Harvard Business Review*, March-April 1958. Copyright © 1958 by the President and Fellows of Harvard College; all rights reserved.
Fig. 5-2   The Managerial Grid figure from *The New Managerial Grid*, by Robert R. Blake and Jane Srygley Mouton. Houston: Gulf Publishing Company, Copyright © 1978, page 11. Reproduced by permission.
Fig. 5-3, 5-4, 5-5   Paul Hersey, Kenneth H. Blanchard, *Management of Organizational Behavior: Utilizing Human Resources*, 2d edition, © 1972, pp. 121, 135, 142. Reprinted by permission of Prentice-Hall, Inc., Englewood Cliffs, New Jersey.
Fig. 9-1, 9-2   Adapted from "A Set of Categories for the Analysis of Small Group Interaction" by Robert F. Bales in *American Sociological Review*. © 1948 American Sociological Association. Used by permission of the American Sociological Association and the author.

10 9 8 7 6 5 4 3 2 1

CONTENTS

PREFACE

Human beings spend a considerable portion of their waking hours communicating with each other. Much of that time is spent communicating in groups.

If we were to ask for a list of groups to which you belong, you would probably list several groups composed of friends, relatives, family, employees, and students. However, if we were to ask you to list the ways those same groups influence your behavior, you probably would not find it as easy a task to complete. Acquiring an understanding of the roles groups play in molding our lives requires careful observation and a framework of knowledge into which we can place our experiences. Unfortunately, most group participants lack this framework.

Communication in groups is so commonplace that we rarely pay attention to its pervasive influence. Just as a fish takes the water around it for granted, we take communication in groups for granted. And, just as the fish dies when out of water for long, we cease to function effectively when we fail to understand or utilize the communication process in groups properly.

We all need to know not only what groups we belong to, but also how we are influenced by them and how we can communicate more effectively within them. Colleges have recognized for some time the importance of studying the behavior of people in groups. Courses have been developed to study the entire range of group activity from the family to large social groups.

A common focus in the study of group behavior has been the group communication process. Sociology classes spend a great deal of time looking at the basic interaction of people in group environments. Many social psychology courses are devoted to the study of personality differences among group participants. Students in business classes study the effects of communication on work groups. And speech communication classes range from group discussion courses dealing exclusively with the acquisition of practical communication skills to the study of communication in group decision making.

For the most part, textbooks on group communication have tended to take either a theoretical or a practical bias in their presentation of material. In the former, students are introduced to a number of theoretical concepts and the research literature that describes those concepts. Books that operate from a practical bias are generally written in a how-to format. Such books are performance-oriented and deal with specific types of groups and the kinds of communicative behavior that are appropriate to each.

Of course, a text need not take only one approach. Our general purpose in writing this book has been to address both perspectives. We attempted to integrate theoretical-conceptual positions about group communication with application of that information to practical problems and situations.

Integrating theory and application is not easy. Therefore, we sought an approach that would provide a framework for our existing knowledge of group communication and at the same time create a method for integrating theory and practice. In response to this goal we developed the group communication process model visually displayed in Chapter 1. Through basing the book on this model and organizing the chapters around it, we hoped to translate the findings of research on group processes into workable ideas for teachers and students. We found it necessary to write casually at times, more technically at others. From time to time we interrupted our discussion to present an exercise that we thought would help students understand the concepts being discussed. At the end of each chapter we provided annotated readings to guide the student or teacher who wanted to learn more about the subjects. Through this approach, we hoped to satisfy teachers and students who we felt wanted and needed both theory and application to become more effective group participants.

In addition to these structural features, we dealt with materials that stand out in small-group texts, research findings, and techniques that are time-tested in actual group practice. For example, the treatment of language and message variables is often omitted from group communication texts. Because of the centrality of message to the entire process of communication in groups, we spent considerable space describing the important factors of language and messages in group deliberations. Since the effectiveness of any group depends upon its participants, we selected and examined several communicator and leadership variables that influence the group communication process. Such factors as roles, rules, cohesiveness, and conflict — important in group settings — have been treated extensively. In our discussion of conflict we explored the implications of conflict in groups and methods of resolving different types of conflict. Because one major task confronting groups is the solution of problems, we devoted an entire chapter to exploring group problem solving, particularly the role of communication in that process. Finally, we explored methods for presenting group discussions and techniques for improving the communication of participants in task or social groups.

The text before you is a second edition. Its content and organization reflect our response to feedback from students, instructors, and reviewers regarding the usefulness of the original text as an educational tool. In preparing this version of the text, we have made a number of significant changes and added new materials which we feel facilitate an understanding of the process of group communication. Our major objective was to improve the overall cohesiveness and interrelationship of concepts.

We began our revision by redesigning the group communication model. We felt it necessary to reinforce in our model the systemic operation of group communication. Our new model required a new sequence for the early chapters of the text. Since the message is the heart and soul of any communicative transaction, Chapters 2 and 3 now concern themselves with verbal and nonverbal messages, respectively. These messages are the products of group participants; hence, Chapter 4 deals with selected communicator characteristics that affect the group communication process. Chapter 5 now extends the discussion of the group communicator by examining the role played by the group leader. Finally, the chapter on problem solving has been shifted to the last section in the text in order to provide greater continuity between problem solving from a theoretical perspective and the actual practice of solving problems. Consequently, group problem solving procedures have been moved to Chapter 10, "Methods of Discussion."

Once the model had been redesigned and the chapters rearranged, we proceeded to add or delete materials to improve the content, quality, and general readability of the text. Chapters 2 and 3 were rewritten to reflect the crucial role of messages in group communication situations. The latest information drawn from research on communicator variables was added to Chapter 4. Chapter 5, "Leadership," was rewritten with specific attention to the communication styles of leaders and their effect on the group communication process. In Chapter 6, "Rules and Roles," we introduced the rule perspective to group communication. In Chapter 11, "Small-Group Techniques," we replaced the section on laboratory training with an examination of two contemporary program planning techniques, nominal group technique (NGT) and Delphi technique. Throughout our revision we attempted to reduce redundancies, provide a more consistent style of presentation, and add examples that the reader can identify with.

This text is the result of a small-group effort. The four authors, each with definite ideas regarding the group communication process, met and discussed for hours on end the materials to be included in the text. At times we were in agreement, at others in conflict. However, the format and materials contained have been accepted by all. We hope you will find the concepts discussed useful in your group experiences.

We wish to acknowledge the assistance of our reviewers who provided a number of excellent ideas and comments which were included in the final manuscript. We also want to thank Alan Lowe, speech communication editor, for his help in this revision and Gretchen Hargis for her outstanding editorial work.

I

AN
ORIENTATION

* * *

CHAPTER 1
AN INTRODUCTION

In this chapter we explore the nature and functions of groups. We deal primarily with communication processes in small groups, examining the nature of communication and then considering the relationship of communication to the group process. We end with an examination of a group communication process model. Each element of the model—messages, communicators, climate, and control—is described and its role in the model identified.

* * *

1

AN INTRODUCTION

PREVIEW

* **What are the functions of groups?**

  They influence beliefs, values, feelings, and patterns of behavior.
  They fulfill many basic needs.
  They may have an impact beyond their immediate membership.
  They affect the strength of our democratic society.

* **What is a group?**

  A group consists of two or more persons interacting with one another in such a way that each person is influenced by each other person.

* **What is communication?**

  Communication is a process in which a message acts as a linkage between people.

* **What are the components of the group communication process?**

  Messages
  Communicators
  Climate
  Control

* **What are the characteristics of the group communication process?**

  Communication occurs in a system.
  Communication dimensions are both causes and effects.
  Communication is dynamic.
  Communication is complex.

THE WORLD we live in is oriented toward group activity. Most people belong to an average of five or six groups at any one time. How many academic, religious, athletic, social, economic, or political groups form a part of your life?

We are changing organisms, and our group associations necessarily change. Most of us are born into a family that plays a dominant role in our formative years. Then we go to preschool, kindergarten, and elementary school. We may join the Boy Scouts or Girl Scouts, an athletic league, the YWCA or YMCA. In high school we belong to the band, the science club, tennis team, or pep club. In college we may join a sorority or fraternity, the Newman Club, the psychology club, or the debate team. We may be nominated to Phi Beta Kappa. If we can afford it, we may live in a singles-only luxury apartment. After college, we may join organizations such as the Chamber of Commerce and professional groups such as the American Bar Association and the International Communication Association. All the while, we might spend many hours working with the PTA and various religious, political, civic, and youth organizations and belong to discussion clubs. To relax we may have cocktails and dinner at our country club and then pay for the bounties of the good life at Weight Watchers. Our list could go on and on; the number of existing small groups has been estimated to be as high as four or five billion.

THE FUNCTIONS OF GROUPS

Groups have a strong impact on our lives. Most of our beliefs, values, feelings, and habit patterns stem from our experiences in various groups, beginning with the family. Were your religious or political views, for example, influenced by your family group? What other attitudes, values, or actions have been influenced by groups to which you have belonged?

Besides exerting influence, groups can satisfy many, if not most, of our basic needs (Maslow, 1954). Except for *physiological* needs, such as the need for food and rest, most of our needs may be gratified by membership in a group. We may satisfy *security* needs, such as the need for physical well-being and the need for a future free from danger, by joining various health and retirement groups. Also, groups typically have established ways of operating that create an atmosphere of stability and confidence. Our *social* needs—those yearnings to gather with people and to give and receive affection—obviously can be fulfilled only by group membership. *Prestige* needs—the desire to be recognized—can be satisfied in groups. Finally, group membership may gratify the need for *self-actualization*. This drive to fulfill one's highest potential, to find more significance in life, is what leads some men and women to seek political office or to work for human rights or to create works of art.

Groups may have an influence beyond their immediate membership. Government agencies as well as numerous groups in education, industry, and the military affect millions of people. A peace settlement between Israel and other Arab nations in the Middle East would affect not only people living in those countries but also millions of people beyond those boundaries. The pursuit of such an accord has already involved thousands of hours of negotiation by numerous Israeli, Egyptian, and other national groups.

The strength of our democratic society depends on the efficient operation of the many groups comprising it. Today, more than at any other time in our history, schools and churches, businesses and unions, together with government bodies and various citizen groups must function well if the larger system is to work successfully. Yet our society is so closely interrelated that no group can act independently. Our democracy requires a coordinated interplay of its innumerable groups.

* * *

Communication Diary   1-1

1. Which of your beliefs, values, and patterns of behavior have been influenced by groups?
2. What basic needs have you fulfilled through group membership?
3. What groups to which you belong or have belonged have had an impact beyond the membership of the group?

THE NATURE OF GROUPS

What is a *group*? Groups have been defined in terms of perceptions, motivations, goals, organization, interdependency, and interaction of group members. No one definition has proved satisfactory to all scholars in the area of group processes. For our purposes we will use the following definition:

A *group* is *two or more persons* who are *interacting with one another* in such a manner that each person *influences and is influenced by* each other person (Shaw, 1976).

This definition emphasizes interaction in the form of mutual influence. Hence, collections of individuals (called aggregates) are not necessarily groups. For example, Person A, wishing to speak with Person B, may see and approach B, but unless B is also influenced to approach A, interaction does not occur: A and B do not constitute a group. Similarly, passersby on a street who begin to congregate around someone looking up at a building would not constitute a group unless the original spectator began to be influenced by the others who have gathered—began to talk with them, for example, about the object of their attention.

Although interaction has been stressed as the distinguishing feature of a group, other characteristics are also very important. For the most part, we will be interested in groups that (1) are relatively permanent, (2) have a common purpose, and (3) have an identifiable group structure.

Since we will be dealing primarily with communication processes in *small* groups, we should now answer the question: What is a small group? There is no clear line of demarcation between small groups and large groups. A group containing fewer than ten members will generally be considered a small group, and one containing a hundred members is certainly a large group, but a group containing between ten and thirty members is hard to classify. Although we are indirectly interested in the dynamics of communication in large groups, the bulk of the literature on group behavior in communication and social psychology is based on research studies using five or fewer members. Fortunately, most groups in everyday affairs fall within these limits.

THE NATURE OF COMMUNICATION

A curious thing about communication is that in spite of all the time people spend communicating, they usually make little effort to study it. Perhaps because communication is so much a part of our daily lives, so much a part of being human, people take it for granted. Most people are unaware of the workings of communication—*how* and *why* individuals communicate as they do. But so what, one might ask, why bother studying communication?

Why Study Communication?

A primary benefit is that you come to *understand yourself better as a person.* Communication is the process primarily responsible for your becoming the person you are. Your personality—whether introverted or extroverted, aggressive or submissive, outgoing or shy, friendly or distant, trusting or suspicious, and so forth—is shaped by the communicative experiences you've had, especially during your early years. The total impression of who you are— your self-concept—is determined mostly by communicative experiences you've had with people important to you, people whom social scientists call *significant others*.

A second benefit—perhaps of more immediate importance to you in this class—is that you come to *understand yourself better as a communicator*. Knowing what you're like as a person—your personality, values, motives, and attitudes—should help you understand your responses to the messages of others. You should better recognize why you are more open to certain suggestions and information than to others, why you are more receptive to some individuals and relatively closed to others. You should also recognize why you say the things you do, why you act one way toward some people and another way toward others, why you say a lot under certain conditions and very little under others. You should come to recognize how your verbal and nonverbal messages reflect who you are and convey who you are to others. Your messages reflect your attitudes, values, and personality—in short, your self-concept.

Study of the communication process should give you insights into how your communicative behavior affects others. It should also make you more astute in discerning the motives and values of others in their communication with you. Put simply, studying the process of communication should help you understand and improve your day-to-day communication with friends and workers and in groups.

What Is Communication?

In the remainder of this chapter we want to increase our natural understanding of communication and perhaps correct any misconceptions we have about it. Our aim is to understand what is essential to communicative behavior. We want to be able to identify the basic components or variables operating in any act of communication, especially communication in a group. Without such knowledge it is impossible to determine why communication is effective or ineffective or to do something about a problem or a communication breakdown.

Most people have an intuitive notion of what communication is. We think of it as the act of imparting, transmitting, or interchanging thoughts, opinions, or information by speech or writing. Let us modify this conception slightly.

Communication is a process in which a message acts as a linkage between people.

The role of the message as a linkage between people is the essence of the communication process. Communication is essentially the *relationship* set up by the sending and receiving of messages.

This text stresses the critical function of communication in affecting social interaction in the group. No matter what the nature of the group or its purpose, the tool it uses to establish social interaction to achieve its goals is communication. Communication is the glue that holds the group structure together; it is the enzyme that allows the group process to function. Without communication, groups could not exist; without communication, people could not interact.

A Model of Communication

A model is a way of representing an object, idea, or process. It allows us to clarify complexity by giving only the necessary details. It provides a frame of reference, a vantage point from which we can look at, examine, and describe complicated relationships.

Communication, however, is not something physical like a lunar rover. It is an activity, a process. We cannot use a replica to depict communication; we have to construct a different kind of model. Nevertheless, any model we construct should enable us to identify, describe, or categorize the relevant components of the process.

Numerous communication models exist. It is helpful to recognize that they are arbitrary creations of the people who developed them. If we remember this fact, we will avoid the fruitless search for the *correct* model of communication.

Bear in mind, also, that any model we build may have weaknesses. Perhaps the most serious is the possibility of oversimplifying and misrepresenting the process in order to make it more manageable or understandable. With this caution, let us start with a very simple model of communication.

The model we propose has two basic components: people and messages (Figure 1–1). Although we can conceive of single individuals communicating with themselves about clouds, stop signs,

Person A   **Person B**

FIGURE 1-1.   Model of communication.

and even rocks, we are going to consider only cases involving at least two people—the encoder and the decoder.

Encoder refers to the person creating the message.

Decoder refers to the person receiving and translating the message.

Message refers to the meanings—thoughts and feelings—sent by the encoder and received by the decoder. These meanings take the form of verbal and nonverbal stimuli, which are actually perceived as sound and light waves; they in turn are translated back into thoughts and feelings.

Most of the time encoding is accomplished so effortlessly that we fail to realize how incredibly complex it really is. As encoders we all develop sounds, words, sentences, and paragraphs as well as an array of nonverbal signals: posture, facial reactions, gestures, and intonation. Speaking is probably the most complex activity we engage in. It requires thought combined with incredibly fine, coordinated activities of the diaphragm, lungs, larynx, tongue, pharynx, nasopharynx, teeth, and lips. Under stress—for example, when giving a speech to a strange audience—a person may not be able to speak at all or at least not well.

In attributing significance to a message, we should recognize that meaning is not something "out there" but something within us. "Meanings are in people" is a basic phrase in communication (Berlo, 1960, p. 175). Meaning is not in the message. Meaning is an active, creative, and subjective activity. Qualities and experiences we bring to a situation bear directly on the nature of the meaning we create. Thus, an identical message may produce distinctly different meanings in two listeners. For example, a student representing the women's dorms on a university committee considering a 24-hour visitation policy for women's rooms may perceive the pleas of a faculty member opposing such a policy to be grossly discriminating, male chauvinistic, and highly ineffective. Another student, representing the university religious council, may perceive the request to be in the best interests of the women involved and very sensible. Obviously, the meaning is not *inherent* in the message.

How the Model Functions

In the model there is a two-way exchange of messages. Person A encodes a message and sends it to Person B. After decoding the message, B encodes his or her own message and sends it back to A. This message is called *feedback*.

As the second message in a temporal sequence, *feedback* serves the vital function of providing senders of initial messages with information about the effects produced by messages. Thus, their senders can continue, backtrack, or do whatever seems appropriate.

Without feedback, people must simply hope that their messages are getting through. Thus, Person A's future messages are modified by B's feedback. Likewise, Person B's future messages are affected by the messages received from A. Persons A and B are said to be in a system.

We have discussed the processing of messages as if it occurred in sequence; that is, a person is alternately either a speaker or a listener. In actuality, decoding and encoding go on at the same time within each person. Person A *sends* a message and *simultaneously receives* Person B's verbal and nonverbal messages. Messages serve as the linkage between the two parties.

Although we have introduced new terms—*encoding* and *decoding*—the model may appear pretty simple. One may be led to believe that when we strip away the jargon, the process of communication between two people is not very complex. Not true. Consider this situation: Person A is trying to communicate with Person B. Initially, A has the task of encoding a message that will adequately express the meaning to be conveyed. Creating words and sentences that express our precise meanings is very difficult, to which many of us will attest when we recall how difficult it is to handle an essay question on an examination. Try, for example, to define the word *time*. We all know what it means. But we have the devil's time trying to express its meaning precisely, especially without using the word *time* itself. This problem is especially apparent when the ideas to be expressed are involved and complex.

Add to this task the problem of creating a message with the other person in mind. This orientation is called a receiver orientation. Person A has to be thinking of Person B while creating the message: B's familiarity or lack of familiarity with the material, B's interest, age, and level of education, as well as B's race, socioeconomic background, and so forth. A message that may be suitable for a college graduate may be misunderstood by someone with only an elementary school education.

Assume now that Person A has created a message considering all of these factors—let us say a sentence. At this point, A has to be very alert to the feedback that B provides upon receiving the original message. B may indicate through words, facial expression, or both, that the sentence was not understood or that it was understood but unappreciated or even rejected. In subsequent sentences A will also have to attend to this feedback.

Finally, added to this three-part process is the fact that, as Person A speaks and listens to his or her own sentences, they must be satisfactory, or A has to make adjustments.

COMMUNICATION AND THE GROUP PROCESS

So far, we have been considering a simple model of communication, although we have discovered that the simple process of Person A talking to Person B is not so simple after all. Let us now consider an expanded model of communication, one more appropriate to the group-communication process.

As illustrated in Figure 1-2, our group model has four fundamental dimensions: messages, communicators, climate, and control. As in all models, these dimensions are arbitrary; they were created to help us perceive the complex communication that occurs within groups. Although each dimension is identified as a

FIGURE 1-2.   Group communication process model.

separate entity, they overlap. Nevertheless, we believe such analytical distinctions have much to offer the student of the communication process.

These four dimensions form the basic material to be covered in this text. Hence, our aim here is not to deal exhaustively with all the possible variables in each of the component dimensions. Rather, we hope to give a broad perspective by illustrating some of the major factors operating within the model and by highlighting the contents of the appropriate chapter.

The Message

The first major dimension of our group communication model is the *message*. As noted earlier, messages are the means by which people interact in groups. This linkage between individuals through messages is the heart of the communication process. By message, we mean any communication factor that operates to link communicators. Messages include gestures, markings, commands, threatening nonverbal cues, or a tension release such as loud laughter.

Messages may be analyzed from two broad perspectives—their *verbal* and *nonverbal* features.

VERBAL FEATURES. The term *verbal* refers to the use of *words* or *language* to convey meaning. Verbal messages fulfill many functions within a group—including furnishing information, initiating proposals, aiding in the choice of strategy to solve a problem, motivating members within a group, and furnishing feedback on the results of group activity. Verbal messages reflect varying communication styles: controlling, equalitarian, structuring, dynamic, relinquishing, and withdrawing. Certain verbal message forms reflect defensiveness and create barriers to effective communication, but various message skills can be used to overcome these barriers and to improve group interaction. All of these elements will be discussed in Chapter 2, "Verbal Messages in Small-Group Communication."

NONVERBAL FEATURES. *Nonverbal* messages fulfill eight functions: repeating, contradicting, substituting, complementing, accenting, regulating, identifying, and indicating. For example, accompanying a person's words or verbal signals is a string of *physical* and *vocal* cues (Knapp, 1972). They are usually employed to reinforce or emphasize the verbal cues. When these nonverbal cues are in conflict with the words, problems in interpretation may arise. One of the interesting aspects of communicative response is that when verbal and nonverbal cues are in conflict, we often pay more attention to the nonverbal cues. We have all heard the committee chairperson begin the meeting by saying—with shaky voice, face immobile and perspiration-beaded, and body rigid— how nice it was to be there. We didn't believe it, did we?

We will discuss these ideas further in Chapter 3, "Nonverbal Messages in Small-Group Communication."

Communicators

Communicators in a small group are affected by many factors as they send and receive messages. We will deal with these factors in Chapter 4, "The Communicator," Chapter 5, "Leadership in Small Groups," and Chapter 6, "Rules and Roles."

THE COMMUNICATOR. Perhaps the most basic and pervasive communicator variable is *self-concept*. Self-concept is the overall view we have of ourselves. It involves how we see ourselves in relation to other people, places, things, and ideas. Self-concept is important because it affects the way we respond to others. For instance, if we have a secure and confident self-concept, we communicate differently than if we see ourselves as incompetent and ineffectual.

Three variables having much to do with communication are attitudes, motives, and values. Attitudes—favorable or unfavorable evaluations we have of people, objects, ideas, or behavior—may be the most important of the factors (Cohen, 1964; Zimbardo and Ebbesen, 1969). For example, a woman who has an extremely positive stance toward the women's movement is not likely to be persuaded to change her mind on the issue. On a subject that is not so important to her, she is likely to be more flexible.

Likewise, motives—needs or drives—may have much to do with communicative behavior. Individuals may be very obnoxious during a group deliberation, constantly interrupting or calling attention to themselves. They may be driven to this behavior because of strong needs for recognition, needs that they feel cannot be satisfied in any other way.

Values—enduring concepts of what is good and bad—also may be very important. Students involved in a discussion about uncontrolled population increase may respond very coldly to abortion as a solution, no matter how economical or practical. They may be Catholic and believe that aborting a fetus is murder.

Because of the way we are socialized, sex and racial background are significant communicator variables in our culture. Men and women are taught to communicate differently. Men are taught to be more assertive than women, for instance, and this difference in socialization affects a variety of behaviors within a group, including conformity, competitiveness, and the potential to attain positions of leadership within a group. A person's race is a major influence on that individual's self-concept, which, in turn, directly affects the person's communicative behavior. All of us have attitudes about people of a certain sex and race as well as age, appearance, socioeconomic background, and so on. Depending on whether the attitude is favorable or unfavorable, our communication within a group may be difficult or easy.

Along with sex and ethnicity, personality factors often have much to do with our communicative behavior. The highly dogmatic group member (Rokeach, 1960), for example, has a strong dependency on authority and has difficulty distinguishing between what someone says and who that person is, especially when the speaker is someone perceived as having high status or prestige. Furthermore, a dogmatic person's thinking tends to adhere to a "party line." We generally describe such an individual as closed-minded.

The information and knowledge one possesses have a bearing on communicative behavior in a group. Someone with information that is necessary to the group may become a dominant influence, and an intelligent person may be a force to reckon with because of a capacity to evaluate critically the proposals of others.

LEADERSHIP. The leader is probably the most influential member of the group. Much research has focused on authoritarian and democratic styles of leadership. An authoritarian leader seeks to be central and indispensable to the group and stresses obedience to authority. Authoritarian leadership tends to emerge when speed and efficiency of performance are most important, as in an emergency or when group members don't feel threatened or inferior if they don't know how to handle the task (Gibb, 1969). Authoritarian leaders tend to increase the quantity of work (though not necessarily the quality) among group members but at the same time lower morale (Shaw, 1976). Democratic leaders tend to be most effective when none of the group members feels more competent to deal with the problem and when group members don't feel threatened or inferior if they don't know how to handle the task (Gibb, 1969). By contrast, a democratic leader encourages participation of all group members, shares responsibility, and lessens status differences.

Leaders tend to be either relationship-oriented or task-oriented. *Relationship-oriented* persons view the task situation as a means of gaining good interpersonal relations within the group and thus achieve prominence for themselves. *Task-oriented* leaders tend to be controlling and punitive, and have poor interpersonal relationships. Which leadership style works best? The answer seems to be

* * *

Communication Diary 1-2

1. What communicator characteristics of a helpful nature do you possess?

2. What communicator characteristics of a harmful nature do you possess?

that it depends upon the situation. Task-oriented leaders are most effective when they have legitimate positions of authority and are dealing with clearly defined tasks. Relationship-oriented leaders operate best when tasks are only moderately structured. In a highly structured task situation, a relationship-oriented leader may find a democratic approach inappropriate—perhaps even harmful. A fire department captain, for instance, cannot call for a vote from the fire fighters in order to choose the best approach to handling a three-alarm blaze (Fiedler, 1967). Leaders and situations must be appropriately matched in order for leadership to be effective.

Climate

Climate is the third major dimension of the model. Climate is the nature of the relationships between group members, the processes that affect and result from the give and take between members of a group. Rules and roles (the subject of Chapter 6) help define these relationships and processes. Two other important aspects of climate are cohesiveness (the subject of Chapter 7) and conflict (the subject of Chapter 8).

RULES AND ROLES. Rules are standards of behavior that are expected of group members. Regardless of the group, the expected patterns of behavior are made clear. Departure from group rules may result at first in efforts to bring the deviate back into the fold, but later in the isolation, avoidance, or even expulsion of the offending member.

Roles may be defined as the set of expectations which group members share concerning the behavior of a person who occupies a given position in the group (Hare, 1962). Aside from the leader, other members of the group must perform their roles if the group is to fulfill its purpose or task. In any group, members may play a number of roles or may specialize in certain roles—initiating group action, for example, or resolving group conflict. We may perform one role in one group and a totally different role in another group. The point is that there are multiple roles to be performed in every group, and many people play different roles in different groups.

COHESIVENESS. Cohesiveness refers to the feeling of "we-ness" or togetherness that members feel toward each other and the group as a whole. Cohesiveness is shown by members' sense of identification with the group, their feelings of attraction for group membership or for other members of the group. Cohesivness—generally regarded as a positive characteristic—has a definite bearing on receptivity to influence attempts within the group, on group productivity, and on individual member satisfaction (Shaw, 1976).

CONFLICT.   Most of us give a negative connotation to the word. We think of conflict as something to be avoided. Indeed, it should be avoided if it hinders the efforts of the group to reach an effective solution to a problem or if it leads to social-emotional problems that prevent members from communicating. On the other hand, the best solutions to difficult problems are often those that have been shaped in the forge of conflict.

Control

The final dimension of our group communication model is *control*. In this dimension we are concerned with the methods and techniques for modifying or affecting messages, communicators, or climate—the other elements of our group process model. The focus is on the means that groups can use to accomplish their *purposes* or *tasks*.

GROUP TASKS.   The circumstances that cause individuals to come together into groups are many and varied. Generally, they can be classified into three major categories: (1) information sharing, (2) self-maintenance, and (3) problem solving. These types of tasks are not mutually exclusive. In fact, elements of all three may be present in the same small group. Thus, group task or purpose is primarily a matter of priority. In other words, a group may meet for information sharing and then find it necessary to engage in problem solving because of conflicting information.

A group whose task is primarily to share information has as its primary purpose the communication of, and interaction about, new knowledge. Group members impart information and do not necessarily debate the views expressed in this information. Government leaders, business people, and students who meet to increase their knowledge and understanding of questions of interest to them are participating in information sharing.

Groups concerned with self-maintenance focus on their members as individuals or on the structure of the group itself. Members of such groups are engaged in communication that concerns

member-to-member or member-to-group relationships. They seek to understand themselves and others better. Students discussing problems over coffee or releasing their tensions and frustrations over beer after an examination are common examples. Sometimes a permanent group is formed to provide the tension-releasing opportunity to communicate with others of similar interests. Alcoholics Anonymous, Weight Watchers, and Parents Without Partners are examples of collections of individuals who have found that formal organization into groups provides needed support.

The third major task, problem solving, involves focusing on a difficulty and seeking to alleviate it. Chapter 9 will deal specifically with this group task.

METHODS OF DISCUSSION. Various discussion methods may be used in small groups—each having its own advantages and limitations. They include the panel, round table, symposium-forum, dialogue, colloquy, and lecture-forum. In addition, three procedures have particular relevance for problem solving: (1) the reflective-thinking pattern, (2) the ideal-solution pattern, and (3) the single question pattern. These methods will be discussed in Chapter 10.

SMALL-GROUP TECHNIQUES. Various techniques can be used to aid task accomplishment or to promote an understanding of the processes going on within the small group. These include brainstorming, buzz sessions and Phillips 66, posting, role playing, nominal group technique, and the Delphi technique. These techniques will be discussed in Chapter 11.

* * *

Communication Diary 1-3

1. What information-sharing group experiences have you had?
2. What self-maintenance group experiences have you had?
3. What problem-solving group experiences have you had?

CHARACTERISTICS OF
THE GROUP COMMUNICATION PROCESS

Now that we have taken a broad look at the components of our model, let us examine the characteristics of group communication depicted by the model.

Group communication occurs in a system. A system implies that there is a connection between all of its dimensions. No dimension operates in isolation. A change in one dimension tends to result in changes throughout the system. Likewise, a change in one dimension results from changes elsewhere in the system.

Viewing group communication as a system suggests that no single dimension can be understood in isolation. An understanding of each dimension is necessary to understand the total system.

In the following ten chapters, as we focus on a dimension or one of its elements, we will gain more detailed, concrete information. At the same time, we may lose our perspective of how each component relates to the larger system. It is important, then, not to lose sight of the principle that no single aspect of group communication can be understood except as it relates to the whole.

A clear understanding of the communication process in small groups cannot be obtained without taking cognizance of *all* the component dimensions. Do not assume, however, that each dimension is equally important on every occasion of group communication. Although a single dimension may have a dominating effect on group processes in one discussion, this same dimension's impact may be relatively minor in another discussion.

Group communication dimensions are simultaneously cause and effect. This idea is implied in the concept of communication as a system. For example, we may look at the message as a cause influencing the dimensions of communicator, climate, and control. From another perspective we can also observe how and why certain characteristics of communicators, climate, or control affect the messages that are produced.

Group communication is dynamic. Communication is not an object. Rather, it is a process, an activity occurring over time. Hence, it is constantly changing, constantly in flux. These changes are continuous, irreversible, and unrepeatable. Once spoken, words cannot be unspoken.

Because of the systemic nature of group communication, each change in the various dimensions produces a fluid, flexible, dynamic process.

Group communication is complex. There are two reasons why communication in a group is complex. For one thing, all of the dimensions are operating (interacting) simultaneously. Secondly, characteristics under each of the basic dimensions are continuously changing while interacting.

If you can conceive of group communication with its interplay of dimensions, all constantly changing while interacting, then you have a notion of its complexity. We hope to simplify the complexity to manageable proportions in succeeding chapters.

II

MESSAGES

---

* * *

In this chapter we discuss how verbal messages facilitate and impede group interaction in performing group tasks, and how these messages reflect varying communication styles. We also consider various barriers to communication within a small group; these barriers often occur when group members do not share common meanings for the language being used. The chapter ends with a discussion of language skills that help make group interaction more effective.

In this chapter we consider the various categories of nonverbal messages—including environment, proxemics, chronemics, paralanguage, facial expressions, and kinesics. We also discuss the functions of nonverbal messages—repeating, contradicting, substituting, complementing, accenting, regulating, identifying, and indicating. We close with a consideration of the effects of environment, proxemics, and other categories of nonverbal messages on group interaction.

* * *

2

VERBAL MESSAGES IN SMALL-GROUP COMMUNICATION

PREVIEW

∗ **What is the nature of language?**

Language furnishes us with words for labeling experiences approximately. No language can describe experiences exactly. The word is not the thing. When used, a word may be a reasonably good representation or a horrendously poor one — or somewhere in between.

∗ **What are verbal messages?**

Verbal messages consist of a set of word-labels in a patterned or structured arrangement. The word-labels we use are susceptible to much personal bias.

∗ **What functions do verbal messages serve in small groups?**

Verbal messages serve five functions in small-group interaction: to furnish information upon which the social unit is built, to strengthen and modify programs, to devise and launch strategies, to motivate group members, and to provide feedback for evaluating programs.

∗ **What is a communication style?**

A communication style is a specialized set of interpersonal behaviors that are used in a given situation.

∗ **What are the various types of communication styles that prevail in small groups?**

Six basic communication styles prevail in small groups. They are referred to as controlling style, equalitarian style, structuring style, dynamic style, relinquishing style, and withdrawal style.

∗ **What are some of the characteristics of verbal messages that create barriers to effective communication in groups?**

The difficulties inherent in sharing meanings and impressions can create barriers to effective communication, as can also particular types of messages: those that arouse defensiveness, those that carry evaluative connotations, those that portray closed-mindedness, and those that attempt to manipulate or "put down" others.

✳ **What are the two essential characteristics of effective message sharing in small groups?**

Two essential characteristics of effective message sharing in small groups are trust and feedback responsiveness. Trust enables us to change our defensive postures; feedback receptiveness demonstrates to others that their contributions and suggestions are worthwhile.

CONSIDER the communication dilemma we are all in. A lot of things are always going on around us. The buzzing confusion rarely lets up. However, we cannot afford to be concerned with, or interested in, everything that's going on. How do we extract what interests us? What mental filters do we use? What do we say to ourselves and to others about the things that interest us? How do we interpret? How do we describe?

We express our interpretations and descriptions through language—first covertly, to classify and organize the incoming sensory impressions, and then overtly, to inform other people of these impressions. However, in our descriptions of events or objects or behaviors, we do not always call 'em as we see 'em. Sometimes we call 'em as we feel when we see 'em. Sometimes we call 'em as we see 'em without realizing that we are not seeing things as they really are. We may see those things that we habitually pay attention to, or things that facilitate our objectives at a given moment, or things that we can use as ammunition to justify our claims; and we may overlook everything else.

When we work together in a small group, we need to perceive and receive a constant flow of incoming stimuli—data or messages. The way in which we perceive the messages determines how much we know about the group's goals and the way we feel about ourselves and the group. Furthermore, our knowledge and attitudes influence the types of messages we send and the meanings or understandings those messages evoke.

Understanding is an important factor among members of the small group, for it helps the group achieve its goals. Small-group communication involves sending messages in order to exchange ideas, impressions, suggestions, directives, requests, queries, and commands. Through this exchange, senders attempt to make receivers understand goals, objectives, and issues.

In Chapter 1, we noted that messages may be studied in terms of their verbal features and their nonverbal features.

> The term *verbal* refers to the use of printed or spoken words to evoke meaning or understanding. Verbal messages consist of a set of words in a patterned or structured arrangement.

In this chapter we shall discuss the verbal features of messages. To do this, we shall consider the nature of language, communication styles and their effects, the barriers to communication, and pathways to better communication.

THE NATURE OF LANGUAGE

A few members of a policy-making group advocate teaching sex education in schools. Most of the group's other members respond by labeling them degenerates and weirdos. Are they really? Does the label make these people degenerates and weirdos? Do a thing and a label become the same?

No. The word is not the thing. A word is a name for a thing. When used, a word may be a reasonably good representation or a horrendously poor one—or somewhere in between.

Language is so much with us that it is difficult to appreciate its limitations. How would you describe the floor in your classroom or a tree near the building to someone who has not seen it? What emotion is really being described when a friend speaks of feeling frustrated? At the end of a gruelling task when you declare to the group that you are "extremely exhausted," do you mean that you are desperately in need of hospital care? Or would just a good night's sleep bring you back to face another day?

We must remember that language can merely furnish us with words for labeling experiences approximately. No language can describe experience exactly.

Although they are potentially both useful and useless, harmful and harmless, orienting and disorienting, words make up verbal messages. In turn, verbal messages are the vehicles through which the group controls its movement toward accomplishing a task and maintains harmony among its members. Therefore, we should be very careful about how we use words.

Referents and Word-Labels

How would you report or describe the following incident, which occurred consistently in a group-discussion class? Whenever his discussion group met to discuss a topic, Edgar sat silently, his chin in his hands, not speaking even when invited to do so.

In reporting, we have several choices. Here are a few:

1. "Edgar sits through the entire discussion and never comments. He has behaved in this manner on several occasions."
2. "I have never seen a more looney s.o.b. than Edgar. Those kinds of guys could go off the deep end any moment."
3. "Edgar is trying to make our group look bad. He knows that our grade depends on total participation, and that's why he clams up."

In our first statement we described as much of an event as we were able to perceive. In the succeeding statements we were making judgments about Edgar and guessing at his motives: We risked creating improper understanding in other group members. The verbal behavior apparent in statements (2) and (3) will not bring about the understanding that we should strive for in group communication.

Total understanding depends on whether the message sender and message receiver have similar experiences with objects or *referents* conveyed in the message. Verbal messages are word-labels. The words have no meanings in and of themselves. Rather, words act as triggers to stimulate meanings in us. These meanings are brought about through our past experiences. Having no prior experience with a group member who sits in silence, we conjured up word-labels to fit referents that seemed similar in behavior, and Edgar became some sort of lunatic.

Bias

Words are not forced on us by some Higher Being; they are not magical. We arbitrarily assign them to things and events. We may all agree, for example, to call a tool *tool* rather than *table*. However, the word-labels we use are susceptible to much personal bias. We may call a certain tool a lug wrench at one moment and a gizmo at another. The object is still the same, but the words convey different understanding about it. Far more serious may be our labeling of people, as when one group member calls another "unpatriotic and lacking in dignity as befits a true American."

THE FUNCTIONS OF VERBAL MESSAGES

Verbal messages perform five important functions in the small group. These five functions are:

1. *Social facilitation.* Verbal messages furnish information for informal activities in the group, including the grapevine, scuttlebut, gossip, and phatic communication or social chitchat. Such nonprogrammed activities are vital to the social fabric of a group.
2. *Program development.* Verbal messages launch programs, strengthen ongoing programs, and aid in the adjustment of goals.
3. *Strategy planning.* Verbal messages denote choice of strategy or arguments. Strategy is involved in decision making, and verbal messages help to carry out decisions.
4. *Group motivation.* Verbal messages motivate individuals in the group. Success in motivation depends on the effectiveness of the message.
5. *Program evaluation.* Verbal messages furnish information on the results of group activity. Such feedback is needed by decision makers, group leaders, and others in positions of authority.

Many communication settings are hazy because words cannot adequately represent what they stand for. This haziness creates tension between senders and receivers. Senders may expect their messages to be accepted by certain individuals in the group, but these "targets" may expect the messages to meet their own needs and demands. Tension between group members increases the need to communicate and to be communicated with (Fearing, 1953–1954). Consequently, verbal messages are exchanged in greater quantity and frequency. More verbal messages may be needed to clear up uncertainties concerning a task or to provide members with reasons for their need to participate in the group's activity. Whether the tension is removed or reduced depends on our ability to vary our communication styles.

COMMUNICATION STYLES AND THEIR EFFECTS

Groups are affected by the *communication styles* with which messages are exchanged.

A *communication style* is a specialized set of interpersonal behaviors that are used in a given situation.

Each communication style consists of a constellation of communication behaviors or "traits" that are used to elicit certain responses in certain situations. Moreover, a particular style will be consistently used by a person for similar situations.

As a general rule, we can distinguish one style from another. For example, we have a remarkable ability for differentiating "apple polishers" from "flatterers," from "condescenders" and so on. The appropriateness of a particular style depends on the intent of the sender, the expectations of the receiver, and the "behavior protocols" or requirements of the culture in which the message exchange occurs.

Six basic communication styles prevail in small groups: a controlling style, an equalitarian style, a structuring style, a dynamic style, a relinquishing style, and a withdrawal style (Wofford, Gerloff, and Cummins, 1977). We shall examine these communication styles and their impact on task performance and group behavior. Some communication styles are more effective than others in certain situations. Table 2-1 provides an overview of the styles. You may want to refer to it as you read.

TABLE 2-1 SIX COMMUNICATION STYLES

Style	Communicator	Purpose	Technique
Controlling	Directive, demanding	To persuade others and gain compliance	Use power and authority and sometimes manipulation
Equalitarian	Friendly, warm	To stimulate and draw out others	Stress mutual understanding
Structuring	Objective, detached	To systematize environment; to clarify or establish structure	Cite applicable standards, procedures, or rules
Dynamic	Direct, aggressive	To arouse to action	Be brief and to the point
Relinquishing	Receptive to others' ideas	To shift responsibility to others	Support others' points of view
Withdrawal	Independent	To avoid communication and influence	Talk about something else; use a verbal attack

SOURCE: Adapted from Wofford, Gerloff, and Cummins, 1977, pp. 154–156.

A Controlling Style

A controlling style of communication is one in which the communicator limits and directs the behaviors or thoughts of other people. People who use a controlling style are basically one-way communicators (Figure 2-1). They are not interested in receiving

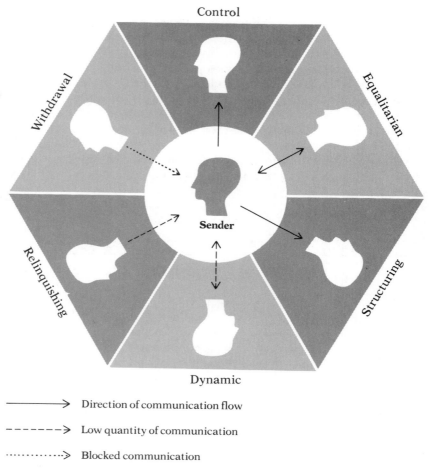

FIGURE 2-1.   Direction and flow of the six communication styles. The equalitarian style and, to a certain extent, the dynamic style involve two-way communication, whereas the other styles are one-way. When a controlling or structuring style is used, the sender takes the initiative and assumes a more active role. In using the withdrawal or relinquishing styles, the sender tends to be passive. (Wofford, Gerloff, and Cummins, 1977, p. 154)

feedback unless it can be used to clarify their own ideas. "Controllers" usually make up their minds before a matter is discussed and are interested only in driving their point across. They do not care about other points of view and generally try to use their authority and power to force compliance with their wishes. They do not try to "sell" others on an idea; they tell others what to do. The *controlling* communicator closely resembles the autocratic leader (see Chapter 5).

A controlling style is very effective when fellow group members view the communicator as an expert on a subject. However, if a communicator who is not competent presumes to take control without consent of the group and starts to give orders, a breakdown in morale, motivation, and performance ensues. Although we are generally willing to submit to a group member whom we perceive as more knowledgeable, competent, and experienced than we are, we are seldom willing to do so for a group member who has equal or lesser capabilities.

The controlling style is used to persuade people to perform effectively and generally takes the form of criticism. Let's look at a case in which a group leader uses the controlling style in a manner that leads to conflict:

Boom-Boom Branigan has been assistant production supervisor of a die-casting group for four years. He is always on the run, checking supplies, eliminating defects, working on schedules with the production people, explaining reasons for substandard parts to the "white-shirts" in quality control. The problem is that whenever Boom-Boom has to leave his group, supervision is interrupted. This situation really annoys the manager, J. Mortimer McNasty. He is further annoyed because he does not always know where Boom-Boom is or why he is not in the assembly area. One day, the manager calls Boom-Boom in, and tells him that henceforth he must check with him (McNasty) whenever he intends to leave the assembly area. Here's a transcript of that confrontation:

MCNASTY: Look here, Boom-Boom. You are spending a helluva lotta time outside your area. As far as I'm concerned, that's bad. It's not the way I want things around here. From now on this is how it's going to be: You check with me first whenever you have to go on some crazy mission anywhere in this plant. You got me?

BOOM-BOOM: Well, you're the boss, Mr. McNasty . . . but I don't know why you want me to report to you every time. I'd have to come to you pretty near fifty times a day. You know that I'm on the run most of the time.

MCNASTY: Never mind that. Just do as I say. I don't have time to go into all the reasons. As a matter of fact, I think the reasons are obvious enough. Tomorrow, you report to me. Okay?

BOOM-BOOM: (sighing loudly as he prepares to leave) Mr. McNasty, this is unreasonable. *You* are unreasonable. Furthermore, you are crazier than I think you are if you really believe that I'm going to come running to you to *beg* for permission every time I have to go down the line. Do you know what? I quit. I sure as hell quit!

Not all controlling communication is as abrasive and threatening as McNasty's. It can be benevolent and gentle. Unfortunately, a controlling style often has negative overtones, and generally evokes negative emotions in the receiver. Like most other people, Boom-Boom Branigan does not respond well to this approach; it simply evokes a defensive reaction from him.

In a series of field studies at General Electric, E. Kay, J. French, and H. Meyer (1962) analyzed the effects of criticisms used by group leaders to improve group performance. The researchers recorded the number and the nature of criticisms and assessed the percentage of the group goals achieved during a twelve-week period. Results showed that constant criticism and controlling had a disastrous effect on goal achievement, especially among group

members with low self-esteem. The researchers conclude that a positive approach in discussing performance is more effective than a critical one. Criticism should be expressed tactfully in a nonevaluative, problem-oriented way.

The controlling style is appropriate in crises such as evacuating a burning building: tasks must be performed immediately and there is no time for building morale and a team spirit.

According to V. Vroom and F. Mann (1960), the controlling style may also be effective when we work with people who lack motivation. We will expand on this topic in Chapter 5 when we discuss group leadership.

The Equalitarian Style

The equalitarian style is marked by a two-way flow of verbal message with influence flowing from one group member to another. In equalitarian message exchanges, members stimulate each other to plan, set goals, take action, or think. The discussion

is open, with each person expressing ideas in a relaxed and informal atmosphere that promotes acceptance and mutual understanding. In such a group, individuals are characterized as having a high concern both for good relationships and for task performance. The communicator with an equalitarian style does not assume personal superiority or expertise but is willing to receive and to give information.

The equalitarian style facilitates group communication by drawing out the ideas of other members. It is effective for fostering empathy and cooperation among group members. It is also effective when there is time for thorough discussion and when decisions on complex problems are being made, because then additional information, which no one person would have, can be brought out.

Let us reconstruct the McNasty-Branigan episode to see what happens when verbal messages are carefully and thoughtfully put together in an equalitarian style:

MCNASTY: I realize that you've got a helluva lot of running around to do every day. And quite frankly, Boom-Boom, I don't know how you do it day after day. But when you are not there, supervision really suffers. It *really* breaks down. You know, I think that both of us will have to work something out here.

BOOM-BOOM: I've been worried about that, too, Mr. McNasty. I lie awake nights thinking about it. I get to thinking that maybe we need one or two more group leaders to give me a hand whenever I've got to go down the line.

MCNASTY: You've got a good idea there, Boom-Boom. But it may take us quite some time to look into the leadership problem. Let me look into it, and I'll try to get some data to back up my request for more leaders. Those guys upstairs like to see hard facts before they talk with me. *In the meantime, I think it would help if you look around for me before you go down the line.* In that way I can keep my eyes open for any problems until you get back. If you'd do that from now on, it should help you and me to keep things going right on schedule.

BOOM-BOOM: As you say, Mr. McNasty. I'll remember to give you the old on-the-road sign whenever I've got to hit the trail.

In the first dialogue, McNasty did not give a reason for his request or criticism. In the second dialogue, he gives Boom-Boom a good reason for the request, and he does not belittle Boom-Boom's suggested solution. The result is goodwill, cooperation, and a feeling of accomplishment.

The equalitarian style is not effective among group members who are overly dependent, nor is it effective in crises.

The Structuring Style

A structuring style uses verbal messages to establish order, organization, scheduling, and structure. Messages involving this style seldom express strong emotion; the communicator appears objective and detached. This type of communicator is basically interested in influencing others by discussing with them the goals, standards, schedules, rules, or procedures that apply to the situation at hand.

Messages incorporating a structuring style are necessary when the group must deal with complex tasks. A structuring style is used first to establish procedures, goals, objectives, and policies. After the task has been launched, structuring messages must still flow from the leader(s) in order to clarify and interpret issues. Job descriptions, operating manuals, and policy statements also require structured verbal messages.

Researchers such as R. Stogdill and A. Coons of the bureau of Business Research at Ohio State University discovered a dimension of effective leadership that they labeled "initiating struc-

ture.'' Efficient initiators of structure are group members who draft verbal messages that establish goals, outline the necessary assignments, and provide answers when questions are raised.

Although the structuring style is necessary for proper conduct on tasks, communicators in such situations should occasionally use the equalitarian style in order to allow some relaxation.

The Dynamic Style

The dynamic style is used by a communicator who is highly active and aggressive, largely because the task environment requires action-oriented, aggressive involvement. It is the style of cheerleaders, coaches, sales leaders, and campaign directors; its primary purpose is to stimulate group members. The message exchange is usually frank and open. According to J. Wofford, E. Gerloff, and R. Cummins (1977), the communications of the dynamic style are not deep and philosophical but are oriented to tackling immediate problems.

At the beginning of a project, a group member may say: "We all know that this is a difficult project and that the next few days will really wear us down. But tackling difficult projects is what we're all about. Everybody knows what we can do, and that's why they

asked us to do this job. So go home, get a good night's sleep, come back tomorrow, and let's start showin' 'em what this team is made of!" This is a succinct and straightforward statement by a pragmatic person. No attempt is made to spell out procedures about what's to be done. Rather, the communicator is intent on boosting group morale.

The dynamic style is effective in dealing with frequent crises if the group members are mature and competent enough to handle the problems. Practically all coaches can deliver pep talks, but not every team can win. Wofford (1971) contends that when the group members feel inadequate to perform in the manner called for by the communicator, they may feel frustrated.

The Relinquishing Style

The relinquishing style involves a declaration of willingness to subordinate one's position to that of another person. Although given the right to command, the communicator is willing to defer to the judgment of another person. Using the relinquishing style, the communicator assumes a receptive rather than a directive position and shows interest in the contributions of other people.

This communication style is often used by the group member or leader who is interested in team building. Notice the team-building intent in this verbal behavior: "I know that most of you

believe that you should not speak up because you have just joined the group. But I want you to know that Arlene, Georgie, and I don't have all the answers. We want fresh ideas about how to tackle this project. And so the three of us are going to back off a bit and let all of you bright, new people take a fresh look at the problem. Make some decision, and we'll help you implement it." Relinquishing authority is a sound method for getting others to assume responsibility.

Verbal messages uttered in a relinquishing style usually express confidence in others. Therefore, they are particularly effective when working with people who are clearly more knowledgeable, experienced, and understanding, and who are willing to assume responsibility. Communicators should not use a relinquishing style, however, when they want to avoid a responsibility that is rightfully theirs. They are likely to lose the respect of the other group members if such shirking becomes apparent. The style may have a negative effect also on people who tend to be very dependent on others in the group. Such individuals are likely to feel frustration and resentment.

The Withdrawal Style

A withdrawal style constitutes a rather impoverished behavior; it involves avoiding interaction. The group member simply does not want to communicate and may withdraw by joking about serious things or resorting to diversionary tactics. The person as-

sumes an independent stance either to perform the task alone or to allow others to do so.

Withdrawal messages are typified by the following: "Look, you guys already know that I don't want to be involved in this issue!" "What do you mean, we should discuss the issue. You know darn well there's no issue to be discussed. It's not going to matter one way or the other!" "Just leave me out of this discussion!" The individual in each example is not relinquishing responsibility by giving it to others but is indicating a desire to avoid all communication on the subject.

Although a withdrawal style appears to be the worst communication behavior among the six styles, it can be effective in rare instances. It may be expedient to be quiet and withdraw tactfully from a discussion when participation would be injurious to oneself or another person. However, since withdrawing usually does not facilitate the group's search for solutions, it is of limited value. Withdrawing would be of even less value if done with hostility and aggressiveness toward other group members.

* * *

Exercise 2-1
COMMUNICATION STYLES

In the conversation below, evaluate each statement by a C, E, S, D, R, W, indicating whether it is a control, equalitarian, structuring, dynamic, relinquishing, or withdrawal statement.

A director of a fund-raising campaign (Alice) and one of her "project captains" (Bill) are discussing problems associated with the campaign and are trying to make some improvements.

_____ ALICE: Bill, the first duty for your group is to "zone" the various territories and to find out how the telephone campaign is going.

_____ BILL: Yes, I think I should definitely get around to that today. Our number of pledges seems to be decreasing, and I need to get to the bottom of it. What do you think?

_____ ALICE: I'll leave that entirely up to you, Bill. You know that I don't want to tell you how to do your job.

_____ BILL: Alice, I've gotten some very good feedback from businessmen in town, and the follow-up on them looks pretty good. I think we should put them on top of our list.

———— ALICE: Businessmen, businessmen . . . Everytime it's the businessmen. You overrate those guys. I know you've been sold on the idea of canvassing businessmen from the very beginning, Bill, but you are off on a wild-goose chase. You've put a lot of effort into that idea and yet your donations from them is only a trickle. I want to make it clear that not only am I encouraging your people to stop canvassing the business sector, but I'm telling you to stop wasting your time with them. Stick with the students, the faculty, and the alumni. And, that's an order!

———— BILL: If that's what you want, all right, boss. I'll go along with you on it.

———— ALICE: Bill, you have a tendency to come up with some really wild schemes. What's the matter with you, anyway?

———— BILL: Look, I thought that a campaign in the business sector would go, but since you feel so strongly about it, let's drop it. Maybe I should come back when you're not so emotional.

———— ALICE: Hold it! I'm not being emotional. I just happen to believe that businessmen don't give money to anything unless you promise to give them publicity. Let's not waste time and energy on losers.

———— BILL: I like to ride a winner, too!

———— ALICE: What do you think of the campaign-button drive in our project?

———— BILL: That drive was launched the wrong way. We should make it standard procedure to find out from suppliers whether they can really get the printing done on time. We should tell them what *we* want, rather than let them dictate to us. As it is, we don't have enough buttons; and at a 50 percent profit on each button, we're losing money.

———— ALICE: You're right, Bill. I told Debbie to make sure that the "buttons" guy could make good on the order, but she never listens.

———— BILL: It surely would make things easier for us. Keep after Debbie. We have to have a serious talk with that "button man."

* * *

Exercise 2-2

EFFECTS OF COMMUNICATION STYLES

Almost from the first day of summer camp Elmer was critical of his fellow counselors. A hard worker, Elmer was annoyed by what he saw as their excessive card playing and volleyball games, and their lack of concern for monitoring the campers. On the third day of camp, Quincey, one of the other counselors, approached Elmer in a friendly manner and said, "Look, buddy, you keep working your head off, and nobody will have any fun here. Cool it, man. These campers aren't prisoners. They can look out for themselves." That began a feud that lasted for three weeks. Quincey became the target of Elmer's anger, and Quincey responded in kind. Elmer became less and less involved with the other counselors; he stopped going to meetings. The disharmony was having a negative effect on the camp's activities.

1. The class is divided into groups of six to eight members.

2. For 10 to 15 minutes, each group discusses the topic "How would you as a manager resolve the conflict between Elmer and Quincey?" The discussions are tape-recorded or videotaped.

3. The tape is replayed for each group. Using Table A, each group member identifies the style of communication being used by each participant and notes the reaction that the group had for the communication item.

4. The group categorizes, evaluates, and discusses each item and its effects. The tape should be stopped at regular intervals to discuss the communication items.

TABLE A   CLASSIFYING COMMUNICATION ITEMS BY STYLE, RESPONSE, AND EFFECT

Communi- cation Item	Communi- cation Style	Response		Effect	
		Positive	Negative	Facilitated Discussion	Hindered Discussion
1.					
2.					
3.					
4.					
5.					

TABLE A continued

Communi-cation Item	Communi-cation Style	Response		Effect	
		Positive	Negative	Facilitated Discussion	Hindered Discussion
6.					
7.					
8.					
9.					
10.					
11.					
12.					
13.					
14.					
15.					
16.					
17.					
18.					
19.					
20.					
21.					
22.					
23.					
24.					
25.					
26.					
27.					
28.					
29.					
30.					

BARRIERS TO COMMUNICATION

All of us who work in groups must contend with barriers to communication. Many such barriers result from attaching different meanings to verbal messages. Others result from various types of communication that may provoke defensiveness.

Message Meaning

Difficulties in communication between individuals can arise because no two persons see or hear in exactly the same way. We all have eyes and ears but the intellectual and emotional makeup of each person is unique. P. Warr and C. Knapper (1968) conceive of these differences in terms of three components of perception: attributive, expectancy, and affective. Perceptions are formed by the dynamic interaction of all three components. We give everything we perceive particular characteristics. These, in turn, create certain expectancies and result in emotions that influence later perceptions. Thoughout this process, attributes, expectancies, and emotions are influenced by whatever language categories we use in talking to ourselves.

THE ATTRIBUTIVE COMPONENT. This component is the act of assigning characteristics to a person or object being perceived—for instance, size, weight, color, intelligence, and behavior. We attribute such qualities and also draw inferences from them. Thus, perception involves categorization. The characteristics we assign to a person or event take their meaning from the language category into which we place the object, and other characteristics within this category are also attributed to the object.

For instance, we might label as group leader someone who took charge of a group discussion and conducted it efficiently. We attribute the individual's behavior to the language category *leader.* Because we usually perceive leaders as knowledgeable, we might assume that the person who acts as leader is also knowledgeable.

THE EXPECTANCY COMPONENT. This component is closely related to the attributive one. Perception involves more than simply placing people or events into categories; it involves expectations arising from these categories. When we attach characteristics to something we perceive, we develop expectancies about it.

For example, if we have an unpleasant experience with a group member, we might label that person a troublemaker. Once we have categorized the person this way, each contact with this group member will be difficult. This phenomenon can be called a *set*. The set influences all our future perceptions of someone or something, continually reinforcing what we first attribute to the individual or event.

THE AFFECTIVE COMPONENT.   We not only classify and make predictions about people, objects, and events, but we also react to them emotionally. Several studies indicate that all of our perceptions have emotional qualities (Warr and Knapper, 1968). We may feel attraction, repulsion, respect, disdain, or sympathy about what we see. These feelings affect our perceptions strongly and, in time, influence subsequent perceptions and interactions. This affective component may stem from what we now perceive and from interactions that are likely to follow; it may arise from past associations with what we perceive; or it may come from feelings aroused by the language categories into which we place the object.

Individual Experience and Message Meaning

It is impossible to predict exactly how each individual will encode, transmit, or decode a message. Communicators may take independent, inner-directed action, or they may be affected by factors not under their control (Pigors and Myers, 1969), such as cultural heritage, social environment, and previous experiences. For example, when a supervisor receives a written order that must be disseminated verbally to co-workers, his or her previous experiences influence the spoken form. Each worker's response depends on the individual's perception of what the supervisor said. The workers' prior experiences provide them with their own unique perception and frames of reference.

In Plato's *Phaedrus*, Socrates points out that one must talk to others in terms of receivers' experiences; that is, one must use a manager's language when talking to managers, and so on. If receivers fail to comprehend the language, repetition is worthless. A message can be clarified only in relation to a receiver's experiences. Peter Drucker (1970, p. 7) says, "To communicate a concept is impossible unless the recipient can perceive it; that is, unless it is within his perception." Disagreement or conflict is likely to occur as a result of incongruity in perceptions. What A sees vividly, B does not see at all; therefore, what A argues has no pertinence to B's concerns, and vice versa.

Remember the story of the three blind men and the elephant? Each man felt a different part of the animal—trunk, tail, and ears—and proceeded to describe the entire beast. Each man's description was different. Each one's experience of the elephant was incomplete, and so his attempt to describe it accurately was doomed to fail. Accurate communication can take place only when one knows what the receiver can see and why. Experiences with people, places, objects, and ideas give meaning to what is taken in.

Not only are our perceptions unique for each of us, they are always changing. Furthermore, meanings for words or nonverbal symbols change throughout our lives. Experiences alter the contexts within which we interpret messages. As we pointed out earlier, in our discussion of language, "the meanings of words are not in the words. They are in us . . . . No word ever has exactly the same meaning twice" (Hayakawa, 1949, p. 6).

Defense-Arousing Communication

Messages, comments, statements, or communications that tend to make us defensive can be placed in four main categories of communication: evaluative, dogmatic, manipulative, and exhibitionistic. Group members who resort to these types of communication may be expressing their own defensiveness. "Evaluating" another person is often done in self-defense. Individuals may label others as pushy or aggressive simply because they are insecure in a particular situation. Dogmatic people may be so busy defending their own viewpoints that they spend little or no time receiving others' ideas. Some people use manipulative communication because they do not believe that their own ideas are good enough to be accepted. Exhibitionistic communicators are defending their self-concept; they feel it is important that others know of their superiority so that they can continue to believe in it themselves.

EVALUATIVE COMMUNICATION. Evaluative communication is characterized by negative labels and terms to refer to or address members of the group. Such labels are usually derived from stereotypes. *Sloppy, stupid, a real creep* are examples of negative stereotypes. Even the positive labels that are attributed from positive evaluations may be stereotypes. After all, once a person is labeled—positively or negatively—it becomes difficult to get away from the label. People continue to see only the label.

Let's listen in on a verbal exchange between a group leader and one of the group members. Listen for the evaluative communication, and look for the traces of defensiveness that the communication provokes. The conversation concerns a meeting in which they both participated.

MEMBER: I guess you'd call that a meeting, eh? You guys really know how to waste people's time! You are one hell of a sorry group leader.
LEADER: Ah, shut up. You don't realize how sensitive this issue is. You can't just rush in "hog wild" and change things overnight. I thought it was a darn good meeting. And I am not the only one who thinks so.
MEMBER: Well, maybe we can't rush into things . . . but we're sure as hell moving like corn syrup on a February morning in Iowa. We haven't even gotten down to the nitty-gritty with this thing.
LEADER: Well, you have to handle a group like ours with kid gloves! Put on the pressure, start tightening up, and setting some deadlines and everybody starts bitching. Buncha pansies.
MEMBER: Wait a minute, fella. Who are you calling a pansy? I didn't know you were so thin-skinned. You know what they say: If you can't stand the heat, you'd better get out of the kitchen. Man, I don't want to pick a fight with you, but I really don't see any progress.
LEADER: O. K. Then back off. Look, if I do things the way you want me to, we'd be getting into all kinds of trouble.
MEMBER: All right, wise guy, . . . what's *my* way?
LEADER: How the hell would I know?

That's a bad situation, isn't it? They could go on like that for hours, and nothing productive would be accomplished. The entire exchange resulted from an evaluative comment: "I guess you'd call that a meeting, eh?" Immediately, the group leader became defensive, and the rest of the conversation went downhill.

A reconstruction of the same conversation but without the evaluative messages might have a different effect:

MEMBER: Man, I'm telling you, I'm really fed up with that meeting. (Describing feelings)

LEADER: I know what you mean. It's hard to get a handle on the problem.

MEMBER: I wonder what we could do to turn things around. We're going to run out of time.

LEADER: I don't know. What do you think? Got any bright ideas? Anything that we haven't thought of?

MEMBER: Not offhand.

LEADER: There's got to be something that we're overlooking.

MEMBER: You could be right. Why don't we sleep on it and come back tomorrow for another crack at it.

LEADER: Good idea.

In this conversation, nobody uses labels, and there is hardly an overt evaluation in the message exchange. Conceivably, both people are frustrated, but they manage to concentrate on the problem rather than make value judgments.

DOGMATIC COMMUNICATION. Dogmatic communication is characterized by the tendency to "discuss" things in terms of either–or statements. Dogmatic people usually are not interested in hearing others' viewpoints and tend to resist feedback unless it supports their point of view. Dogmatic communication is perhaps the most difficult barrier to overcome, and, according to Milton Rokeach (1960), dogmatism itself is very difficult to change. Dogmatism is another term for chronic closed-mindedness. Discussions with dogmatic or closed-minded people usually degenerate into heated debates. In their minds, they are always right; others are always wrong. It is easy to see how such message exchanges lead to defensive climates in the group.

Dogmatic communicators are poor listeners because they are too busy dressing up their own arguments. Also, because of the rigidity of their thinking, dogmatic communicators cannot exercise much creativity in dealing with issues as they arise.

MANIPULATIVE COMMUNICATION. Has anyone ever tried to sell you something "in your own best interest," but somehow you knew that the person was not really interested in your welfare? How did that communication affect you? Most people find it offensive. Nobody likes to be manipulated into behaving in a prescribed manner. As J. Wofford and associates (1977, p. 179) put it: "Manipulative communication excites the control issue, and the reaction to the communication is based on not wanting to be controlled rather than on the content of the communication."

Frequently, group members or leaders will call for ideas or suggestions and may even conduct democratic discussions, only to distort the ideas later or make choices in such a way as to influence a group decision in favor of their preference. However, the manipulator's influence deteriorates rapidly when other group members become aware that they are being manipulated. A common result is that such members withdraw from group participation.

The manipulator's real message is: "I can't trust you to make the right decisions, but I'll let you feel that you are really necessary in this process." Needless to say, the group members are likely to spend most of their time refuting that hidden message, and they refuse to go along with the charade.

EXHIBITIONISTIC COMMUNICATION. Group members who enjoy boasting and bragging about their knowledge, experience, expertise, triumphs, and accomplishments may be characterized as exhibitionists. They are forever praising themselves and convincing others of how important their contributions are. Exhibitionistic communication arouses defenses in other people because, by implying superiority, the communicator is also putting down everybody else.

Exhibitionistic communication is not an effective strategy. A person who is truly talented does not have to "go on exhibition"; a talented individual is usually recognized and appreciated by others. Once the other group members come to know the useful roles the talented person plays, they are eager to listen and seek that person's advice on crucial matters.

PATHWAYS TO EFFECTIVE MESSAGE SHARING IN SMALL GROUPS

The best way to increase effective communication is to increase self-confidence and to decrease defensiveness. We have to know the difference between confronting others constructively and pro-

* * *

Exercise 2-3
BARRIERS TO COMMUNICATION

The maintenance department at the United Paper Mills has a history of difficulties. Recently, things have gotten worse. It is known, for example, that several employees are spending company time on their own projects and using company materials. Many supervisors have apparently given up trying to discipline workers because they feel that the company will not back them up.

Jerry is a newly promoted maintenance supervisor. His crew works pretty well, but he sometimes has difficulties when workers under him are changed to other crews and supervisors because of absenteeism and rush jobs. Wednesday he caught one of his workers, Hal, quitting early. He told him that quitting time was not for another hour and he expected him to work until then. Hal did but seemed disgruntled.

The next day Hal was assigned to another supervisor and, sure enough, Jerry saw him quitting early again. Hal saw Jerry but paid no attention to him. Jerry knew that some of the other supervisors "looked the other way" when workers quit early and suspected that Hal's supervisor for that day would not want to know about Hal's quitting early.

1. What can Jerry do?

2. Role-play a discussion between Jerry and Hal.

3. Role-play a discussion between Jerry and Hal's supervisor for that day.

4. What issues are at stake here? What are the barriers to communication?

---

voking defensiveness. We do this best when we describe our own position as it really is and encourage other people to describe their position honestly.

Two of the essential markers on the pathway to effective message sharing are *trust* and *feedback receptiveness*.

Trust

We are not willing to communicate accurately and openly with others unless we trust them. We must be convinced that our comments, expressions, and opinions will be received without defensiveness or retaliation. We all like to have the assurance that everyone can disagree without becoming unfriendly. How do we develop this trust in a group?

Trust starts when we declare our intention to be fair in dealing with other group members. It grows when others see that we do indeed honor our commitment to accurate message sharing. By making an effort to change our defensive postures, we move from a *destructive trust* cycle to a *constructive trust* cycle.

As shown in Figure 2-2, person A's trust for B results in more accurate and more open communication with B. This open communication provides A with another opportunity to trust B. If A responds with integrity, B will feel more confident to increase self-disclosure. And so the constructive cycle builds in a positive direction.

The second cycle is not so favorable. It can begin with a lack of trust by A for B. Since A does not trust B, their communication tends to be guarded and may be deceptive. Person A probably responds by being less supportive of B. Person B responds by having less trust for A and by being less open, more cautious, and more deceptive. This results in a continuing response of less support and less effective communication.

Either A or B can break the destructive cycle. Person A can do so by being consistently honest, fair, supportive, and nonpunitive even though B is being deceptive. In seeing A's response, B will then begin to give more open and accurate messages. Person B can break the cycle by being more open and disclosing more

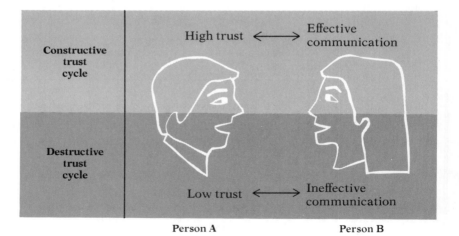

FIGURE 2-2. Trust cycles in communication. (After Haney, 1973)

thoughts and feelings in spite of believing that A may use this against B. In seeing this openness, A will become more supportive. The result is the constructive trust cycle.

Trust is a key ingredient of communication effectiveness and ultimately of organizational effectiveness. Group members and leaders strive to build up trust among themselves.

Feedback

Feedback permissiveness, responsiveness, and receptiveness are crucial factors in the enrichment of group communication. All members should encourage a climate in which (1) everyone feels free to give feedback (feedback permissiveness); (2) everyone is willing to get feedback, whether positive or negative (feedback responsiveness); and (3) everyone is willing to act upon the suggestions entailed in the feedback (feedback receptiveness). A few guidelines may help us recognize how messages can be tailored to create an efficient feedback environment:

1. *Feedback should be descriptive rather than evaluative.* A judgmental, evaluative tone should be avoided. Group members should describe their feelings or emotions without casting aspersions on the "offender." Saying, "I am upset about the way things are going," is more acceptable than saying, "You people are really driving me out of my mind!" The first statement merely describes a feeling; the second statement blames others for the feeling.
2. *Feedback should be specific rather than general.* Group communication should tell all members exactly what's going well or what's going wrong.
3. *Feedback should be directed toward behavior that the receiver can do something about.* This guideline is an extension of the preceding one. Such feedback is more likely to be constructive and less likely to provoke defensiveness. "I am not going to vote for you because you 'politicians' just don't give a darn about the students on campus," does not tell the receiver what sort of behavior is expected.
4. *Feedback should be solicited rather than imposed.* However, if one group member demands feedback from others, they may withhold it. A climate that *permits* and *encourages* feedback is necessary.
5. *Feedback should be given as early as possible.* People tend to forget quickly. When not given promptly, feedback loses much of its specificity and may become so general as to be useless.
6. *Feedback should enable the receiver to understand the information.* The receiver should rephrase what's being said. "See if I am getting you correctly. What you're saying is . . ." "Would you kindly say that again?"

* * *

Exercise 2-4

FEEDBACK

Your instructor will appoint a class member to describe two pictures.

1. During the description of the first picture you are to make no sounds and ask no questions. The sender of the descriptive message turns away from the class so that visual cues are minimized.

2. During the description of the second picture you may make any sound or statement or ask any question you wish. The sender receives any feedback you want to send.

3. Describe your impressions, reactions, or feelings in each of the two situations.

SUMMARY

Verbal messages consist of words in a patterned or structured arrangement.

There are six basic communication styles: controlling, equalitarian, structuring, dynamic, relinquishing, and withdrawal. Each of these exerts a unique influence on human responsiveness in small groups. If we understand the features that distinguish one communication style from another, we can better identify, categorize, and evaluate group communication behavior. An understanding of these styles also helps enrich group participation and group leadership.

Although the equalitarian style is the most useful for building healthy group interaction, no one style is best for every situation. Communicators should employ a style that accomplishes the objective and that fits the expectations and abilities of fellow group members. As we discuss leadership, roles, and status in other chapters, the close connection of these factors with communication styles will become apparent.

No matter how skillful we may be at sending and receiving messages, breakdowns in communication are inevitable. Misunderstandings may occur because of a faulty use of, or response to, verbal messages. Certain types of language may also make us defensive and so lead to breakdowns in group interaction.

Effective feedback is descriptive, specific, and directed toward behavior that the receiver can deal with. Timing, clarity, and openness must be encouraged. In order to maintain an efficient feedback system, we should ask the proper questions at the proper time. Above all, the most important method for gaining accurate, constant feedback is a communication style that shows that we are willing to receive suggestions and respond to them to the best of our ability.

ADDITIONAL READINGS

Collins, B., and Guetzkow, H. *A Social Psychology of Group Processes for Decision-Making.* New York: John Wiley, 1964. Chapter 9 contains a helpful discussion of the issues involved in group communication and interaction. The discussion on pages 183–87 deals with the manner in which group members respond to messages.

Haney, W. *Communication and Organizational Behavior: Text and Cases.* Homewood, Ill.: Richard D. Irwin, 1973. This book provides an excellent collection of case studies that may be used for class discussion of the impact of message styles.

McCroskey, J.; Larson, C.; and Knapp, M. *An Introduction to Interpersonal Communication.* Englewood Cliffs, N.J.: Prentice-Hall, 1971. Chapter 8 deals with verbal message variables in interpersonal influence. This chapter gives a good review of scientific findings.

Mortensen, C. D. *Communication: The Study of Human Interaction.* New York: McGraw-Hill, 1972. Chapter 5 details an extensive review of studies of the dynamics of verbal interaction. Students will find this material most helpful.

Scheidel, T. M. *Speech Communication and Human Interaction.* Glenview, Ill.: Scott, Foresman, 1972. See chapter 6 for a discussion of the interaction between language and perception. Chapter 6 also presents ample coverage of the nature of language.

Scott, W. G., and Mitchell, T. *Organization Theory: A Structural and Behavioral Analysis.* Homewood, Ill.: Irwin and The Dorsey Press, 1972. Chapter 8 discusses communication processes in the organization. The section entitled, "Appendix: Notes on Communication Dysfunctions" (pp. 157–64) is valuable reading material.

3

NONVERBAL MESSAGES IN SMALL-GROUP COMMUNICATION

PREVIEW

✳ **Why is an understanding of nonverbal messages crucial to the success of small-group interaction?**

An understanding of nonverbal messages is crucial to the success of small-group communication because such messages communicate our desires, intentions, attitudes, orientations, roles, responses, and feelings.

✳ **What are the various kinds of nonverbal messages that affect interaction in the group?**

The various kinds of nonverbal messages affecting interaction in the group may be listed under six categories: environment, proxemics, chronemics, paralanguage, facial expressions, and kinesics.

✳ **What functions do nonverbal messages perform in small-group interaction?**

Nonverbal messages perform eight functions in small-group interaction: to repeat, contradict, substitute for, complement, or accent verbal messages; to regulate the flow of communication and interaction; to identify interpersonal relationships; or to indicate status relationships.

✳ **How do nonverbal messages influence interaction and communication in the small-group process?**

Nonverbal messages influence the behaviors of group members in several ways. A few of the possible effects are:

Environment (material components such as the shape and size of the room, lighting, furniture, color of the walls) affect group members' attitudes, performance, and interactions.

Proxemics (spatial distance among group members, seating arrangements, encroachment or invasion of personal space) exert considerable influence on patterns of communication and interaction in the group.

Chronemics (time) can indicate status and importance.

Paralanguage (how something is said) provides clues about a speaker's intention or emotion.

Facial expression (especially eye contact) can enhance or inhibit effective group interaction.

Kinesics (body movements) tell how people are dealing with their feelings and how much cohesion there is in a group.

SPOKEN words—verbal messages—constitute only a minor portion of the messages that trigger communication in the small group. The major portion is derived from what we are sometimes unaware of—nonverbal messages.

Nonverbal messages are communication triggers that spring from our behavior in the presence of others. They are present even when we behave unintentionally.

Every glance, twitch of an eyebrow, nod of the head, or movement of the hand is a nonverbal message that can be interpreted by others.

Since we are always behaving, either consciously or unconsciously, we cannot keep from communicating as long as we are under the scrutiny of others. Inert Edgar, seated impassively at the discussion table while everyone else is jabbering is "communicating" as much as motor-mouth Morton, who volunteers an opinion on every issue. Both are a bother to the group because we attach meaning to their behavior.

Researchers have found that we obtain approximately 35 percent of meaning from the verbal messages that we read or hear, whereas approximately 65 percent is triggered by nonverbal messages. In short, we communicate the most not by what we say, but by what we do while speaking. Nonverbal messages communicate our desires, intentions, attitudes, orientations, roles, responses, and feelings. As participants in group activities, we cannot afford to misread, misunderstand, or misperceive these vital signs.

Because an understanding of nonverbal messages is crucial to the success of small-group interaction, we need to identify the various categories of nonverbal messages, understand their different functions in the small-group communication process, and assess their effects on the group.

CATEGORIES OF NONVERBAL MESSAGES

How can we detect true messages in small-group communication? For example, how can we know when a person is interested in discussing a particular issue? How can we tell when a group member is angry or scared—in spite of the person's words to the contrary?

In order to learn what people are really saying, we must do more than listen to their words. We must read the nonverbal language cues that individuals intentionally or unintentionally display. There are times when people cannot find words to express an emotion or when they try to hide their feelings. Recall, for example, the frustration of being unable to tell someone exactly how angry you were; maybe you simply sighed, shrugged your shoulders, and walked away. Or recall being in a social group for the first time and trying not to show how awkward you felt. How successful were you? What signs betrayed your real feelings?

Whenever you need to know how a person really feels, concentrate on the face and the shifts and postures of the body. Faces in particular are good indices of emotional states because they emit expressions that are relatively standard in any given culture. There are certain conventional ways of looking scared, or appearing to be really interested, or showing awkardness. Some psychologists (for example, Tomkins and McCarter, 1964) suggest that certain telltale signs reliably reveal internal emotional states or responses.

The various kinds of nonverbal messages affecting interaction in the group come under six categories: environment, proxemics, chronemics, paralanguage, facial expressions, and kinesics.

We call these categories nonverbal messages because each has the power to affect people's moods and behavior.

1. *Environment.* Environment refers to the physical setting in which communication occurs. It includes room color and lighting, general attractiveness of the surroundings, temperature, and the like.
2. *Proxemics.* Proxemics are related to environment, but refer specifically to the placement or position of group members in relation to one another. Proxemics deal with physical distance and seating arrangements.
3. *Chronemics.* Chronemics refer to the impact of clocks and calendars on people. In the American society time is viewed as an object that can be packaged, saved, or wasted. It is an extremely important nonverbal variable in organizations. We punch time clocks, schedule meetings, argue over 30- to 40-hour workweeks, set due dates, and have specific pay periods. We take coffee breaks and eat lunch at preset times. We interpret people's proficiency by their ability to complete a job within a specified time. Some people infer the attitudes of group members by whether they are prompt or tardy.
4. *Paralanguage.* Paralanguage concerns the *way* in which something is said rather than *what* is said. G. L. Trager (1958) divides paralanguage into two parts: vocal qualities (for example, range, pitch, rhythm, rate, and resonance), and vocalizations (for example, laughing, crying, sighing, vocalized pauses, and silent pauses).

5. *Facial Expressions.* Facial expressions include movement of the facial features, especially the eyes.
6. *Kinesics.* Kinesics are body movements that include postures, gestures, and movement of the head and limbs. P. Ekman and W. Friesen (1969) recognize five types of kinesic expressions: emblems, illustrators, regulators, affect displays, and adaptors. *Emblems* are gestures that are equivalent to verbal messages because their meaning is recognized by the individuals involved. For example, the quick movement of one's index finger against one's throat may signify to some people that it's time to quit working. *Illustrators* complement and reinforce verbal messages. We illustrate when we flag a cab with our arms while yelling "Taxi!" *Regulators* control oral interaction by providing the communicator with instructions. Backing away slowly while someone is speaking to us, or looking at our watch frequently while in a meeting may constitute regulating. *Affect displays* are unconscious, emotional responses that generally appear on the face, such as blushing, perspiring, frowning, or glaring. *Adaptors* are learned actions that have an instrumental purpose. Senders are often not aware that they are performing an action, but alert observers can get valuable clues from it. For example, the nervous wiggling of the feet may be a sign of boredom or disinterest.

FUNCTIONS OF NONVERBAL MESSAGES

Each of the six types of nonverbal messages operates simultaneously with verbal messages. A person says something and gives nonverbal cues that indicate what the person really means. Nonverbal messages serve eight functions. J. Baird and S. Weinberg (1977) label them *repeating, contradicting, substituting, complementing, accenting,* and *regulating.* J. Wofford, E. Gerloff, and R. Cummins (1977) add another, which they label *identifying,* and we add still another, *indicating.*

These eight functions operate in all small-group communication. As effective group communicators, we should become familiar with them in various situations. If we develop an awareness of how people use and react to them, we will gain insights into the relationships between group members.

Repeating

Nonverbal messages play a major role in restating or repeating the content of our verbal messages. Whenever we have to direct someone to a particular place or object, we not only give directions verbally, but we also *point* the way. When we say, "Please pick up the box in the corner by that cabinet," we have the urge to motion either with our hand or our head. This repeating is helpful in that it restates the message and makes it doubly clear.

Contradicting

Nonverbal messages that contradict verbal messages help us to zero in on what's really happening among group members. Since the nonverbal message is much more difficult to control, it is probably closer to a person's real feeling. Senders are often unaware that they are sending contradictory messages. The contradiction of nonverbal and verbal messages constitutes what we call game-playing, in which one person deliberately but unsuccessfully attempts to "con" someone else.

Substituting

Any gesture, emblem, or sign that takes the place of a verbal utterance or expression is a substitute. A circle made by the thumb and the index finger is a substitute for "Everything is all right." Shrugging our shoulders, opening our hands, and raising our eyebrows acts as a substitute for "I don't know what the hell this guy is talking about, do you?"

Complementing

Some nonverbal messages complement or elaborate on verbal statements. "Please bring me a piece of string about *this* long," is usually attended by a length-indicating gesture using the palms of both hands. When the verbal message is an emotional statement, such as "I like you very much" or "The smell of this varnish really upsets me," it is usually accompanied by facial expressions, posture, and gestures that indicate the magnitude of the emotion or feelings.

Accenting

Some nonverbal messages accent the verbal message. "Listen, if you come back before this group one more time and insinuate that I am a liar, I'm gonna take you outside and kick your butt from now 'til Sunday." Is the speaker kidding? Tone of expression and gestures can accentuate seriousness. The deliberate pointing of an index finger; the slow, soft manner of speaking are some telltale signs of earnestness.

* * *

Exercise 3-1

OBSERVING ANOTHER PERSON'S BEHAVIOR

You and a classmate are each to conduct five short interviews with students on campus. On one interview you will be the interviewer and your classmate will be the observer; on the next interview you will switch roles.

As the interviewer, you approach a fellow student and say that you are part of a survey team and would like to ask four or five questions pertaining to value profiles on the college campus. Then you ask each of the five following questions. Be sure to ask "Why?" or "Why not?" after each "Yes" or "No" response.

1. Have you ever cheated while taking an examination for a class? Why? Why not?

2. Do you consider yourself to be an attractive person? Why? Why not?

3. Do you consider yourself to be a polished, refined, cultured person? Why? Why not?

4. One of the Ten Commandments says "Thou shalt not steal." Do you steal? Why? Why not?

5. If some of your acquaintances were asked to describe you, would they characterize you as bright, so-so, or not very bright? Why? Why not?

As the observer, you pretend to record the answers, but actually record the nonverbal behavior of the person being interviewed.

1. Does the interviewee look directly at the interviewer?

2. Are the person's eye movements erratic? Does the person maintain eye contact?

3. Are there nonverbal cues that contradict what the interviewee is saying? Describe them.

4. Are there traces of nervousness, discomfort, and the like? Describe them.

5. Do you get the impression that the person is lying? What convinces you?

Regulating

Some nonverbal messages control or direct the flow of communication in the group. Have you ever participated in a group discussion that proceeded in an orderly way even though the leader appeared to exercise minimal control? Only one individual spoke at a time; others anticipated a speaker's concluding statement and began speaking as if on cue. Actually, all this was probably being orchestrated through the leader's eyebrow motions, shifts of posture, eye contact, hand movements, and head nodding. Even motor-mouth Morton can be controlled by denying him the customary eye contact for a prolonged period and withholding feedback. To encourage a group member to continue speaking—particularly someone presenting information that facilitates goal achievement—we can give a few quick nods. To give someone a chance to interject a point, we can gesture with an open hand and raise our eyebrows quickly, directing the group's attention toward that person. We can also use hand movements to slow down a speeding speaker or hasten along a rambling one. The fact that group members respond appropriately to these signals gives ample evidence that many nonverbal message cues are culturally shared and understood.

Identifying

Nonverbal messages may help us to detect interpersonal conflicts between group members. Who talks to whom, who interrupts whom, who listens to whom, and the frequency of eye contact are easily detected clues. These uncomplicated nonverbal messages are likely to identify members' interpersonal relationships. Awareness of such clues is invaluable in promoting cooperation among group members.

Indicating

Leaders who want to influence compliant behavior from others may use nonverbal communication to underscore their status. The size of one's office, having a personal secretary, the seating arrangement at a meeting (the high-status person generally sits at the end of the table), requiring subordinates to come to one's office for discussions, interrupting another person's activities, having the last word in a conversation, and monopolizing the conversation are some nonverbal indicators of status or power. They are saying, "I am more important or more powerful than you—pay me the proper respect." Often people do accept nonverbal displays of status, although they may resist more obvious control. The manager who wants to facilitate open communication, however, should eliminate displays of status.

EFFECTS OF NONVERBAL MESSAGES

Relatively few of the many aspects of nonverbal messages that determine group behavior have been examined systematically in small groups. We will restrict our consideration to those aspects that have been studied extensively enough to permit relatively safe conclusions about their effects on the small group. These include the six types of verbal messages identified at the beginning of this chapter: environment proxemics, chronemics, paralanguage, facial expressions, and kinesics.

Environment

Among the aspects of environment that influence the small group, the material components appear to be the most significant: shape and size of the room, lighting, furniture, color of

the walls, and so on. For example, it has been shown that people work more efficiently when lighting is evenly distributed. In one work situation, researchers observed that when the walls were painted cool blue, group members complained of being cold although the temperature was set at 70 degrees; when the thermostat was raised to 75 degrees, they still complained of being cold. When the wall color was changed to "warm yellow and restful green," the group members complained of being too warm at a 75-degree room temperature (Seghers, 1948).

In addition to color and lighting, the general appearance of the area in which a group works influences its members. Researchers found that people reported more fatigue, monotony, headaches, discontent, hostility, irritation, and room avoidance in "ugly" rooms than in "nice" rooms (Mintz, 1956). J. Baird and S. Weinberg (1977, p. 44) argue that "the feelings aroused in us in our surroundings may be transferred to the people who are present. If the room makes us feel good, we tend to respond well to other people; if the room makes us feel uncomfortable, we find it more difficult to interact well with others. . . . Finding a room which is attractive to all group members seems to be another measure that will contribute to group cohesiveness."

Proxemics

The distance among group members and the seating arrangement have a considerable influence on group communication.

SOCIAL DISTANCE. Speaking and listening are facilitated when group members feel that they are separated from one another by comfortable distances. The amount of distance each individual needs to communicate comfortably is dictated largely by personality. Extroverts are more comfortable in close quarters than are introverts (Williams, 1963).

We sometimes use social distance to communicate feelings. Increasing the distance between ourselves and others in a group may communicate dislike, detachment, avoidance, rejection, fear, contempt, or anger. Decreasing the distance communicates a willingness to be drawn into fellowship, a liking for those around us, or feelings of security.

Edward T. Hall (1959) suggests that distance between communicators is sometimes dictated by the kinds of messages being exchanged. We would violate social protocol if we stood 50 feet away from another person and blurted out confidential information. Similarly, exchanging neutral or nonpersonal information does not warrant standing too close.

In addition, the degree of familiarity between the communicators in a group affects social distance. We tend to maintain greater distance between ourselves and people we don't know. Conversely, the more established the friendship, the greater is the tolerance for proximity and physical contact (Mortenson, 1972, p. 233).

INVASION OF PERSONAL SPACE.   Encroachment or invasion of one's personal space or territory generally evokes defensiveness, and even aggression in certain situations. The manner of aggression depends on the person whose space is being invaded and the manner of the intrusion. Robert Sommer (1969, p. 35) reports some research that was conducted by N. Russo (1967):

> There were wide individual differences in the ways victims reacted— there is no single reaction to someone's sitting too close; there are defensive gestures, shifts in posture, and attempts to move away. If these fail or are ignored by the invader, or if he shifts position too, the victim eventually takes flight. . . . There was a dearth of direct verbal response to the invasions. . . . Only one of the eighty students asked the invader to move over.

Defensive gestures include turning one's head away from the invader, using an elbow as a barrier, placing books or other personal objects in the invader's path, ignoring the invader, leaving the area, and even uttering obscenities.

In small groups, invasion of personal space is sometimes caused by crowding. Crowding forces us to limit our customary territorial behavior. There is evidence that crowding affects interpersonal orientations in the group. One study (reported by Knapp, 1972) assessed the reactions of men and women to crowded conditions in a mock jury trial. Men liked other members less, considered them less friendly, gave more sentences to defendants, and thought other members in the crowded room would make poor jury members. They found the experience unpleasant and became more suspicious and antagonistic. Women, however, were more lenient in the sentences handed down and considered others to be more friendly and likable.

SEATING ARRANGEMENT.   Where do individuals prefer to sit? Why do they have seating preferences? Seating arrangements in the small group determine who will be drawn into communication and interaction patterns, the amount of interaction that occurs, and the emergence of leadership.

As early as 1961, Robert Sommer conducted research to find out where people tend to sit in discussion groups. He found that individuals prefer to sit across from each other (obliquely opposite) rather than side by side, unless the distance across is too great for comfortable conversation. One possible explanation for this preference turned up in a study of eye contact conducted by M. Argyle and J. Dean (1965): Individuals sitting side by side found themselves too close to study one another as much as they wanted to. The closer people sat to each other, the less eye contact there was. Argyle and Dean also found when eye contact increased among people sitting close to each other, tension also increased.

A. Hare and R. Bales (1963) found that (1) seating position influences the amount a person interacts and (2) people who are inclined to dominate discussion tend to choose central seats (Figure 3.1). Individuals who sat in these positions also tended to receive more communication from other group members. These so called high-talking seats are identified with status, because members of the group are likely to perceive as leaders those individuals who talk most.

Because leaders are usually those who direct interaction and make decisions, it is understandable that they would choose the most advantageous position from which to use eye contact for signaling, gaining feedback, exhibiting dominance or authority, and challenging the positions or arguments advanced in the group. B. Steinzor (1950) points out that if a person happens to be in a spatial position which increases the chances of his being more completely observed, the stimulus value of his ideas and statements increases by virtue of his greater physical and impressive impact on others.

FIGURE 3-1. At a rectangular table, the central seats are generally the end seats and those in the middle on the sides—the darker shaded seats in the diagram.

The very centrality of the high-talking seats tends to discourage from sitting there those who suffer a high level of anxiety. Anxious individuals avoid these seats because they do not relish the increase in eye contact that accompanies such positions.

These findings furnish vital information that could make us more effective in groups. Many stressful encounters could be avoided through proper seating arrangements. Two people who tend to monopolize a discussion might be less inclined to do so if they sat next to each other. If the group requires a high level of interaction and participation, it might be advantageous to have an expressive individual sit opposite a quiet person in order to encourage the quiet person to speak more. Those who feel uncomfortable under the gaze of others could be seated in less central positions.

Chronemics

In our society we are conscious of time, and we regulate our lives by it. The alarm clock or the clock radio wakes us up; on our way to work or school we check our watches frequently or listen to the car radio. We punch time cards when we get to work. During the day, we listen for class bells or buzzers, and so on.

Edward T. Hall (1959) has broken use of time into three categories: informal, formal, and technical. In informal use time is expressed in general terms, such as *a while* or *later*. Formal time is measured with a calendar or a clock. A supervisor may tell an employee to do a job at a particular time, and it is done at that time. Technical time is precise and is measured exactly. For example, a solar year is 365 days, 5 hours, 48 minutes, and 45.51 seconds.

Our punctuality shows whether we are using informal or formal time. Technical time is used mainly in the physical sciences, and rarely influences daily communication. Our experiences and personalities influence our punctuality. Some people are compulsive and anxious; others are oblivious of time. Halpin (1966) notes that most organizations develop informal tolerance ranges for lateness; to keep a person waiting beyond the tolerance limit is a subtle way of insulting him or her. However, the handling of promptness and lateness can vary with the culture and with the functions of the meeting.

We attach different meanings to time. For example, time is related to status. The duration of one's meeting with a superior suggests one's status within a group. The longer the meeting, the more important the subject of discussion and the higher the status of the discussants. The longer the time allowed a person to respond to a message, the higher that person's perceived status. Similarly, a person is more likely to be punctual with a boss than with peers.

The nicest compliment that members of a group may give is "You've got time for everyone." That's the goal of effective use of time as a nonverbal message in the small group process.

Paralanguage

During a particularly hectic discussion over whether to donate money from the general fund of the Student Association to a scholarship for needy students, Thaddeus Fish III delivered an impassioned argument against the proposal. When he finished, the floor was given to Casper Smirkerman, who asked that the

executive board of the S.A. pay tribute to Mr. Fish, "a man who is truly blessed with a sense of priorities, as can be witnessed from his having voted to donate $500 to the Annual Turtle Race just last week!" Fish III sprang to his feet complaining that his integrity was being impugned. When the chairman reminded him that Mr. Smirkerman had intended to pay tribute, Mr. Fish, enraged, advised the chairman: "Sir, it isn't *what* Smirkerman said; it is *how* he said it."

How something is said does give a clue about the speaker's intention or emotion. Vocal cues furnish nonverbal messages that we can use to clarify verbal messages. It makes a difference whether we say something loudly or softly, in a high-pitched voice or a low-pitched voice, fast or slow. Generally, increased loudness is a sign of mounting anger, hostility, or alarm; and increased softness may convey grief, frustration, helplessness, disappointment, or powerlessness. A high-pitched voice may indicate alarm, annoyance, anxiety, fear, threat; lowered pitch may be used to emphasize certain points. Someone who drawls, "Of course, Elsa is a nice girl," may mean just the opposite; however, increasing tempo would help eliminate the contradiction.

R. Pittenger and H. Smith (1967) suggest that when "Well," "Yep," and "Nope" are uttered in a clipped manner, the person is usually saying, "It's my turn to talk now." Furthermore, they suggest, "No" or "Nope" with a clip does not generally mean negation. For example, "No, you are damned right" indicates basic agreement, along with an opinion that the previous speaker did not carry the argument far enough.

C. D. Mortensen (1972) suggests that vocal cues expressing excitement and interest help promote the importance of what is being said, just as a confident tone of voice enhances a person's credibility among the members of the group.

It is important that we understand the manner in which others depend on our vocal cues for an understanding of our moods, personality, and feelings toward the task and fellow group members.

Facial Expressions

Emotions are displayed largely by the face and head. When we are excited or interested, our eyebrows move downward; our eyes look intent, and we assume a listening posture. We manifest enjoyment with broad smiles and smiling eyes. Surprise or startle sends the eyebrows upward, and we blink our eyes momentarily

as if attempting to focus. In distress or anguish, our eyebrows arch, our mouths turn down, and we cry. Fear or terror does remarkable things to the countenance: Eyes become fixed in a frozen stare; the face grows pale and sweaty; the body trembles; and hair bristles. Contempt or disgust brings a sneer, which tightens the upper lip and lifts it upward. When angry, we frown, clench our jaw, narrow our eyes, and our face becomes flushed or red (Tomkins and McCarter, 1964).

As C. D. Mortensen (1972, p. 222) puts it, "The face is a visible source of [emotional] leakage." He reports some research conducted by D. Huenegardt and S. Finanda (1969) in which a subject was instructed not to show any emotion while watching a film designed to arouse emotional stress. When interviewed later, the subject was certain that he had been able to conceal his feelings. However, photographs taken without his knowledge revealed several emotions; in spite of his efforts, changes in his facial expression betrayed his responses.

In group situations members position themselves to maximize eye contact. However, as group interaction progresses, eye contact may decrease in certain situations and increase in others. Members avoid eye contact when they become highly ego-involved or when they are being "crowded." Highly personal or threatening and embarrassing discussions result in more silence and less eye contact than do nonthreatening ones. Little mutual eye contact in a group that talks together frequently is a symptom of difficulties that inhibit effective group interaction; group members may not be listening to one another, which results in less eye contact and more looking away (Argyle and Kendon, 1967). When power coalitions develop in groups, members who see themselves as having more influence spend more time looking at their fellow members as they speak than do individuals who see themselves as having less influence (Weisbrod, 1967).

How does personality correlate with eye contact? R. Exline and L. Winters (1965) found that those who suffer from emotional problems or from strong guilt feelings tend to maintain or encourage very little eye contact. Researchers also tell us that people who think in abstract terms engage others in more eye contact than those who think concretely. Also, members who are dependent on others for reinforcement tend to maintain more eye contact than those who feel less need for reinforcement (Argyle and Kendon, 1967). People tend to increase eye contact when they seek approval or recognition (Efran and Broughton, 1966).

Kinesics

Researchers say that body movements hint at *responses to feelings* rather than the feelings themselves. Body movements tell us how people are dealing with their feelings at a given moment, whereas their face or head may show their feelings themselves (Ekman and Friesen, 1969). The face displays the *nature* of the emotion; the body displays the *intensity* of the emotion.

Various body movements offer cues that can be interpreted with great accuracy. But our ability to interpret them depends on our sensitivity to how we ourselves generally behave when we feel angry, elated, fearful, insecure, or some other emotion. Figure 3-2 shows nonverbal behaviors in various situations. Try to act out some of these behaviors. Can you think of others?

Body movements give vital signs that we need to recognize when we participate in or supervise group activities. For example, if pressure is being exerted on a group member, it is important that we know when to ease it. How can we tell when a particular person is feeling too much stress or tension? The person tends to fidget, shift, or change posture frequently (Dittman, 1962; Sainsbury, 1955). While the body grows restless the person's hands display a consistent movement, such as a rubbing of the palms.

P. Ekman and W. Friesen (1969) give us a few other valuable pointers. A person uncertain about an issue, decision, or event may resort to a shrug of the shoulders. A person signaling an intent to answer a direct question tends to reach out with an open hand.

Kinesics can be used to assess how well a discussion group interacts as a whole. When individuals feel knowledgeable and comfortable about a topic, their body movements tend to be fre-

Defensiveness
Arms crossed on chest
Crossing legs
Fistlike gestures
Pointing index finger
Karate chops

Suspicion
Arms crossed
Sideways glance
Touching, rubbing nose
Rubbing eyes
Buttoning coat—drawing away

Frustration
Short breaths
"Tsk" sound
Tightly clenched hands
Wringing hands
Fistlike gestures
Pointing index finger
Rubbing hand through hair
Rubbing back of neck

Nervousness
Clearing throat
"Whew" sound
Whistling
Cigaret smoking
Picking or pinching flesh
Fidgeting in chair
Hand covering mouth while speaking
Not looking at other person
Tugging at pants while seated
Jingling money in pockets
Tugging at ear
Perspiration, wringing of hands

Insecurity
Pinching flesh
Chewing pen, pencil
Thumb over thumb, rubbing
Biting fingernails
Hands in pockets

Evaluation
Hand-to-face festures
Head tilted
Stroking chin
Peering over glasses
Taking glasses off—cleaning
Glasses earpiece in mouth
Pipe smoker gestures
Putting hand to bridge of nose

Confidence
Steepled hands
Hands behind back
Back stiffened
Hands in coat pockets with thumbs out
Hands on lapels of coat

Cooperation
Upper body in sprinter's position
Open hands
Sitting on edge of chair
Hand-to-face gestures
Unbuttoning coat
Tilted head

Openness
Open hands
Unbuttoned coat

FIGURE 3-2. Attitudes communicated nonverbally. (Ricki Fulman in Rosenfeld and Civikly, 1976, p. 120)

quent, vigorous, zestful, and enthusiastic. When the topic is unfamiliar or tension-provoking, body movements tend to be more inhibited. Kinesics also show the amount of camaraderie and cohesion within a group. When group members feel friendly toward one another, they exhibit relaxed posture and increased eye contact. Members reach forward or draw closer to one another. Conversely, when there is friction among members, postures are tense, and members lean away from one another (Baxter, Winter, and Hammer, 1968; Mehrabian, 1971).

* * *

Exercise 3-2
COMMUNICATING NONVERBALLY

Sit or stand facing another person and try to communicate without words. Choose an attitude or emotion—such as defensiveness, anger, disappointment, eagerness, or nonchalance—and express it using kinesics and facial expressions. Can your partner identify the emotion? Switch roles and see how well you can interpret your partner's expressions.

This exercise can be conducted by having each student receive a sealed statement of an emotion or attitude and then act it out for the class. Each class member jots down on a sheet of paper secretly a guess as to the emotion or attitude being portrayed. The good actors are those who receive agreement from 50 percent or more of the class.

SUMMARY

We have touched on a few of the vital components of nonverbal messages in small groups. Communication involves more than transmission of words, but many communicators pay more attention to verbal components than to the nonverbal aspects. We have discussed six categories of nonverbal messages—environment, proxemics, chronemics, paralanguage, facial expressions, and kinesics—and we have described eight functions that nonverbal messages perform as they operate simultaneously with verbal messages. Nonverbal messages repeat, contradict, substitute for, complement, or accent verbal messages; regulate the flow of communication in the group, identify members' interpersonal relationships; or indicate status relationships. We have described the various effects of nonverbal messages on group behavior.

Group communicators should familiarize themselves with the various types of nonverbal behavior and develop ways of dealing with nonverbal messages to enhance effective group communication.

ADDITIONAL READINGS

Brooks, William. *Speech Communication.* Dubuque, Iowa: W. C. Brown, 1971. Chapter 6 covers the various types of nonverbal communication and offers an excellent comparison between nonverbal and verbal communication.

Knapp, Mark. *Nonverbal Communication in Human Interaction.* New York: Holt, Rinehart & Winston, 1972. Chapters 2, 4, 5, and 6 offer excellent discussions of the influence of environmental factors on human communication, the effects of physical behavior on human communication, the effects of the face and eyes on human communication, and the effects of the vocal cues which accompany verbal communication.

Mehrabian, Albert. *Silent Messages.* Belmont, Calif.: Wadsworth, 1971. Chapter 2 describes the way in which power, status, and fearlessness are communicated through nonverbal messages.

Mortensen, C. David. *Communication: The Study of Human Interaction.* New York: McGraw-Hill, 1972. Chapter 6 presents a comprehensive discussion of the components of nonverbal interaction. The chapter details many research findings which should prove very helpful.

Sommer, Robert. *Personal Space: The Behavioral Basis of Design.* Englewood Cliffs, N.J.: Prentice-Hall, 1969. This is interesting reading on the effects of physical structure of the areas in which people work and live on human response behavior.

III

COMMUNICATORS

---

* * *

CHAPTER 4
THE COMMUNICATOR

This chapter examines how the personal characteristics of group members affect communication in the group. Seven factors are considered: (1) self-concept, which refers to perceptions of our social reality; (2) credibility, which refers to evaluative perceptions we have of other group members; (3) attitudes, which are tendencies to make favorable or unfavorable evaluations about ideas, things, and behavior; (4) the impact of sex roles; (5) ethnicity, which refers to racial background; (6) personality, which may be thought of as tendencies to respond to certain classes of stimuli in particular ways; and (7) the influence of communicator intelligence upon group behavior.

CHAPTER 5
LEADERSHIP
IN SMALL GROUPS

This chapter examines characteristics of the communication of effective leaders. These characteristics interact with the characteristics and expectations of a group. The effectiveness of a leader depends largely on the personality and needs of group members; it involves a concern for both task and human relations. In this chapter we also examine leadership styles and the managerial Grid®. This Grid notes combinations and choices of leadership styles; it can be an aid in evaluating leadership within a small group. Finally, we consider the life cycle theory of leadership.

* * *

4

THE
COMMUNICATOR

* **What communicator characteristics have an impact on group processes?**

  Among the communicator characteristics that affect group processes are self-concept, credibility, attitudes, sex, ethnicity, personality, and intelligence.

* **What is self-concept?**

  Self-concept refers to our perceptions of our social identity.

* **What is credibility?**

  Credibility refers to the evaluative perceptions we have of the competence and trustworthiness of group members.

* **How do attitudes affect group processes?**

  Attitudes (the tendencies to judge concepts, persons, objects, and behaviors in a favorable or unfavorable manner) reflect a person's ego involvement, which can help or hinder group communication.

* **How does a person's sex affect group processes?**

  Sex roles influence leadership, conformity, and competitiveness within groups.

* **How does ethnicity affect group processes?**

  A person's racial background affects self-concept and credibility.

* **What aspects of personality affect group processes?**

  Six personality traits (the tendencies to respond to certain classes of stimuli in particular ways) are most relevant: authoritarianism and dogmatism, social sensitivity, ascendent tendencies, self-reliance and dependability, unconventionality, and emotional stability.

* **What role does intelligence play in group processes?**

  Intelligence, the ability to understand and solve problems, can be very important in task-related activities and in group leadership.

COMMUNICATOR characteristics are perhaps the most important dimension of group communication, for what a communicator does or is capable of doing has a great effect on how the group operates. Qualities we bring to the group affect whether we will lead or accept someone else's influence, enhance cohesiveness or foster conflicts, help solve problems or impede solutions, and so on. Because all variables within the communication system affect one another, qualities of the communicator influence other dimensions—messages, group climate, and control. In turn, communicators are affected by these dimensions.

Social scientists do not know how every communicator variable affects, and is affected by, variables of other dimensions. They do recognize that the dimensions affect one another. In this chapter we will emphasize factors that research has shown to have some impact, as well as factors that reflect the authors' biases. These factors are self-concept, credibility, attitudes, sex, ethnicity, personality, and intelligence. We hope that our examination of these characteristics will help you to understand better the role of communicator factors in affecting group processes.

SELF-CONCEPT

Self-concept is perhaps the most basic, significant, and broadly conceived communicator variable. It's the view we have of ourselves, or, more accurately, our perception of our *social identity.*

Self-concept involves the relationship we see between ourselves and other people, places, things, and ideas.

Self-concept does not develop in isolation. It develops through interaction with others and is shaped by how other people see us and behave toward us. The way we determine who we are is to observe who others perceive us to be. You couldn't determine, for example, that you are quite likable except through interacting with others and observing their responses to you.

What makes self-concept important is that *it affects the way we respond to and talk to others.* We have already observed that self-concept is shaped by how others perceive us and act toward us. Our self-concept, in turn, affects our communicative behavior toward others (Cushman and Craig, 1976). For example, when a self-confident person joins a group, that person is likely to make

an impact on the other group members. If they perceive that the confidence is well-founded—based on competence—they are likely to communicate in ways that reinforce the person's confidence. Conversely, if through past experience a person feels incompetent or indecisive, this self-concept will probably make the person's initial communicative behavior tentative and cause the other members of the group not to regard the person as a potential group leader. Such mutual influence continues throughout our lives in a constantly evolving, dynamic process.

Although social scientists agree about the significance and function of self-concept in our interactive or communicative behavior, they disagree about the exact components. We will examine some of the most important variables that can be thought of as aspects of our self-concept or that have a strong bearing on its development.

CREDIBILITY

Group members are not inherently credible—no one is.

Credibility is the evaluation we give others.

It ranges from high (positive) to low (negative). Members perceived to have high credibility strongly influence crucial aspects of a group's life.

Although credibility is a single construct, it typically operates in combination with other variables. It is affected by the purpose of a discussion, for example, or by differences among group members. (For a more complete review—than what follows—of the interaction of credibility with other variables, see Simons, 1973.)

Determinants of Credibility

We often have personal knowledge of group members that affects our responses to them within the group. Prior knowledge of group members may predispose us favorably or unfavorably toward them. As a result, we may be willing or unwilling to listen to them and may automatically accept or reject their ideas, quite apart from what they actually say.

In the absence of personal knowledge, other factors affect us— such as a member's reputation, appearance, occupation, education, wealth, ethnic background, religion, or marital status. Because of their reputation, certain people may never become leaders and certain other people may have leadership thrust upon them.

Do any characteristics invariably lead to high or low credibility? Consider these descriptions of two people. One has a bachelor's degree in applied physics from the California Institute of Technology. He comes from a family prominent in industry. He lives in a comfortable home in the wealthy suburb of San Marino. He's intelligent, fluent, and personable—and a double for Robert Redford besides. Our second member of the cast lives in the Watts district of Los Angeles. She had to quit school after the ninth grade to help support her family. She's divorced, the sole support of four young children, and on welfare. And she's black.

We might assume that the man from Cal Tech would have higher credibility than the welfare mother from Watts. But suppose these two individuals are members of a citizen committee

appointed by the mayor to investigate the effects of poverty on the quality of life of inner-city residents. Can we see why the physicist would not be a particularly credible group member, whereas the high school dropout would? Suppose our two individuals were members of a research team developing new smog-control devices. The characteristics of both communicators remain constant, but each one's credibility would be perceived differently in each situation.

What communicators actually say and do in the group interacts with their characteristics to influence our perceptions of their credibility. A beautiful woman with blond hair might have low credibility because of the stereotype of the beautiful-but-dumb blond: We expect her to be somewhat slow-witted and shallow. We expect the same of the star tackle on the football team; we assume that he only knows how to grunt and run into people. But if the blonde woman and the athlete turn out to be articulate, insightful, and dynamic members of a committee to increase student influence in creating classes, their credibility would probably rise dramatically. Their communicative behavior—expression, quality of reasoning, organization of ideas, delivery, and language—would modify our initial perceptions of credibility based on stereotypes.

Competence and Trustworthiness

When we evaluate group members' credibility, we take into account certain characteristics that combine to form basic factors. Two of these factors have been consistently identified in research: competence (or authoritativeness) and trustworthiness (or safety).

Group members are said to have *competence* if they are perceived to be knowledgeable about the discussion topic and demonstrate general ability. *Trustworthiness* is a result of our perceptions of honesty, lack of ulterior motives, sense of fair play, concern for others, and the like.

We must emphasize that, as with credibility, we perceive these qualities in people—whether or not the people actually are competent and trustworthy. Successful con artists become rich precisely because they are able to persuade their victims that they possess both high competence and trustworthiness.

Competence and trustworthiness are not necessarily equally important in affecting group behavior. The nature of the discussion and the characteristics of other group members determine the relative importance of these two factors. For example, if the discussion requires special expertise, knowledge, and skill, then competence is very important. However, there are groups in which superior competence is irrelevant or even detrimental. Such a group might be concerned primarily with establishing cohesiveness and openness in discussion, as often happens in group therapy. The members emphasize the common elements that help them identify with each other. In this case, perceptions of high trustworthiness are crucial. A member who is perceived to be superior in competence could be looked on as separate from others in the group. Competence then becomes a barrier.

Evidence suggests that perceptions of competence and trustworthiness are very important in affecting acceptance of opinions (Cohen, 1964). If we are perceived as having low credibility, we have little chance of getting our ideas accepted, even if they have merit. Perceptions of low credibility seem to inhibit the ability of objectively evaluating a statement's intrinsic merit.

✳ ✳ ✳

Exercise 4-1
DETERMINANTS OF CREDIBILITY

Form a leaderless group of five to eight classmates in order to discuss determinants of credibility.

1. What kinds of prior determinants of credibility are perceived as significant for members of the group? Why are they significant?
2. What kinds of ongoing determinants are perceived as significant? Why?
3. Compare the importance of prior versus ongoing determinants.
4. What kinds of behaviors are group members likely to exhibit toward those who exhibit these characteristics?

ATTITUDES

Attitudes play a major role in the processing and ultimate acceptance of information.

Attitudes are tendencies to evaluate a symbol, person, object, or behavior in a favorable or unfavorable manner.

These predispositions have a strong influence on our behavior, especially when we act as receivers.

The Nature of Attitudes

At its simplest, an attitude can be conceived of as a point on a continuum of response options ranging from favorable to unfavorable. For example, this might be Vera's response to the topic "The need for student input in hiring new faculty."

good ____ _X_ ____ ____ ____ ____ bad

If Tom's response looked the same, we might conclude that Vera and Tom have similar attitudes toward the topic. However, what if an attitude represents more than a point on a continuum? C. W.

Sherif, M. Sherif, and R. E. Nebergall (1965) assert that an attitude consists also of latitudes of acceptance, rejection, and noncommitment. To indicate these positions on the continuum, we can use A for acceptable positions, U for unacceptable positions, and N for noncommitment.

If we add to Vera's and Tom's attitude responses indications of latitudes, we might get a picture like this:

Vera good _A_ _X_ _U_ _U_ _U_ _U_ _U_ bad
Tom good _A_ _X_ _A_ _N_ _N_ _U_ _U_ bad

We can now see that Vera and Tom do not have similar attitudes. Although both have identical most acceptable positions (X), their latitudes differ. Vera's responses show that she rejects all positions aside from her most acceptable position and the one position more extreme than hers. Tom has a much smaller latitude of rejection and larger latitudes of acceptance and noncommitment.

Ego Involvement

A large latitude of rejection and relatively small latitudes of acceptance and noncommitment (such as Vera has) indicate high ego involvement in a position. For a person who has low ego involvement (like Tom), few positions on the continuum are unacceptable, while most are either acceptable or noncommittal.

Most people are highly involved with personal matters. For many college students, these might be career choice, a particular class, marijuana, the next football game, their car, and the opposite sex.

What kinds of behaviors are likely when a group task concerns topics of high ego involvement to the members? Numerous studies have shown that highly involved people tend to retain their most acceptable stands, even when exposed to messages espousing a contrary position. Low-involved individuals, on the other hand, tend to change their most acceptable position more readily to conform to positions advocated in a counterattitudinal or belief-discrepant message (Sherif, Sherif, and Nebergall, 1965).

Members highly involved in their positions are not likely to work harmoniously with members espousing contrary views. In a study of conflict resolution, for example, pairs of highly involved and low-involved individuals espousing opposing stands on an issue were given the task of negotiating an agreement (Sereno and Mortensen, 1969). Opposing, highly involved individuals tended not to reach consensus, whereas opposing, low-involved individuals readily did. Because they were not involved in the issue and consequently didn't care one way or the other, low-involved individuals tended to give in and to modify their stands, facilitating agreement.

Because highly involved people tend to have a latitude of rejection that takes up most of the continuum, it is very difficult to get them to accept any position other than the one they hold. A position that departs appreciably from their most acceptable position is likely to fall in their latitude of rejection. However, if we take a stand that's at the boundary of their latitude of rejection and make it clear that we're not asking them to abandon their most acceptable position but only to listen to what we say and to suspend judgment for a while, highly involved people may change a rejection position to one of noncommitment. With continuing efforts, we may change the noncommitment position to an acceptable one. Once their latitude of acceptance increases, it becomes more possible to change their most acceptable position. In short, when communicating with group members who are highly involved in their positions, we must take stands that don't differ widely from theirs and gradually nudge them over to our point of view (Sereno and Bodaken, 1975).

* * *

Exercise 4-2
EGO INVOLVEMENT

Form a leaderless group of five to eight classmates in order to discuss ego involvement.

1. List the topics about which members are highly involved— topics that are especially meaningful, significant, and relevant to them.
2. Probe the reasons for their involvement in these topics. Analyze the nature of and motivation for their involvement in these topics.
3. Discuss the impact that high involvement in these topics might have on various dimensions of group communication such as cohesiveness, attraction, conflict, acceptance of differing opinions, and resistance to group conformity pressures.

SEX

Culture determines the roles considered appropriate for each sex, and these different roles often emphasize different behaviors for men and women. Although there has been a strong movement in our society toward equality between women and men, research indicates that small-group interaction is usually characterized by a lack of equality. Perhaps the most obvious example of this lack of equality is group leadership. Men traditionally have easier access to positions of leadership in a group. It has been suggested that men may be more influential because of their assertive–aggressive tendencies; they tend to be more active in groups. They initiate more verbal acts, make more suggestions, and defend their ideas more tenaciously (Baird, 1976). In addition, men differ from women in interrupting behavior. Interruption often functions as an indication of dominance, and research indicates that men interrupt more than women (Zimmerman and West, 1975). These differences in communication behaviors increase the likelihood that men, rather than women, will emerge as leaders in a group.

The degree to which people conform to norms also seems to be affected by sex-role training. Women tend to conform more to group norms than do men (Baird, 1976). Men tend to conform if they can accomplish the group task more quickly by doing so (Tuddenham, MacBride, and Zahn, 1958).

Our cultural sex-role training affects other communication behaviors. For example, it is more acceptable for a man to engage in conflict behaviors than for a woman to do so (Bernard, 1973). Men are also more likely to exhibit competitive rather than cooperative behavior. Because women are taught to cooperate, they are more likely than men to adopt systems and methods through which everyone in the group will benefit (Uesugi and Vinacke, 1963). Women are also usually more concerned with establishing harmonious interpersonal relationships, whereas men are more involved with task requirements (Berg and Bass, 1961). Women are taught to relieve tension, to comply with others' desires, to be agreeable, to concur with others (Bernard, 1973). These behaviors contribute to the group's social-emotional dimension. In contrast, men are taught to be independent, assertive, and inquisitive— qualities that facilitate ascendance to leadership.

Although some of the behaviors women are taught to exhibit have a positive effect on the group, it would be healthier if both men and women were taught to be sensitive to others, to develop and reveal their competence, and to respect the competence of others, regardless of sex. These differences in communication behaviors will probably lessen in time. Because these sex-role behaviors are learned rather than innate, they can be changed. The increasing impact of the women's movement on our culture will likely be beneficial.

ETHNICITY

Group members may have ethnic stereotypes that help or hinder an individual's potential for acceptance and leadership within the group. Race can affect perceptions of credibility because people tend to think of races in stereotypes. Although these stereotypes may be positive, those concerning minority and ethnic groups tend to be negative. Perceptions of competence, intelligence, honesty, trustworthiness, and even ambition are closely linked with race.

In addition, race is intimately connected to the development of self-concept. Many members of ethnic minorities have directly or indirectly experienced prejudice. Such experiences affect their self-concepts and subsequently their concepts of how they should act with people outside their ethnic group. They may be open or withdrawn, aggressive or submissive, hostile or friendly, competitive or cooperative, trusting or wary, and so on. Members of various races may use different communication rules in small-group interaction. Many Asian Americans, for example, are socialized to be less assertive in their communication than members of other ethnic groups. Since assertiveness in communication is one factor positively correlated with leadership, this communicative behavior limits the potential of such individuals for becoming leaders.

PERSONALITY

The study of personality has long fascinated social scientists.

Current thinking views *personality* in terms of individual dispositions or tendencies to respond to given classes of stimuli in particular ways.

Although they have a certain stability, these tendencies should not be considered rigid. Rather, personality should be viewed as dynamic in that we are constantly monitoring and adapting to our environment. This view of personality reflects a distinct change from earlier conceptions that treated personality as pre-dispositions to behave in consistent and fixed ways in many different situations (Swensen, 1973).

We can consider personality as individual needs. From this perspective, we can think of ourselves as having to be authoritarian, ascendant, self-reliant, and so forth. When these needs are somewhat stable tendencies or dispositions, they are called *traits.*

An extremely large number of personality traits have been identified. Theorists and researchers give varied names to similar ones and similar names to different ones. Of the multitude of characteristics, six broad categories can be identified: authoritarianism and dogmatism, social sensitivity, ascendant tendencies, self-reliance and dependability, unconventionality, and emotional stability.

Before we analyze the six categories of personality traits, a few words of caution are in order. First, personality attributes are not typified by their presence or absence; they exist on a continuum. All people exhibit them to greater or lesser degrees. Second, although an analysis of personality traits is helpful in gaining insights into why individuals in groups behave as they do, most social behavior is influenced by other factors in addition to a particular trait. Behavior is affected by both personality and situational factors (Gergen, 1974).

Authoritarianism and Dogmatism

Authoritarian or dogmatic people believe that there should be status and power differences between people. As group leaders, they are likely to be firm, demanding, and directive. They are not likely to accept others' ideas, particularly when such ideas go against group norms, because they believe that norms and roles should be strictly adhered to (Shaw, 1976). Therefore, although authoritarians may exhibit strength when they are in positions of leadership, they will also exhibit what may be called weak behavior, such as lack of independence.

When in subordinate group positions, authoritarian group members tend to be submissive and compliant. They tend to agree with the group leader, although the leader may espouse a position they don't favor. As group members, they accept their submissive behavior as natural and appropriate (Adorno et al., 1950). One of the interesting characteristics of authoritarians is that they have trouble distinguishing between who the leader is and what the leader says (Rokeach, 1960).

High authoritarians tend to accept the leader's ideas not because of their intrinsic merit but because of the belief that leaders should be followed. Nonauthoritarians, on the other hand, reject both the superior and subordinate role. They are not likely to accept the ideas of a leader without examining them critically. They are able to distinguish between what people say and who they are.

Social Sensitivity

This trait is exhibited by insight into others' feelings. Group members who have this capacity have what is called the ability to empathize. This trait seems to be moderately related to leadership success (Bell and Hall, 1954), acceptance by the group (Cattell and Stice, 1960), amount of participation (Bass et al., 1953), and group effectiveness (Greer, 1955). Persons with low sensitivity to others tend to lack the requisites for social-emotional leadership within a group. Insensitivity to the feelings of others may contribute to their lack of acceptance by members of the group. This, in turn, diminishes their potential for participation because other group members may try to limit the extent of their contributions. This ultimately will affect their potential for increasing group productivity and efficiency.

Ascendant Tendencies

Group members high in this characteristic wish to assert themselves and exert dominance over others. They tend to emerge as leaders and influence group decisions (Borg, 1960). Dominance also exhibits itself by harmful social behavior. Ascendant personalities tend to make remarks that build themselves up at the expense of others (Cattell and Stice, 1960). They also tend to exhibit rigid behavior (Borg, 1960), which seems to work against success in dealing with others, especially in terms of engendering social support. These contradictory effects show up in the inconsistent results produced by research of this personality characteristic.

AUTHORITARIAN / SOCIAL SENSITIVITY / ASCENDANT / SELF-RELIANT / UNCONVEN-TIONAL / EMOTIONAL STABILITY

Self-Reliance and Dependability

These group members demonstrate a sense of responsibility. They manifest such characteristics as integrity, self-esteem, self-reliance, and self-control. Not surprisingly, they are likely to emerge as leaders and to be successful in helping the group accomplish its task (Stogdill, 1948; Haythorn, 1953). Can we see why the member high on this trait also is likely to be more attractive to others, more popular, more active, and so forth?

Persons with low self-esteem tend to be highly susceptible to influence attempts by others (Hovland and Janis, 1959). This is especially true when the communicator attempting the influence has higher self-esteem. Members with low self-esteem are especially susceptible to appeals employing threat. And as might be expected, high self-esteem is associated with resistance to influence attempts by others and resistance to threatening appeals.

Unconventionality

This trait is exhibited by a lack of behavioral stability and control. Unconventional group members do not behave in expected ways. They seem disinterested in the group's task. Lowered group productivity usually results, primarily because this behavior tends to irritate the group and distract it from its task (Haythorn, 1953). Needless to say, such persons rarely emerge as group leaders.

Emotional Stability

This trait has been studied more than any other. All behaviors associated with emotional or mental well-being are included here.

ANXIETY. The most extensively studied index of emotional stability is *anxiety*, a general worry about some uncertain event. Anxious people feel a vague unease, a nagging worry, but they usually cannot point to a specific cause for it. As group members,

* * *

Exercise 4-3
PERSONALITY ATTRIBUTES

Form a small leaderless group of five to eight classmates. Of the six broad classes of personality attributes—authoritarianism and dogmatism, social sensitivity, ascendant tendencies, self-reliance and dependability, unconventionality, and emotional stability—discuss those that seem most relevant to *task* and *social-emotional* behaviors within the group.

1. What personality traits seem necessary for getting a job done?

2. What aspects of task accomplishment are likely to be positively affected by these characteristics? Why?

3. What personality attributes are likely to hurt task fulfillment? Why?

4. What personality factors seem vital for the maintenance of a cooperative, comfortable, and relaxed atmosphere within the group? Why?

5. What personality variables are likely to disrupt a cooperative, comfortable, and relaxed atmosphere among group members? Why?

6. To what extent do specific attributes improve *both* task and social-emotional aspects of group life?

7. To what extent do particular attributes help one aspect while hurting the other?

8. What means might be taken to handle disruptive personalities?

anxious people are unusually dependent on the group; yet they expect less of the group. Research indicates that anxious members exhibit no behaviors having a positive effect on the group (Shaw, 1976).

In addition to general anxiety, group members may have *oral communication apprehension,* a fear associated with either real or anticipated communication with another person or persons. People with high communication apprehension avoid talking with others in order to avoid the anxiety they associate with such communication. Communication apprehension is broken down into two types. *Trait apprehension* is characterized by fear of different types of oral communication activities, from talking to a single person or within a small group to giving a speech before a large crowd. *State apprehension* is specific to a given oral communicative situation, such as giving a speech to a group of strangers or interviewing an important person. Although most people experience state apprehension, trait apprehension is not characteristic of most well-adjusted persons (McCroskey, 1977).

ADJUSTMENT. This personality characteristic refers to the degree to which individuals relate in an adequate way to their environment, including people. They appear to have emotional control and emotional stability. Adjustment may be related to group effectiveness, development of cohesiveness, high morale, and group motivation (Shaw, 1976).

INTELLIGENCE

Attitudes and personality characteristics may determine what people are predisposed to do; intelligence may determine what group members are capable of doing. Regardless of their attitudes, unintelligent group members cannot analyze and comprehend a difficult, abstract problem.

Intelligence is a capacity to deal with a variety of situations and problems. It shows itself through an ability to analyze and solve problems, see relationships, evaluate critically, reach sound conclusions, and so on. The highly intelligent individual tends to participate more and to be more active in the group (Bass et al., 1953). Not surprisingly, leaders tend to be more intelligent than the average group member (Stogdill, 1948). Studies also indicate that intelligence is associated with group popularity, although the correlation is very low (Mann, 1959).

Intelligence appears to be negatively correlated with conformity (Nakamura, 1958). Highly intelligent group members tend not to conform to group norms as closely as less endowed members. In addition, they seem less likely to accept influence attempts by leaders and other group members. However, group members with low intelligence may also resist attempts to influence them to change their ideas or behavior. Apparently, low intelligence makes them resistant to normal appeals using logic, evidence, and so forth.

SUMMARY

As members of small groups, we should be conscious of ways that communicator characteristics shape group processes. *Self-concept*—our perception of who we are—is perhaps the most basic, significant, and broadly conceptualized communicator characteristic influencing behavior within groups. *Credibility*—our perception of competence and trustworthiness in others—is one of the more crucial communicator variables influencing group behavior because we react one way to group members we perceive to be competent and trustworthy, and another way to group members we perceive differently. *Attitudes* that we bring to a group determine to a great extent the group's potential for conflict as well as for productivity. Cultural influences bear most strongly on the *sex* variable: Different cultures expect different roles of men and women. *Ethnicity* may have an effect on credibility and has a strong relationship to self-concept. *Personality* characteristics affect the amount of participation, conformity and competition, leadership, and group productivity. Finally, *intelligence* plays an especially dominant role in task-related activities and in group leadership.

These communicator characteristics are not the only ones that influence small-group processes. Our selection here was guided mostly by the availability of research. Also, we discussed characteristics in their extreme forms, although all communicators exhibit these characteristics to a greater or lesser extent. Furthermore, these characteristics mesh constantly with changes in message, situational context, and interaction variables.

ADDITIONAL READINGS

Mortensen, C. David. *Communication: The Study of Human Interaction.* New York: McGraw-Hill, 1972. Chapter 4, "Psychological Orientation," discusses fundamental psychological processes operating within communicators. The chapter includes an examination of the nature and role of credibility and ego involvement in communication.

Shaw, Marvin E. *Group Dynamics: The Psychology of Small Group Behavior.* 2d ed. New York: McGraw-Hill, 1976. Chapter 6, "The Personal Environment of Groups," surveys the experimental literature on characteristics people bring with them to a group and the influence these exert upon group process.

5

LEADERSHIP
IN SMALL
GROUPS

* **What is leadership?**

  Leadership is the process of influencing the activities of individuals in a group toward goal achievement in a given situation. The leadership process is a function of three variables: leader, follower, and situation.

* **What is the major determinant of our personality as group leaders?**

  Our personality as leaders is not denoted by how we think we behave in certain situations but by how the members of our group perceive our behavior.

* **What is the significance of expectations to the overall pattern of effective leadership?**

  When all group members (including the leader) perceive and accept one another's roles and behaviors, they have shared expectations — a prerequisite for success in small-group communication.

* **What is the impact of group members' personality and needs on leadership?**

  The leader's effectiveness depends largely on the group members' personality and needs.

* **What are the two major determinants of leadership style?**

  The two major determinants of leadership style are concern for people and concern for production.

* **What are the five styles of leadership?**

  The five styles of leaders that may be identified are country club leadership, impoverished leadership, middle-of-the-road leadership, team leadership, and task-centered leadership.

* **What factors should be considered when choosing a leadership style?**

  When choosing a style of leadership we should realize that each situation has unique characteristics. Some situations may call for team leadership, while other situations may call for task-centered leadership, and so on.

* **What is a style range?**

   Style range is denoted by a leader's ability to adapt to various styles. The greater the adaptability, the greater the potential to be effective in a variety of situations.

* **What is the relationship between flexibility, effectiveness, and appropriateness of leadership style?**

   Flexibility alone does not guarantee effectiveness. Leadership behavior appropriate to a given situation is called effective; leadership behavior inappropriate to a given situation is called ineffective.

* **What is the usefulness of the life cycle theory of leadership in describing how leaders should adapt to various situations and groups?**

   Life cycle theory proposes that as the level of motivation or maturity increases among group members, the leader's behavior should become less production-oriented and more people-oriented.

SUCCESSFUL groups (that is, groups in which tasks are accomplished efficiently, and in which people interrelate harmoniously) are often distinguished from unsuccessful groups by dynamic, effective leadership. However, such leadership is scarce. In every enterprise—commercial, civic, religious, political, or educational—there is an endless search for individuals who have the ability to lead effectively. In this chapter, we will discuss the various factors that contribute to the "ability" to lead.

WHAT IS LEADERSHIP?

From 1900 to 1956, research on group leadership was confined largely to the search for so-called leadership traits. Certain characteristics, such as intelligence and assertiveness, were believed absolutely essential for effective leadership. Those who held to the so-called *trait approach* did not place much value on leadership training; they contended that individuals who were not born leaders would not profit from it and that those who were born to lead did not need training.

Findings were neither consistent nor conclusive. After reviewing the research, E. Jennings (1961, p. 2) concluded that "fifty years of study have failed to produce one personality trait or set of qualities that can be used to distinguish leaders from nonleaders." What the search did find, however, was that leadership is a dynamic process, varying with changes in leaders, followers, and situations. This finding resulted in a *situational approach* to leadership study. This approach emphasizes the observed behavior—not inborn abilities or potential—of those who are required to lead and of their group members, as well as the situations and conditions under which they must work together. A convenient way to define a leader would then be:

A *leader* is a person who performs or demonstrates leadership behaviors (that is, behaviors that have been labeled "leadership behaviors").

What constitutes leadership behaviors depends on the perception of the person categorizing the behaviors.

H. Koontz and C. O'Donnell (1972, p. 557) state that leadership is "the art of inducing subordinates to accomplish their assignments with zeal and confidence." R. Tannenbaum, I. Weschler, and F. Massarik (1959, p. 24) define leadership as "interpersonal influence exercised in a situation, and directed, through the communication process, toward the attainment of a specialized goal or goals." The major elements of several definitions might be combined as follows:

Leadership is the process of influencing the activities of individuals in a group toward goal achievement in a given situation. In other words, the leadership process is a function of three variables: *leader, follower,* and *situation.*

The discussion throughout this chapter is based on the situational approach. With this approach we begin to see that people can be trained to adapt their leadership styles to fit group needs in various situations. In order to explore the various principles, strategies, and techniques of small-group leadership, we will look at (1) the interaction between leader personality and group needs and expectations, (2) leader biases toward either getting the task done or making sure that the group members are happy, (3) five basic leadership styles, (4) factors in choosing an effective leadership style, and (5) the life cycle theory of leadership and how group maturity relates to leadership style.

PERSONALITY, EXPECTATIONS, AND NEEDS

What do subordinates, colleagues, and supervisors find predictable about your behavior as a leader? As we observed in Chapter 4, personality is an individual's consistent behavior patterns as perceived by others. These patterns become established as the person responds in the same manner under a variety of circumstances; they develop over time and through experience.

Our personality as leaders is not denoted by how we think we behave in certain situations but, rather, by how the members of our group perceive our behavior. There may be discrepancies between our self-perceptions and other people's perceptions of us. We like to think of ourselves as "fantastic" leaders and are generally disappointed to learn of our flaws or shortcomings. However, what we believe or feel about ourselves is not as important as how other people perceive us. If group members see a leader as a hard-nosed taskmaster, it makes little difference whether that person sees himself or herself as tolerant and humane. The group members' response will be dictated by what they see, and they will treat the leader with the coldness that hard-nosed taskmasters often provoke.

As a leader, what expectations do you have of yourself and others? What do you think you should do under various circumstances, and how do you think subordinates, colleagues, and supervisors should respond? We define *expectations* here as the perceptions of appropriate behavior and responses based on roles and circumstances within the group. When all group members (including the leader) perceive and accept one another's roles and behaviors, they have *shared expectations*—a prerequisite for success in small-group communication.

Group members are the most crucial element in the leadership process because they accept or reject leadership and determine the amount of power or influence a leader may exercise. If leaders do not fulfill their duties, such as "providing orientations, evaluations, and suggestions about the situation when these are demanded by group members, other members will assume these tasks and remove their power" (Burke, 1966, p. 237). Although a person appointed or designated a leader has probably shown leadership tendencies in the group, he or she may not be able to exert effective power or influence over the other members in certain situations. If the members do not want an individual as their leader, that person's attempts to control and guide the group toward goal achievement may be ineffective.

As we will see later when we discuss choosing a leadership style, the leader's effectiveness depends largely on the group members' personalities and needs. For example, if group members want to work independently and if the leader interferes with their work habits, the members will resist. If group members tend to be submissive and over-reliant on leadership for information or instructions and if the leader lets them figure things out for themselves, they may feel frustrated and think the leader ineffective. In both of these examples the group expectations and needs have been violated or unfulfilled.

When group and leader expectations are incompatible, the leader should adapt—temporarily—to the group's needs in order to gain members' confidence. Later the leader may be able to convince the group that other expectations would be more suitable for goal achievement.

* * *

Exercise 5-1
PERSONALITY, EXPECTATIONS, AND NEEDS

As you observe yourself in the role of leader in some situations and a group member in others, you can develop an awareness of the factors that either frustrate or facilitate effective leadership and group member satisfaction.

1. List seven group situations in which you occupied a leadership position.

   a. In which situations were you *effective*—by your estimation and/or that of others? For each situation, note some reasons why you were effective.

   b. In which situations were you *ineffective*—by your estimation and/or that of others? For each situation, note some reasons why you were ineffective.

2. List seven group situations in which you were required to follow the directives of a leader.

   a. In which situations were you *satisfied* with the leadership given? For each situation, note some reasons why you were satisfied.

   b. In which situations were you *not satisfied* with the leadership given? For each situation, note some reasons why you were *not* satisfied.

LEADERSHIP STYLES

Because leadership, by our definition, involves influencing the activities of a group toward goal achievement, a leader must be concerned about both group members *(human relations)*, and goal achievement *(production)*. Some leaders tend to focus on only one of these aspects to the neglect of the other, which leads to poor group performance. Leaders capable of blending the concerns for sound human relations and efficient production are more effective. Such blending is not as simple as it may appear, and leadership style plays an important role in a leader's success.

The People-Production Continuum

An excessively high concern for group members to the neglect of task accomplishment is manifested in what we call an ultrademocratic leadership style. Under such leadership, the group members are allowed to do whatever they want. Ultrademocratic leaders believe that there is no need to exert authority because people are generally motivated, mature, responsible, and "turned on" to work and that the sole aim of leadership is to keep everybody happy. They establish no policies or procedures; they create no controversy; and they expect to be well-liked.

Autocratic leaders, on the other hand, are excessively concerned with production. Under this type of leadership, the group is told what to do and how to do it, with little or no deviation from the leaders' orders and little or no opportunity to make decisions. Autocratic leaders believe that power belongs to them, that people are basically lazy, stupid, immature, and undependable, and that a leader must constantly enforce rules and procedures, regardless of the discomfort or unhappiness that probably results in the group.

Both extremes of leadership style are ineffective, especially when used by inexperienced leaders. Fortunately, there are useful, effective alternatives between these two extremes. R. Tannenbaum and W. Schmidt (1958) developed a continuum of leader behaviors (Figure 5-1). At the democratic end of their continuum are leadership styles consistent with a reasonable human-relations approach. The group leader permits the group to function within limits that he or she has defined, attempts to keep interpersonal relations pleasant, . . . arbitrates disputes, . . . provides encouragement, . . . gives the minority a chance to be heard, . . . stimulates self-direction, . . . and increases the interdependence among mem-

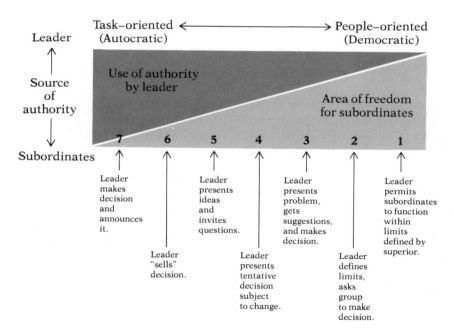

bers. The Tannenbaum-Schmidt continuum does not include the ultrademocratic style of leadership, because this type of leadership is considered a "backing away from" leadership or a non-leadership.

We can use the characteristics from both ends of the continuum as reference points against which to compare other styles. At one extreme, a leader might use a "hard sell" approach by confronting the group with a decision, ignoring members' ideas and suggestions, and pressuring the group to accept the decision as the only means of achieving a goal; at the other extreme, a leader might use a "consulting" approach by presenting the problem to the group, allowing members to suggest procedures to be followed, and considering the suggestions prior to arriving at a decision. Each behavior contributes to a different type of group climate in terms of the amount of power or authority enforced by the leader and the amount of freedom or license that group members are allowed in decision making.

Some leaders tend to be both people-oriented (democratic) and production-oriented (autocrat)—a fine balance, indeed; and some leaders, interestingly enough, try to lead without a concern for either people or production. Leadership behaviors or styles fall under several categories involving "pure" extremes and many combinations.

The Managerial Grid

R. Blake and J. Mouton (1964, 1978) have devised a managerial Grid®, which shows various combinations of leadership behavior. These behaviors can be found among leaders or managers in small groups as well as among leaders or managers in large corporations.

Blake's and Mouton's managerial Grid uses the same two orientations that the people-production continuum does. These two orientations are plotted on two separate axes as shown in Figure 5-2.

Concern for production is illustrated on the horizontal axis, and concern for people is illustrated on the vertical axis. The numbers (1–9) along each axis describe the degree of concern—from low to high—shown by leaders. For example, a leader with a rating of 9 on the horizontal axis may be described as extremely concerned about the amount of work a group should perform, whereas a rating of 9 on the vertical axis suggests a high concern for group members.

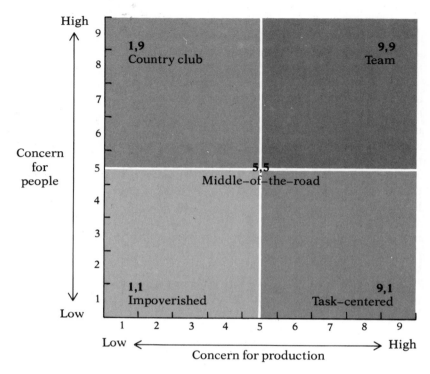

FIGURE 5-2. The managerial Grid leadership styles. (Adapted from Blake and Mouton, 1978, p. 11)

The communication behavior of leaders in groups can be visualized on the managerial Grid. A leader, for example, might describe his or her behavior in the following manner:

"When conflict develops in my group over a crucial issue, I would try to stop it by trying to convince my group members that they are wasting valuable time, that they are making a big fuss over a minor issue, and that they ought to quit fighting and get on with the task."

"When conflicts or squabbles over procedures arise in my group, I find it best to mind my own business; I simply get away from the group and keep my mouth shut until the conflict is over, no matter how long it takes."

A leader who manifests the first communication behavior would appear to have a relatively low concern for people and a relatively high concern for production. A leader who manifests the second communication behavior does not appear to care about the well-being of the group and is not concerned about getting the task done. Table 5-1 gives some more examples of possible leadership behaviors in group situations and where those behaviors might fit on the Grid.

Figure 5-2 shows five leadership styles: country club (1, 9, upper left corner), impoverished (1, 1, lower left corner), middle-of-the-road (5, 5, center), team-centered (9, 9, upper right corner), and task-centered (9, 1, lower right corner).

COUNTRY CLUB LEADERSHIP. Individuals who demonstrate high concern for people and low concern for group production or performance are classified as country club leaders. Under this kind of leadership, production is sacrificed or de-emphasized in favor of social relations, good fellowship, and fraternity. Leaders give thoughtful attention to group members' needs, and try to develop a comfortable, friendly, working organization. They assume that contented people will produce well.

Leaders who resort to the country club leadership style often use the relinquishing style or pattern of communication which we discussed in Chapter 2. They frequently submit to the desires of group members, comply with other individuals' points of view, assume a supporting role, and shift responsibility to others.

IMPOVERISHED LEADERSHIP. Impoverished leaders have little concern for both people and production. Their basic attitude is "don't rock the boat under any circumstance." Impoverished leaders not only exert minimal effort at getting work done, but also show minimal concern for personal relationships in the group. They choose to be unfriendly and lazy or grouchy and obstinate. Impoverished leaders believe that high-quality work can never be achieved because people are lazy, apathetic, and indifferent, and that whenever people get together, conflict is inevitable.

Impoverished leadership is characterized by the withdrawal pattern of communication. There is usually very little purposeful communication between the leader and group members, few attempts to influence activities, and little or no interest in confronting issues and solving problems.

MIDDLE-OF-THE-ROAD LEADERSHIP. Middle-of-the-road leaders behave like "dampened pendulums," not swinging too far one way or the other. They push enough to get average work and yield

TABLE 5-1 VARIOUS LEADERSHIP BEHAVIORS

Group Situation	Possible Leadership Behaviors	Grid Type
A. Emergence of conflict and arguments	1. Slug it out with the group and try to get a point across.	9, 1
	2. Retreat, shut up, and wait until they stop, regardless of how long it takes.	1, 1
	3. Ham it up! Tell a funny story. Get the members to see that they are making a big deal out of nothing.	1, 9
	4. Hammer out a "compromise" between the parties to the conflict, and get on with the job.	5, 5
	5. Communicate the feelings and information available so that all members can arrive at some understanding.	9, 9
B. Giving feedback to the group	1. Hit them over the head with the facts until they get the point through their thick skulls.	9, 1
	2. Never give feedback, because people don't really listen.	1, 1
	3. Give feedback only if it will make them feel good.	1, 9
	4. Give both negative and positive feedback, but make an effort to balance it.	5, 5
	5. Try to build a climate of trust so that both leader and group will be comfortable regardless of the kind of feedback.	9, 9
C. Leader's choice	1. Tell the group exactly what to do, when to do it, and let them work at it until they are finished.	9, 1
	2. Just like to get "the hell out of there," and let whatever happens happen.	1, 1
	3. Cover up any hint of conflict or problems and keep 'em smiling.	1, 9
	4. Balance things, give them a certain amount of time to work on the task, and a certain amount of time for horsing around, and rotate it that way.	5, 5
	5. Cultivate an environment where "work" and "good vibes" can proceed simultaneously, while maintaining efficiency.	9, 9

enough to maintain some group morale. Middle-of-the-road leaders have moderate concern for both people and production. Such balanced behavior is not enthusiastic about either group performance or member satisfaction.

This general lack of enthusiasm is reflected in the communication style. Middle-of-the-road leaders utilize a smidgen of all of the communication styles—controlling, equalitarian, structuring, dynamic, relinquishing, and withdrawal—that were discussed in Chapter 3.

TEAM LEADERSHIP. Team leaders have high concern both for group members and for production. In working with the group (as opposed to "leading" the group) they meet with group members, present the scope of the task, get their reactions and ideas, build on those ideas, and generally excite the group into being committed to each task. Both the leader and the group members set up procedures and policies and assign individual responsibilities. The team—for this is what the group really is—sets goals and flexible schedules. When interpersonal problems arise in the work relationships, leaders who use the team approach recognize the problems and confront them directly; they deal with and work through conflict as it appears.

Both equalitarian and dynamic styles of communication are instrumental in achieving team leadership. The communication is two-way, free, fluid, friendly, and warm in an atmosphere of mutal understanding and personal interest. Leaders and group members participate equally in drawing out thoughts and ideas. In such an atmosphere of mutual understanding, the communication style is dynamic; the communicators are usually frank and direct, and the messages are pragmatic and action-oriented.

TASK-CENTERED LEADERSHIP. Task-centered leaders express little concern for people and a great deal of concern for the tasks. For this leader, work is the name of the game. Task-centered leaders and country club leaders are opposites. The country clubber strives to produce smiles; the task master strives to produce sweat. Results are the only thing for task-centered leaders. They view any problems that get in the way of production, especially personal problems, as nuisances that must be quickly suppressed without emotion. They see group members as production tools, obligated to do as they are told. Task-centered leaders consider group members who challenge instructions, policies, or procedures insubordinate and uncooperative. They ignore or expel group members who do not comply with orders or regulations.

In task-centered leadership, the controlling style of communication prevails. Controlling is manifested in a one-way flow of communication, a heavy use of power and authority in gaining compliance, and a tendency toward manipulation. A good measure of structuring communication is also used in order to keep group members in line.

CHOOSING A LEADERSHIP STYLE

It would seem that the most desirable leadership behavior is team leadership. We would all like to use the team approach whenever we are called on to lead a group, but does team leadership work in every situation? Are there some situations in which country club leadership is both necessary and effective? Task-centered leadership? Even ultrademocratic leadership?

Our definition of leadership as a function of the leader, the followers, and other situational characteristics precludes the use of a single leadership style. Each group situation has unique characteristics that must be carefully evaluated before an effective leadership style can be adapted to it. Many factors affect the style of leadership behavior, such as cultural customs and traditions and standards of living as well as the levels of motivation and maturity of group members.

Style Range

Leaders differ in their ability to vary their styles—that is, their flexibility or adaptability. Some leaders are limited to one basic style. As a result, they tend to be effective only when their styles are compatible with the group situation. Other leaders can use two or three styles, and still others can use any of the five basic styles. Adaptive leaders have the potential to be effective in a variety of group situations.

According to P. Hersey and K. Blanchard (1972), style range can be illustrated in terms of concern for production and concern for people—the same variables as we have used to define various leadership styles. As shown in Figure 5-3, the size of the circle indicates the range of style. If the circle is small, as in A, then the range of leadership behavior is limited; if the circle is large, as in B, the leader has a wide range of behavior.

The leader in A of Figure 5-3 has a high concern for the people in the group but very little flexibility; in B, the leader has a broad

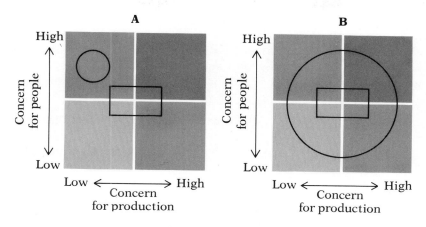

FIGURE 5-3. Style range in terms of concerns for people and production. (Adapted from Hersey and Blanchard, 1972, p. 121)

range of leadership behavior and is able to use any of the five basic styles to some extent. In this example, A may be effective in situations that demand a country club leadership approach, such as coaching or counseling. However, B has the potential to be effective in a wide variety of situations.

Flexibility, Effectiveness, and Appropriateness

Flexibility alone does not guarantee effectiveness. A leader may be able to use all five behaviors but not know where or how to adapt them. Leader B will be effective only if he or she changes style appropriately to fit the situation. For example, when the group needs emotional support, B may be unavailable; when the group needs to have some goals, B may be supportive but frustratingly nondirective; and when group members are really motivated, B may unwittingly exert unnecessary pressure and become too assertive or bossy. In each case B used behavior inappropriate for the environment. A leader needs to be able to understand the group and to evaluate them in terms of both production and people demands.

Leadership behavior appropriate to a given situation and group is called *effective;* leadership behavior inappropriate to a given situation and group is called *ineffective.* If the effectiveness of leadership behavior depends on the situation and group in which it is used, then any of the five basic leadership styles—task-centered, country club, impoverished, middle-of-the-road, and team-centered—may be effective or ineffective. Appropriate leadership behavior means a leader's ability to estimate the demands of a given situation and group and to make the necessary behavioral adjustments—that is, adapt to the situation and group.

Situational Determinants of Flexibility

Some situations warrant high flexibility; others warrant low flexibility. W. J. Reddin (1970) has developed a list of characteristics of situations that call for low flexibility in leadership behaviors, and those that require high flexibility. These characteristics are listed in Table 5-2.

An example of a high-flexibility situation might be the job of a college or university president. Such a person usually deals with many groups—including the board of trustees, an administrative staff, faculty, students, and alumni. With the board of trustees, the president might find it practical to be conciliatory, yet firm. With the administrative staff, he or she might be highly production-oriented—enforcing, planning, organizing, and controlling. With the faculty, a team-centered approach might be effective, with both faculty and president sharing in making policies. The president would probably strive to be "people-oriented" with the students; however, the president might have to take a very firm stand with an individual problem student. In dealing with each of these groups, a different leadership style would be appropriate.

An example of a low-flexibility situation might be the job of drill sergeant. In supervising a large group of draftees in an army

TABLE 5-2 SITUATIONAL DETERMINANTS OF FLEXIBILITY
IN LEADERSHIP STYLES

Determinant	Low-Flexibility Situations	High-Flexibility Situations
Leadership roles	Low-level	High-level
Leadership tasks	Simple	Complex
Group goals	Established	Emerging
Group procedures	Tight	Relaxed
Social/environmental change	Little or none	Rapid or major
Leader	Great authority	Little authority
Group tasks	Routine	Creative

boot camp, this person probably uses the same style with all his recruits. He needs to act toward everyone in a stern manner. Since he is training his recruits for possible battle, he must emphasize and demand strict discipline. Consequently, he might be most effective in using task-centered behaviors in almost every situation.

Group Members as Determinants of Leadership Style

As we mentioned earlier in this chapter, individual group members are the most crucial factor in determining leadership style. The group has the power not only to accept or reject leadership but also to determine how much power the leader will be allowed to exercise. Therefore, effective leadership can emerge only when the leader fully comprehends the character of the group and responds to its psychological needs—its level of motivation and maturity.

A LIFE CYCLE THEORY OF LEADERSHIP. The life cycle theory of leadership (Hersey and Blanchard, 1969) will help us understand how a leader may chose a style to match group needs. Their theory emphasizes leadership behavior in relation to the group members.

Life cycle theory proposes that as the level of "motivatedness," maturity, or achievement increases among the members of a group, the leader's behavior should become less and less structured or production-oriented and a "little" more people-oriented.

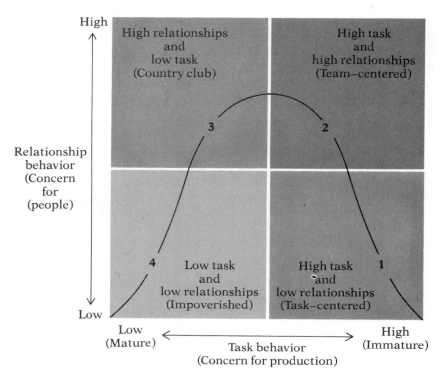

FIGURE 5-4.   Merging of the managerial Grid and the life cycle theory of leadership. Terms from the managerial Grid are included in parentheses. (Adapted from Hersey and Blanchard, 1972, p. 135)

Eventually, even the emphasis on concern for people in the group should decrease. To demonstrate their theory, Hersey and Blanchard provide a diagram (Figure 5-4) that is very much like the managerial Grid, except for minor differences in terminology.

In life cycle theory *maturity* is defined as *achievement motivation:* the group's willingness and ability to take responsibility, and the amount of task-relevant education or experience members possess (McClelland et al., 1961). The theory is concerned with the "psychological age" of the group rather than its chronological age. Life cycle theory suggests that as the group members progress from immaturity to maturity, the leader's behavior should change from (1) high-task–low-relationships to (2) high-task–high-relationships to (3) high-relationships–low-task to (4) low-task–low-relationships. This cycle shows simply that the leader should exert less influence as the group picks up in motivation, ability, and knowledge.

We can think of the leader–group relationship in terms of the parent–child relationship. As the child matures, parents provide less structure, giving the child an opportunity to assume more responsibility. As the child's ability increases, it is reinforced by an increase in socioemotional support. At this point, parents must be careful, because if they allow a child to assume too much responsibility before the child is mature enough to appreciate it, the child may misinterpret this high-relationship orientation as

* * *

Exercise 5-2

EFFECTIVE STYLES OF LEADERSHIP
FOR DIFFERENT GROUP SITUATIONS

What style of leadership would be most effective in creating cohesiveness and efficient productivity in each situation listed below? Using the managerial Grid in Figure 5-2 as a guide, indicate your choice in the blank space at the right. Be prepared to justify the choices you have made in these eight situations.

Group Situations	Type of Leadership Style
1. An evacuation crew at a tunnel disaster.	1. _____
2. A hearing committee concerned with disciplining a group member.	2. _____
3. A study group preparing for a final exam.	3. _____
4. A group of engineers, all of equal skill and rank, working on a project.	4. _____
5. A military commander and his crew at a fire base.	5. _____
6. An assigned discussion in your classroom among classmates.	6. _____
7. A new group to which you have been assigned as leader.	7. _____
8. A quarterback planning a play with second down and three yards to go.	8. _____

permissive. So, with caution, it is appropriate to decrease structure as the child becomes better able to take on responsibility and respond to mutual trust. As the child grows through adolescence into adulthood and psychological maturity develops, there will be less need for socioemotional support from the parents.

Similarly, during the early stages of a group's development, when the group is becoming familiar with a task, a certain amount of structure, guidance, and information about procedures and regulations must be established. At this stage, leader domination is usually helpful if the group is to be molded into an efficient working unit; however, the leader must exercise a great deal of tact and avoid being overly aggressive and bossy.

After the group has developed an appreciable measure of maturity and the leader has assumed the low-task–low relationships style, the leader must be willing to allow the group to adopt

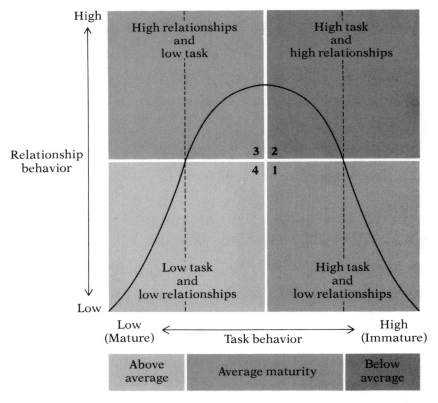

FIGURE 5-5. Maturity levels. (Adapted from Hersey and Blanchard, 1972, p. 142)

a decentralized organizational structure. In this structure, the leader delegates responsibility to group members and allows them to play an equal role in decision making.

LEADERSHIP STYLE AND GROUP MATURITY. By applying a maturity continuum—below-average, average, and above-average—to the life cycle as shown in Figure 5-5, we can determine and prescribe appropriate leadership styles. Figure 5-5 suggests that when working with people of below-average maturity—low in motivation, experience, and willingness—a leader with a high-task style (quadrant 1) would be the most effective. In dealing with people of average maturity, the styles of quadrants 2 and 3 appear to be most appropriate; quadrant 4 has the highest probability of success with people of above-average maturity.

* * *

Exercise 5-3
CHOOSING A LEADERSHIP STYLE

The following presents four different groups whose members are characterized as willing or unwilling (motivation) and mature or immature (ability).

Group	Willingness	Ability	Recommended Leadership Style
A	No	No	_____
B	Yes	No	_____
C	No	Yes	_____
D	Yes	Yes	_____

1. In the column to the right, indicate what you consider to be the best leadership style for dealing with each of these groups. The four styles from which to make your choices are:

> High-Relationships–High-Task
> High-Relationships–Low-Task
> High-Task–Low-Relationships
> Low-Task–Low-Relationships

2. Write a brief justification for your choice of leadership style for each group.

SUMMARY

Leadership involves not only certain kinds of actions in the group, but also the perceptions, reactions, and expectations of group members. Certain kinds of behavior are perceived and characterized as leadership behavior; a leader is expected to exhibit them.

Leadership styles may be characterized by their location on the people–production continuum, which stretches from ultrademocratic leadership to autocratic leadership. Using Blake's and Mouton's managerial Grid, we identified five leadership styles, which vary in the degree to which they emphasize people or production: country club leadership, impoverished leadership, middle-of-the-road leadership, team leadership, and task-centered leadership.

The difference between effective and ineffective leadership behavior is not the actual behavior, but the appropriateness of the behavior to the group situation in which it is used. Effective leaders adapt their behavior to meet the needs of the group and the particular situation. As H. Koontz and C. O'Donnell (1972, p. 242) put it: "The [leader] must be like the musician who changes techniques and approaches to obtain the shadings of total performance desired."

ADDITIONAL READINGS

Bormann, E. G. *Discussion and Group Methods: Theory and Practice.* 2d ed. New York: Harper & Row, 1975. Chapter 10 discusses some of the patterns of interaction that result in the emergence of a leader.

Cartwright, D., and Zander, A., eds. *Group Dynamics: Research and Theory.* 3d ed. New York: Harper & Row, 1968. Part 5 on "Leadership and Performance of Group Functions" presents seven studies involving leadership (see pages 301–98). Studies 25 and 28 present excellent coverage of styles of leadership and situational determinants of leadership, respectively.

Collins, B., and Guetzkow, H. A. *Social Psychology of Group Processes for Decision-Making.* New York: Wiley, 1964. See Chapter 11 for an explanation of leadership traits and the differentiation of leadership roles.

Fiedler, F. *A Theory of Leadership Effectiveness.* New York: McGraw-Hill, 1967. Chapter 3 emphasizes methods for measuring leadership style. Chapter 15, particularly pages 247–55, discusses fundamental aspects of leadership training.

Shaw, M. *Group Dynamics: The Psychology of Small Group Behavior.* 2d ed. New York: McGraw-Hill, 1976. See pages 267–87 for a review of approaches to definitions of leadership, leadership styles, and a listing of 24 hypotheses concerning group structure and member status.

IV

CLIMATE

* * *

CHAPTER 6
RULES AND ROLES

This chapter examines the nature of rules and roles and their functions in small groups. Rules refer to group standards about acceptable and unacceptable behaviors within the group. Roles are the various positions a member occupies within a group and the behaviors required of each position. Both rules and roles develop to provide structure within a group. They are seen as necessary in accomplishing both group task and social-emotional goals. The manner in which rules and roles influence group members, the sending and receiving of messages within the group, and important aspects of group interaction are illustrated.

CHAPTER 7
COHESIVENESS

We begin with a definition of cohesiveness, acknowledging the importance of attraction, motivation, and common goal as forces that keep members in groups. We examine member satisfaction and group productivity as factors relevant to group cohesiveness. Our analysis concludes with an examination of the communicator, message, and situational context as causes or effects of cohesiveness.

CHAPTER 8
CONFLICT

This chapter examines conflict behavior in the small group. We describe conflict on intrapersonal, interpersonal, and intragroup levels. Conflict is discussed as both productive and nonproductive in terms of group function and purpose. We examine conflict as it relates to the communicator, message, and situational context. In conclusion, we note some communication principles pertinent to conflict behavior in the small group.

* * *

6

RULES
AND ROLES

PREVIEW

* **What are rules?**

Rules are standards governing communication behavior in various situations; they specify appropriate, acceptable, and forbidden communication behaviors.

* **What are the major types of rules?**

Constitutive and regulative.

* **What are the major levels of rules?**

Cultural, sociological, and psychological.

* **Why do rules develop in small groups?**

Rules develop because they are perceived as helping task and social-emotional goals.

* **How do rules relate to small-group communication?**

Sociological-level rules govern most of the communication behavior within small groups.
Rules tend to produce conformity.

* **How do rules relate to the communication model?**

Communicator: the relationship of intelligence, authoritarianism, power, and status to rule-conforming behavior.
Message: the relationship of openly expressed standards and praise and criticism to rule-determined behavior; effect of rule deviation upon message behavior within a group.
Climate: relationship of rule conformity to cohesiveness within a group.
Control: relationship of rule conformity to task accomplishment within a group.

* **What are roles?**

Roles refer to the many positions a person occupies and the variety of behaviors tied to each of them.

* **Why do roles develop in small groups?**

As with rules, roles develop to enable the group to accomplish its task and social-emotional activities.

* **How do roles relate to our communication model?**

Communicator: the relationship of attitudes, sex, and personality to role behavior within groups.

Message: the relationship between different roles and message interpretation; "in role" and "out of role" messages and perceptions of personality; sender and receiver roles and message behavior.

Climate: the relationship of role conformity to cohesiveness.

Control: the relationship of role differentiation to group productivity; role behavior and "idiosyncracy credits."

IMAGINE that all of the members of a small group decided independently of the others how they would act. The result would be that coordinated activity within the group—efficient task accomplishment and the development of cohesiveness—would be difficult, if not impossible. Chaos would reign.

Most of us don't realize how much we depend on social structure to help us in our day-to-day communication. We have learned appropriate and inappropriate communicative behavior in various settings. We know that certain messages considered acceptable at a meeting to organize a beer bust are out of place at a meeting of the campus planning committee. We know how we should act when we discuss a business matter with our boss as opposed to how we, as Little League coaches, should talk with our players after the first inning.

Communication can't be studied apart from its context. We can't study people and their messages without regard for the social system in which they exist. We can't study social systems such as small groups without considering the people who comprise them. *Communication is impossible without some structure.* We need structure to be able to predict the behavior of others in a group, to prepare and provide appropriate responses, to achieve group goals, to maintain harmonious relations between group members, and to promote individual well-being.

Rules and roles probably provide the most important sources of social structure within the small group, and they provide the clearest means for predicting behavior within the group. Of all the dimensions of the group communication model, rules and roles have the greatest potential for promoting task accomplishment and personal satisfaction.

RULES

Rules are often described in terms of norms. Indeed, many social psychologists use the words *norms* and *rules* interchangeably
(Homans, 1974; Swensen, 1973). However, the construct of rules
has been developed by communication theorists and deals
explicitly with communication behavior; norms were developed
by social psychologists and sociologists, not specifically to account for communication behavior, although they have been
profitably used to explain certain communication behaviors
within groups. In this discussion, we will use the term *rule*, although other writers may use the term *norm* to refer to the same
phenomenon.

Definition of Rules

Rules govern the ways in which people interact in various situations. They are prescriptions of behavior.

Rules are standards of conduct of the group; they provide a
means for determining what is appropriate communication
behavior in what would otherwise be a chaotic situation.

Deviation from rules is followed by some punishment or negative sanction (Pearce, 1976). The handling of deviation and punishment is rather complex. For example, the range of permissible
behavior varies. Some rules may apply only to selected members,
not to the whole group. Some members may be allowed greater
freedom than others to deviate from rules.

Types of Rules

There are two major types of rules: constitutive and regulative.
Constitutive rules specify the acts that are necessary for a communication transaction to take place (Pearce, 1976). They are
analogous to game rules—unless you know the rules, you can't
play the game. One example of a constitutive rule is that two
people must be involved if communication is to take place—one
to send a message and one to receive it. Another example is that
to communicate people must share in common the meanings for
the symbols they use.
Regulative rules specify those allowable communication acts
from which the person may choose (Pearce, 1976). Some situations require that we be fairly formal; others require that we be

cooperative, friendly, and not too serious; still others allow us to be open and to deal with personal concerns in depth.

There are three major levels at which communication rules operate: cultural, sociological, and psychological. These levels are characterized by different relationships between communicators and by different communication rules.

CULTURAL LEVEL.   Communication rules at the cultural level are based on knowledge shared by the culture as a whole. They allow us to communicate with people we are meeting for the first time. Sometimes they govern the *content* of messages. For example, we talk about familiar topics such as the weather, traffic problems, or food. Intimate and personal discussions are avoided. Other cultural rules dictate the *structure* of the interaction. For instance, there should be short exchanges (rather than long "speeches"), no probing questions, and everyone should be allowed to talk. Cultural-level rules are typically used for brief encounters with strangers or as a necessary preliminary to sociological-level relationships (Miller and Steinberg, 1975).

SOCIOLOGICAL LEVEL. Most of our communicative activity is spent in *sociological*-level relationships. They are like cultural relationships except that the communication rules are based on group membership. They differ with communicators' status, occupation, politics, social affiliations, and so forth. What's considered appropriate communication behavior in a meeting of alumni may be considered out of place in a military organization. It wouldn't be acceptable for a corporal to reply to a captain who gave an order, "Sure thing, Howard."

There are formal and informal sociological-level rules. In *formal* sociological relationships, the range of communication possibilities is rather small. Fairly strict rules govern the ways in which people may communicate with one another in these situations. Organizations that use parliamentary procedure in their deliberations, such as the U.S. Senate, are good examples of groups adhering to formal sociological rules. Other examples include applying for a marriage license or dealing with the registrar about a problem with payment of fees.

Informal sociological communication relationships have many of the same qualities but to a lesser degree. There are still restraints on communication behavior, but communicators have more alternatives. Student–teacher relationships are typically informal sociological ones. Limits are placed on the times, places, and ways in which students and teachers may communicate, but

a good deal of freedom is permitted within these limits. Other examples of informal sociological communication behavior include the communication in neighborhood bars where patrons habitually stop off after work or the meetings of law students studying together for their bar exams. Although there are restraints, the communication is relatively open. Sociological-level relationships may remain at that level or may move to the psychological, or interpersonal, level (Miller and Steinberg, 1975).

PSYCHOLOGICAL LEVEL. At this level people communicate on the basis of personal experience with another person. They respond to each other as unique human beings. To respond to someone in this way requires knowledge of and experience with that person, but it goes beyond knowing the other person's race, major, occupation, and similar characteristics. It requires knowing the other person's likes and dislikes, hopes, fears, strengths and weaknesses, beliefs, values, and other characteristics that are unique and intimate aspects of personality or self-concept. Examples include the communication behavior between good friends and in close marriages.

The rules regarding permitted behaviors at the psychological level may be quite different from those allowed in cultural or sociological relationships. They are typically unique to the communicators. Lovers, for example, may have their own private

"code" or set of communication rules. The content of conversations is often personal and intimate and is characterized by self-disclosure—that is, information about oneself that the other person would not otherwise be able to obtain. Such behavior generally is not appropriate in cultural- and sociological-level relationships.

Development of Rules

Groups that have achieved some measure of permanance or stability develop rules. Some factors are especially relevant in forming rules:

1. The extent to which members find that conformity to rules is rewarding or costly to the group's goals.
2. The extent to which the rule behavior fits the group members' basic values.
3. The extent to which group members observe communicative behaviors that conform to or deviate from the group's rules. Sanctions cannot be applied unless deviations are actually noticed by members of the group or, in a group with an authoritarian leader, by the leader.
4. The extent to which punishment may be imposed.

From this list of factors we can conclude that rules develop because conformity in values and behavior is perceived as improving the outcomes experienced by members of the group.

Rules such as not speaking more than ten minutes, refraining from using obscenities, and avoiding personality attacks are generally used by a group if the members feel that these standards increase productivity or help maintain desired social-emotional conditions within the group. For example, an elementary-school community council comprised of students, faculty, and parents may place a high value on ensuring that subgroups of the council are treated the same at meetings. To prevent status differences from unduly influencing the reception of ideas, the group may decide to use "Mr." or "Ms." before everyone's last name (including the students') or to call members by their first names only. Such a rule would develop because the group members see it as helping them achieve their goal of solving certain educational problems facing the students.

Rules and Small-Group Communication

Communication behavior in small groups—indeed, most of our daily communication behavior—is typically determined by rules operating at the sociological level. Except for groups such as the military services or those using parliamentary procedure, most small groups communicate according to informal sociological-level rules. Some rules pertain to the leader's communication responsibilities. The leader may be expected to solicit information and opinion, test reasoning, keep the discussion on the issue under consideration, productively manage conflict, and so forth. Other rules pertain to members' communication behaviors. They may be expected to keep comments brief, make productive comments that help the group move toward its goal, treat other members with respect, show interest in the matters at hand, not interrupt other members when they have the floor, and so on.

MIXED-LEVELS PROBLEM. Some group members may use psychological-level rules to communicate among themselves. This usage may result in the so-called *mixed-levels problem* (Miller and Steinberg, 1975). For example, during the monthly meeting of a civic organization, two members who are close friends may make comments to one another that other group members resent because they do not understand the friends' comments and expect people not to engage in private conversations at the meeting. Let's take another example. During a break in a meeting of the social committee, Basil, the host, announces that he's made fresh coffee. One of the committee members of long-standing appreciatively responds, "That's great, Flash, would you bring me a cup?" Another older member also replies, "Yeah, me too, Flash." Freddie, the newest member of the group, follows suit with, "And don't forget me, Flash." When the meeting resumes after the break, the other members are colder and less receptive to Freddie's ideas. Freddie presumed he could communicate using a personal and somewhat intimate form of address, and the other group members felt that his communication behavior violated a rule of appropriateness.

CONFORMITY. One of the consequences of rule-governed behavior in small groups is that *rules tend to produce conformity*. Conformity may be of two types. People may conform with the majority simply for the sake of agreement, to avoid disapproval and possible punishment; or they may conform because the group standard supports their own attitudes and values.

Some people see conformity as a negative consequence, as leading to loss of individuality, restriction of creativity, and reduction of all members to a mediocre level (Asch, 1951; Milgram, 1964; Whyte, 1957). They use the term only when standards of behavior

they disapprove of are involved. Conforming to standards of behavior they approve of they call "cooperation." As we use the
word, conformity means behavior complying with group standards—whether these be "good" or "bad." However, there are
good reasons for conformity to group rules. They provide order
and the means for coordinating individual behaviors, without
which effective group interaction would be impossible (Homans,
1974).

Rules in Relation to Our Communication Model

Our model can help us understand the relationship between
rules and the communicator, message, climate, and control dimensions within the small group. Like any attempt to break
down the communication process into component parts, our
categorization is arbitrary. For as we observed in Chapter 1,
communication is a process occurring in a system, and all parts
of the system relate to the others. Thus, when we talk about rules
and messages, for instance, of necessity we'll also be discussing
communicators and control. So keep in mind that our purpose is
to place some of the many complex relationships in a readily understandable pattern.

COMMUNICATORS.   Let's look at a few communicator variables
that bear upon rule-determined behavior: intelligence, authoritarianism, power, and status.

Communicators with high intelligence seem to conform to rules
less than individuals with lower intelligence (Crutchfield, 1955;
Nakamura, 1958; Wyer, 1967). This relationship is one we have
probably experienced. Think, for example, of the discussions
you've participated in or observed this term. Wasn't it usually the
more intelligent member who would question or challenge the
group's rules or decisions?

Highly authoritarian individuals tend to conform more than
those who do not have this personality trait (Beloff, 1958;
Crutchfield, 1955; Nadler, 1959). As we noted in Chapter 4, highly
authoritarian people need structure. They believe in the necessity
for rules. As in the soap commercial, we can just hear them say,
"I'm glad I follow the group's rules. Aren't you glad you follow
them? Don't you wish everybody did?"

A somewhat surprising finding is that people in power sometimes conform more closely to the rules of their groups than do
people with less power; but not surprisingly, under some cir-

cumstances members with power are allowed to deviate from accepted rules more than their less influential associates. We allow our leaders to bend the rules to get the job done.

A closely related variable is status—the prestige accompanying a group position such as that of leader. People with average status conform to a greater extent than those with high or low status (Harvey and Consalvi, 1960; Hollander, 1958; Gergen and Taylor, 1969). The high-status members (such as the leader) have certain powers and rights that allow them to break the rules while other group members wink at their behavior. The low-status members have nothing to lose, and so they are also likely to break rules. Thus, it is the communicator of average status who conforms most closely to group rules.

MESSAGES.   A classic series of experiments have demonstrated that group rules have much to do with responses made to a variety of messages. This research asked people to do such things as judge apparent movement of a stimulus (Sherif and Sherif, 1956) and determine which of three vertical lines is the same length as a standard line presented at the same time (Asch, 1951). In these experiments, the individual is usually asked to make these judgments in the presence of others, whose standards are openly declared. The typical finding is that a substantial portion of individuals are consistently influenced by the group. They adjust their own judgments to conform to those of the group, especially when the stimulus is difficult to judge—that is, when the person has problems in making objective judgments about the stimulus. We can readily see, for example, how an engineering major might tend to conform to standards agreed on by a group of English majors in a discussion evaluating the works of modern poets. Yet it must be admitted that some people conform to standards made by the group even when they *know* the group's standards are *wrong*.

Rules also help determine how praise and criticism are given and received. For example, rules in our culture are biased in favor of giving praise; there seems to be a strong norm toward saving face. We tend to be very careful when we make negative evaluations in our groups, because we know we can easily offend people. Furthermore, the status of the person giving the praise or criticism is a crucial factor. Evaluations made by a superior to a subordinate tend to be interpreted by group members most favorably; praise or criticism of a peer by another peer is judged next most favorably; and judgments by a subordinate of a superior least favorably. This research (Deutsch, 1971) supports the inference that the meaning group members intend to communicate depends on what they assume the rules to be. Understanding and misunderstanding within a small group may reflect the accuracy with which rules have been perceived and the degree to which they are part of the message-sending and message-receiving behavior of the group members.

Some interesting studies show how deviation from group rules affects the pattern of messages sent within a group. In one experiment (Schachter, 1951), for example, in a small-group setting, confederates fulfilled three experimental conditions: the *mode*, who expressed the group's position, the *deviate*, who took a stand at the opposite extreme from the mode, and the *slider*, who first took an opposed stand but later came around to the group's position. The group's first series of messages was directed primarily toward the deviates and sliders. The number of messages to the sliders, however, decreased as they approached the modal group position. Messages to the deviates (who maintained an opposing stance) increased up to a point and then decreased dramatically. The general picture that emerged was one of increasing attempts to get the deviates to conform to the group's position, followed by complete acceptance if they did, and rejection and isolation if they did not.

The effects of rules upon group behavior, especially responses to messages, are not restricted to laboratory research. Support has also been found in field settings. Studies have been done on whether people obeyed or violated traffic signals (Lefkowitz, Blake, and Mouton, 1955), whether they did or did not signal when driving (Barch, Trumbo, and Nangel, 1957), whether they

* * *

Communication Diary 6-1

1. Discuss your general tendencies and feelings about conformity to group standards.

2. Identify rules you believe to be important for improved social relations and task accomplishment. Discuss the reasons for your choices.

3. Identify rules you believe to be unimportant or detrimental to improved social relations and task accomplishment. Discuss the reasons for your choices.

did or did not exhibit volunteering behavior (Rosenbaum and Blake, 1955), whether they conformed to "Do Not Enter" signs (Freed et al., 1955), and so forth. In these studies, what individuals perceived to be rules for the behavior strongly affected their own behavior. In the famous Bennington study, T. M. Newcomb (1943) showed that through their college years, students accepting the college community as a dominant reference group moved in the direction of commonly held liberal attitudes.

CLIMATE. As we described our communication model in Chapter 1, one of the important aspects of the climate dimension is cohesiveness. When cohesiveness within the group is high, greater pressure is exerted to maintain the group's rules. Members of highly cohesive groups are very sensitive to failure to act according to group rules. Religious orders, for instance, typically are very touchy about maintaining their rules. When rules are violated, overt pressure for conformity will be applied.

CONTROL. Rules have an influence, though somewhat roundabout, upon accomplishing tasks such as problem solving. The pattern goes something like this: Group rules cause members to become more alike in their attitudes and consequently more effective in their communication within the group; better communication helps in attaining group goals, which increases interpersonal liking; this, in turn, raises the interaction rate above that required for the attainment of group goals; the high communication rate leads to a further increase in value and attitudinal similarity among group members; and so on.

Rules affect task accomplishment in another way. They act as substitutes for the exercise of personal influence. They produce simpler and more efficient patterns of behavior and save the wear and tear that would be involved in producing these behaviors through personal persuasion alone.

ROLES

Rules and roles are not mutually exclusive constructs; they overlap. Although some rules within a group apply to all members, others pertain only to certain individuals or subgroups of persons within the group. These rules pertaining to certain individuals within the group provide a method for identifying different roles within a group. Group members are said to be in the same role if the same rules apply to their behavior.

Roles refer to the many positions a person occupies and the variety of behaviors tied to each of them. Roles may be viewed in terms of whether they are expected *(role expectations)* or enacted *(role performance).*

> A *role* may be thought of either as a set of expectations people have about required behaviors or as the actual behavior engaged in by the person.

Role behavior is generally agreed upon not only by the occupant of the position but also by other members of the group. Roles are the organized patterns of social relationships into which the individual must fit. It is assumed that there is considerable agreement about what someone in a certain position should do and that most people within the group are inclined to play these roles. To the degree that there are differences between role expectation and role performance, conflict and group dysfunction become more likely.

Each position in a group has many required role behaviors. The group task leader, for instance, may be required to assign jobs, draw inferences, test soundness of reasoning, and so on. The group social-emotional leader may have the functions of encouraging members and releasing tensions when conflicts arise.

In addition to obligations, roles also have rights or rewards and costs. For the leadership role, rewards include satisfactions gained from successful achievement of group goals and satisfactions inherent in the leadership activity itself. Furthermore, the leader's role has a high degree of status. On the other hand, costs include effort spent, worry over failure, criticism and blame, and the emotional distance required. A follower's rewards may come from sharing a leader's sense of achievement, satisfying the need to depend on someone, identifying with a strong leader, and being free of the costs of assuming a leadership role. The follower, however, has lower status, less control over the group's functions, and none of the advantages of leadership.

As we said in Chapter 1, people play different roles in different groups. A student may be also a parent, a provider, and a community leader. The quiet follower in a discussion class may be a

team leader on the athletic field. The role a person plays in a particular group reflects both personal choice and others' expectations.

A single role within a small group cannot be considered apart from other roles in the group. Several related roles comprise a social system—in this case, small group. Each position in a group has one or more counterpositions; in other words, roles require complementary functions. Rights and duties of one role tend to be the "other side" of those of associated roles. One can't be a husband without having a wife, a father without having children, a group leader without having followers.

Although some roles encompass a small portion of a person's total behavior, others may be all-encompassing. Performing the behaviors required as president of the United States consumes much more of an individual's total behavior than acting as supervisor for a school club. Behaviors associated with the role of male or female or members of a religious order encompass nearly all of any particular individual's activities, no matter what the group may be. Males, females, and members of religious orders are expected to conform to certain rules of behavior regardless of the group to which they belong.

There are two basic types of roles: those associated with task dimensions and those associated with social or group maintenance dimensions of the group. Many theorists and researchers have described what they perceive to be critical roles in a group. As you can see in Table 6-1, some theorists agree on certain roles (such as those of initiator and evaluator), but they differ on the scope and specificity of the roles they propose. Because roles tend to be recategorized by researchers, depending on the aspects of group behavior they are concerned with, the quest for an objectively defined or commonly accepted list of roles is not likely to succeed.

Role Formation

Roles tend to develop whenever a group continues for some time and has group activities to perform. To accomplish these activities, divisions of responsibility come about. Different members of the group are made responsible for various group activities. Some roles are designed to achieve group tasks, such as information exchange, solution formation, and answer exchange. Other roles have as their purpose the development and continuation of a harmonious group atmosphere.

Roles may be established by chance, by appointment, or because an individual withholds information to the group. In the first case, someone's role might be established without any intention on the person's part. Due to prior training or experience an individual may have skills needed by the group. For instance, a church committee composed of members of the congregation might be considering the establishment of a Bingo game as a way of raising money for church projects. If one of the group members happens to be an attorney with expertise in the legal ramifications inherent in such an endeavor, it would not be surprising if the group conferred a leadership role upon that person for this project.

A person's role might also be established by appointment. Teachers and military officers, for example, have their roles fairly well defined for them. They are expected to perform certain leadership task behaviors within the groups in which they work. In most organizations, roles within specific units or sections are typically well-defined—persons with higher status tend to have greater leadership responsibilities and power.

TABLE 6-1 CATEGORIES OF ROLES SUGGESTED BY VARIOUS RESEARCHERS

Type of Role	E. G. Bormann (1975)	K. D. Benne and P. Sheats (1948)	H. Guetzkow (in Cartwright and Zander, 1968)	D. Cartwright and A. Zander (1960)
Task roles	Initiating action Doing routine chores Testing soundness of information Dividing up group work and assigning jobs Gathering information Following orders and doing the job assigned Suggesting ways to do a job Drawing inferences Evaluating inferences and plans of action	Initiator-contributor Information seeker Opinion seeker Information giver Elaborator Coordinator Orienter Evaluator-critic Energizer Procedural technician Recorder	Keyman—receiving information, formulating solutions, and sending answers Endman—sending information others do not have and later receiving answers Relayers—passing on both missing information and answers received	Initiating action Keeping member attention on goal Clarifying issues Developing procedural plan Evaluating quality of work done Making expert information available
Social roles	Being funny Releasing tension	Encourager Harmonizer Compromiser Gatekeeper and expediter Standard setter Group observer and commentator Follower		Keeping interpersonal relations pleasant Arbitrating disputes Providing encouragement Giving minority a chance to be heard Stimulating self-direction Increasing interdependence of group members

A leadership role could even be established by deliberately withholding information important to the group. Returning to our example of the Bingo game, if the attorney really wanted to achieve a leadership role within the committee, she might let the group struggle for a while with the red tape, and then through her "diligent and hard effort" get the project approved. The group would probably be so grateful that they'd insist that she take on a leadership role.

A good deal of research on role formation—especially that of leader—has been done by E. G. Bormann (1975) and his students at the University of Minnesota. Bormann worked with groups that were given various tasks but had no assigned leader. After several hours of discussion, members began to specialize in particular roles. Discussants did not automatically assume roles, but rather worked out their roles jointly. A given individual tried various role functions and received encouragement or discouragement from the group; the process was a dynamic series of trial-and-error episodes. Some members gained status and esteem.

The clarity with which positions are perceived by occupants, aspirants, and counterposition occupants affects role learning in the group. People who aspire to be group leaders often perceive the roles needed in the group and plan how they can assume their chosen role. There are generally three ways:

1. Propose that they be leader.
2. Make a specific proposal about a course of action the group should take. If the group agrees, the door is open for more suggestions, whereupon the group gradually comes to accept the individual as its leader.
3. Make a general, abstract proposal about group action. Positive group responses to such proposals clear the path for assumption of leadership.

Although leaders who are task specialists may be liked initially because they satisfy the members' need for leadership, they may also arouse envy because of their prestige, and create resentment because they necessarily talk a lot and make other members attend to the task. The more leaders talk, the more uncertain other members become toward them. Eventually members transfer some liking from a task-oriented leader to people who are less active and who express their negative feelings. These social-emotional specialists are the best-liked members of the group. They symbolize the values and attitudes that have been upset, curbed, or threatened by the necessity of fulfilling the task.

What happens when group members do not fulfill their expected roles? Members may be excused for deviant behavior if they have already proven themselves. Persons who make helpful contributions to the group may store up what are called idiosyncrasy credits (Hollander, 1958), which allow the person to depart somewhat from the prescribed role behaviors. For instance, a member who has earned the right to group leadership through previous contributions to the group will be allowed to violate a standard as long as the behavior does not harm the group. Leaders may be forgiven if they sometimes lose their cool, because the group members realize the strain they are under. If, however, the actions hurt the group, members react with greater hostility than when a lower-status person behaves the same way. Indeed, when role behavior departs too much from the expected role, the occupant of the role, not surprisingly, is often forced out.

* * *

Exercise 6-1
TYPES OF ROLES

Observe a problem-solving group discussion. Classify the role behaviors that you see.

1. What task roles seem to be demonstrated? How do they affect the work of the group?

2. What social roles seem to be operating? How do they influence the atmosphere of the group?

3. Do any task roles affect the social-emotional aspects of the group? What effects do they have?

4. Do any social roles help or hinder the group's task fulfillment?

5. Were any roles missing that should have been performed?

6. How do you feel about the relative importance of task versus social roles in problem-solving groups?

Role Conflict

Conflict over roles may occur between people (*interpersonal* conflict) or within one person (*intrapersonal* conflict). Members of a small group, for example, may disagree on what kinds of behaviors are included in a given role, particularly that of leader. Some may feel the leader has the right to make decisions for the group; others may feel the leader may suggest courses of action, but only the group can decide. They may also disagree on the situations to which the role applies or whether the role behavior is required or simply preferred.

Intrapersonal conflict may occur because of conflicting differences in successive roles a member must play, or because a member must play two or more different roles simultaneously. For example, many graduate teaching assistants find that having to be both teacher and student generates a painful identity crisis. Intrapersonal conflict may also develop because the rights associated with a position may not be sufficiently rewarding to motivate group members to carry out the obligations of that position. Many professors, for example, refuse to be appointed department chairpersons because they feel that the rights associated with the position do not compensate for the tension and work associated with it. Intrapersonal conflict may also develop when conformity to the expectations of one role would interfere with goal achievement by a role partner. For example, a group leader might debate internally whether to evaluate a group member's proposal negatively if doing so would interfere with the member's desire to make a substantive contribution to the group.

How is role conflict resolved? The group or organization may use indoctrination manuals and training programs, and rituals and ceremonies to reaffirm the rights and duties of group members. Individuals, too, use certain methods to resolve role strain. They may establish their own ranking of values. In the role of teacher, a person may decide that it's more important to be a disciplinarian than to encourage individuality. A person may rationalize or leave the group. Typically, when role conflict occurs, people resolve it in the direction of greatest attraction: they choose to play the role required by the group having the greatest significance for them.

Roles in Relation to Our Communication Model

As in our consideration of rules, we'll use the dimensions of our model to discuss specific relationships between roles and behavior in small groups.

COMMUNICATORS. Several communicator variables are related to roles: attitudes, sex, and personality.

* * *

Recall a group that had tensions, arguments, and poor task accomplishment. Identify the role conflict that may have triggered the original tensions.

1. Were these role conflicts of an interpersonal or intrapersonal nature?

2. What were some of the social-emotional and task difficulties encountered because of this role conflict?

3. How were these difficulties resolved? Would other methods of resolution have been preferable?

Attitudes. A large series of studies (Miller and Burgoon, 1973) showed that when people assume roles that involve attitudes contrary to their own, they tend to change their attitudes and values to be consistent with those of the new role. Choosing a new role or having a new one forced upon one generates strong psychological pressure toward changes in attitudes and behavior to conform to expectations of the role. For example, in a small office a staff member who takes over for a couple of weeks while an executive goes on vacation may fill the boss's role too well.

Personality. Some people cannot tolerate an unclear social situation; they need specifically defined roles. Most people feel the need for some structure or psychological "closure," and cannot tolerate leaderless groups, especially when the group's purpose is problem solving. However, some people cannot operate in an overly defined (and to them restricted) social structure. In a small group, then, roles should provide some structure but not be so rigid that members feel there is no room for individuality or creativity.

There is evidence that to achieve the leadership role, a group member must not only be intelligent but also have a strong drive to attain the leader role. In this situation, however, a person's ascendant tendencies are even more important than intelligence.

Sex. Men are more likely to emerge as group task leaders than are women. In contrast, women are encouraged to adopt communication patterns that lead to their emergence as social-emotional specialists (Baird, 1976). As cultural norms continue to change, differences in communication patterns should decrease, which should allow group members to emerge in various roles—regardless of sex.

As we noted in our discussion of role formation, it is almost impossible to be both task leader and social-emotional leader of a group. Group resentment prevents fulfillment of both roles. In addition, personalities attracted to and able to perform these roles tend to be dissimilar. The social or group maintenance specialist must like and be liked in order to meet these needs in the group. In contrast, the task specialist must be emotionally aloof. If a person is to guide the group in achieving its aims, the individual cannot become so emotionally attached to other members that power over them cannot be used.

MESSAGES. As communicators playing different roles in diverse groups, we should be aware of the relation between roles and varying levels of message interpretation. As we observed in our discussion of rules and messages, evaluations made by a superior to a subordinate are interpreted most favorably, evaluations by a peer next most favorably, and evaluations by a subordinate least favorably. Research indicates that message meaning depends not only on the authority relationship of source and receiver but also on the setting in which the messages are exchanged and the evaluative content of the message (Barnlund, 1968).

Interestingly, group members tend to interpret messages that are "out of role" as disclosing more of the senders' true selves than "in role" messages (Jones, Davis, and Gergen, 1961). The use

* * *

Communication Diary 6-2

1. What general class of small-group roles do you most enjoy playing—task or social-emotional? Why?

2. What specific role behaviors do you play fairly well? Fairly poorly?

3. Indicate the roles you play in at least three small groups to which you belong. Analyze the reasons for similarities or differences in your role performance in these groups.

of roles apparently inhibits personal interaction. Communicating with another group member as a *person* appears to be unnecessary and unlikely within clearly defined role structures.

As group members, we perform either sender or receiver roles (Zajonc, 1960). In sender roles we tend to use more detail, allow greater complexity, and organize material more tightly than when in receiver roles. As speakers, we tend to get all wrapped up in our own ideas. As receivers, on the other hand, we tend to leave out details, simplify a message, and lose sight of its organization. Apparently, when listening we don't work as hard at getting the other person's messages as we do when creating our own messages. However, both sending and receiving of messages within a group are influenced by role assignments.

CLIMATE. Role conformity tends to increase as group cohesiveness increases. "With few exceptions, the group's cohesiveness increases rather dramatically when roles are stabilized" (Bormann, 1969, p. 192). Stabilization of roles allows group members to know what to expect and what others expect of them. There are fewer conflicting communication exchanges. Members can relax and concentrate on the job without worrying about how people are going to act.

CONTROL. Role structure strongly influences the flow of messages within a group. Members tend to direct more talk to people they consider playing important roles, such as leader. People in more important roles tend to talk more to the whole group. These findings support the conclusion that persons occupying important roles receive the most consideration by other members of the group.

A very important finding on the relation of roles to group task accomplishment is that groups tend to be more successful when roles are clearly defined. For example, a group without an accepted leader will experience role conflict, which decreases productivity. Only after a leader has been selected can the group begin to function effectively and harmoniously. Members become more productive after they have established a system for working together. Differing roles help members understand what communication is appropriate and when. For example, members who are accepted as fulfilling the tension-release role know they should step in whenever conflict gets out of hand and thus help the group be productive again. The more effective the communication, the more likely the group's task needs will be fulfilled.

* * *

Exercise 6-3
PERCEPTIONS OF ROLES

On a sheet of paper, list the five major roles you have played in recent class discussions. Place a check alongside the roles you believe others recognize you as having played. On another sheet of paper, list all class members, including yourself; for each person, write in the two major roles that person has played in class discussions. These sheets are to be collected in class and read aloud. Tally the perceptions that other class members have of major roles you played in previous discussions.

1. How do their perceptions of your roles compare with your perceptions?

2. How might the similarities and differences in perception have helped you make positive contributions in class discussions?

3. How might the similarities and differences in perception have created conflict or problems for you in class discussions?

SUMMARY

In this chapter we have examined the nature of rules and roles and their relevance to communication behavior within groups. *Rules are standards governing appropriate, acceptable, and forbidden communication behaviors.* Rules may be constitutive or regulative, and operate at cultural, sociological, and psychological levels. Rules tend to produce conformity within groups and influence the behavior of individual communicators, meanings given to messages, group climate, and productivity. *Roles refer to the many positions a person occupies and the variety of behaviors tied to each.* As with rules, roles affect communicators, messages, climate, and control.

ADDITIONAL READINGS

Miller, Gerald R., ed. *Explorations in Interpersonal Communication.* Beverly Hills: Sage Publications, 1976. This volume contains an excellent collection of essays on the concept of rules. The essays are for advanced students and should be read only after Miller and Steinberg. The foreward by Miller, and the essays by Pearce, Cushman, and Craig, and Miller and Rogers are particularly relevant.

Miller, Gerald R., and Steinberg, Mark. *Between People: A New Analysis of Interpersonal Communication*. Chicago: Science Research Associates, 1975. Chapters 1 and 2 provide a clear introduction to the concept of communication rules. These chapters discuss the nature, types, and levels of rules, and their relationship to communication behavior.

Shaw, Marvin E. *Group Dynamics: The Psychology of Small Group Behavior*. New York: McGraw-Hill, 1976. A good summary of empirical research findings on the relevance of rules (Shaw uses the term *norms*) and roles to small-group behavior.

7

COHESIVENESS

* **What is cohesiveness?**

   Cohesiveness is a process by which group members are attracted to each other, motivated to remain together, and share a common *perspective* of the group's activity.

* **How does attraction operate in the group?**

   Attraction operates on two levels:
   Interpersonal: amount of attraction that individuals feel for other group *members*.
   Group: amount of attraction individuals feel for the group's *function*.

* **What does group satisfaction depend on?**

   Satisfaction depends on requirements for membership, effective group performance, and material rewards for membership.

* **What is group productivity?**

   Productivity is group outcome in terms of expected results.

* **How does cohesiveness relate to our communication model?**

   Cohesiveness and communication are impossible to separate. The level of cohesiveness affects and is affected by the types of messages sent and the attitudes communicators have toward each other and the task. The quality of group climate and control is directly related to member cohesiveness.

THINK of your favorite group. It may be a work group, a school group, or just a group of friends who get together from time to time. Do *not* think of this group in terms of its jobs, problems, successes, or even its members. Concentrate on the group's *climate*, its *working atmosphere*. Not easy, is it? We tend to appreciate the climate of a group only in comparison with that of other groups. When we describe our "good" or "bad" groups to others, we usually describe how we "feel" working with other group members.

Our attitude toward a group to which we belong depends largely on whether we want to belong to the group and how comfortable we feel working with the group. The climate within which the group works is a very important factor in maintaining group membership: perhaps the best single indicator of climate is the amount of *cohesiveness* in the group. When we understand cohesiveness, we can begin to explain why we like one group more than another. More importantly, we can better understand the kinds of communication taking place within the group.

DEFINITION OF COHESIVENESS

We all have some meaning for the term *cohesiveness.* To some of us it represents an ideal state in which we are happy as group members—probably a state always beyond the reach of many of us. Others of us may best define it by referring to a particular group—perhaps a family, a class, a fraternity, a debate squad. Although we may have trouble pinning down a word definition of cohesiveness, usually we can think of some group that exemplifies it.

B. A. Fisher (1974, p. 31) defines cohesiveness as the "ability of group members to get along, the feeling of loyalty, pride, and commitment of members toward the group." This definition implies that cohesiveness is largely a social product of any group. For example, if a person works for Smith, Inc. for an extended period, we begin to think of that individual as a "Smith person." In other words, cohesiveness is a social outcome of a group, a natural consequence of lasting membership in a group.

In a more general sense, cohesiveness is an outcome of both social and task pressures; a cohesive group can exist for reasons other than social. For example, the motive of an eager, young supervisor who joins a local management association and works hard in the group may be ambition rather than loyalty to and pride in the group.

For the purposes of our discussion, let's use the following definition of cohesiveness:

Cohesiveness is a process in which group members are attracted to each other, motivated to remain together, and share a common perspective of the group's activity.

This definition allows us to think of group cohesiveness as both cause and effect of certain group processes. It also gives us three interrelated aspects of the group process to examine: (1) a person's attraction to the group and other group members, (2) group characteristics that motivate members to stay in the group, and (3) dimensions of the group's purpose that provide members with reasons for sticking together.

* * *

Exercise 7-1
FACTORS DETERMINING COHESIVENESS

Make a list of the groups to which you belong. Rank them using degree of cohesiveness as the prime criterion. For example, the group you perceive to be the most cohesive would be 1, the next most cohesive would be 2, and so on. Now answer the following questions.

1. Is your "most cohesive" group one in which you have held membership longer than in the others?
2. Does your ranking have anything to do with the amount of influence (or lack of influence) that you have in the various groups?
3. Do any of the groups you listed relatively low in cohesiveness contain highly cohesive subgroups?
4. Is the degree of cohesiveness related to the standards of behavior (norms) that operate in the groups?
5. Would these rankings have been the same several weeks ago?

ATTRACTION TO A GROUP

Attraction to a group, or its attractiveness for us, operates at two levels: at the level of the individual members and at the level of the group as a whole. Whether or not we are initially drawn to the group because of other group members or because we want to be affiliated with the group, attraction is a prime determinant of group cohesiveness. Attraction can be either a cause of cohesiveness in a group or an outcome of cohesive group activity.

Attraction has elements of justification (what will I get out of it?) and volition (how free am I to make this choice?). Sometimes we have no choice but to join a group—for example, an assigned work group in a class—but even in those cases, we assess the group's significance for us. We evaluate our groups and their members, and that evaluation plays a large part in the group's cohesiveness.

Regardless of a person's motivation for being attracted to a group or its members, the group must afford that person the opportunity to identify with it and to establish meaningful relationships with other members. Once membership has been attained, the attractiveness becomes a "self-fulfilling prophecy." That is, once members have been accepted by the group, all participants must do what they can to justify that acceptance. Thus, few members leave an organization once membership has been approved.

Interpersonal Attraction

Interpersonal attraction refers to feelings we have for members of a group. We may be drawn to a particular group because we perceive people in that group to be like us or like what we want to be. We may join civic groups, school clubs, or social organizations, for example, because the members have characteristics similar to those we see in ourselves. Of course, interpersonal attraction of this type implies that we know something about the people who belong to a particular group.

We may also be attracted to a group because its members are very different from us. This type of interpersonal attraction can be seen in some people's drive to join elitist groups; they think that membership in these groups will help elevate their own status. Although the members are different from us, they are like what we want to be.

Interpersonal attraction is jeopardized when belonging is involuntary. When members are given a choice in belonging, however, interpersonal attraction is very important in group cohesiveness.

Group Attraction

Group attraction is the appeal a group may have because its goals and objectives are what individuals like or want. This form of attraction emphasizes group purpose, history, operating norms and rules, and its potential for energizing the individual's personal motives or goals. A group may attract individuals because of their drive for security, their altruistic goals, or a number of material factors. Some groups draw members primarily because of their task orientation. For example, the American Civil Liberties Union, Common Cause, and Black Students Union tend to attract people who are interested in the group's function and not necessarily in its interpersonal attractiveness. We join Jogger's Unlimited, the Knights of Columbus, the University Recreation League largely because we want to be identified with the group and its activities; of course, we may also like and admire the members of these groups.

Some students may feel motivated to join a fraternity or sorority because of group attraction. Imagine a first-term freshman at a large university who wants to make friends and establish a social life. Interpersonal attraction is naturally important to this person, but the prime concern is to find a place, so to speak, in the system.

**Interrelationship of Interpersonal
and Group Attraction**

Although people have priorities in terms of attraction in seeking group membership, the two levels of attraction—interpersonal and group—are interrelated. D. Cartwright (1968, p. 95) says that a member's attraction to a group is based on an "assessment of the desirable and undesirable consequences attendant upon membership in the group." This statement refers to our evaluation of both the interpersonal and the group attractiveness. We consider the value of people and group activities in deciding what the group is "worth" to us.

Cartwright (1968) offers the following checklist to determine an individual's attraction to a particular group:

1. Motive base for attraction, consisting of needs for affiliation, recognition, security, money, or other values that can be mediated by groups.
2. Incentive properties of the group, consisting of its goals, programs, characteristics of its members, style of operation, prestige, or other properties of significance for the person's motive base.

3. Expectancy, the subjective probability that membership will actually have beneficial or detrimental consequences.
4. Comparison level—the conception of the level of outcomes that group membership should provide.

This list can help us see how interpersonal and group attraction are related. Individuals have drives for recognition and wealth and choose groups that seem to serve those needs. For example, job applicants may want to sign on with a major corporation with an extensive training program in order to rise to the top of the corporate ladder. We may choose particular academic majors because they seem to offer us more satisfaction than others. In other words, we are determined to achieve personal goals, and we choose groups to serve as mediators of those goals. Once in our groups, we may acknowledge that we like the others who share the group and thus become attracted on an interpersonal level.

To get some idea of the part that attraction—interpersonal or group—plays in a cohesive group, consider the example of a typical job interview. In this interview, the employer and the prospective employee evaluate each other in terms of potential "fit." Each one makes judgments about the other on the basis of personal and group characteristics. On the personal side, judgments are made about social dimensions such as appearance and personality. For group characteristics, competence and capability are important. The prospective employee might not be attracted to the type of person who works for the company but might be attracted to the company's goals and objectives. On the other hand, the interviewee may not like the company's policies much at all but be entirely taken by the co-workers.

We must evaluate the favorable and unfavorable consequences of our choice of group membership. What expectations about the goodness or the badness of a group underlie our choices? Will we be ostracized by our family if we marry into a certain religious group? Will we alienate our friends by joining a certain political group? What are the relative merits of being attracted to certain groups and individuals? How strongly attracted are we to the group members or to the group purpose and function? On the basis of past experience, information about the group's purpose, knowledge of individuals in the group, and our own needs, we must evaluate the wisdom of joining the group.

Our attraction to the individual members of a group or to the group itself depends on variables that allow us to pursue the realization of our own goals.

Incentives

Our attraction to the group is predicated on both our needs and the ability of the group to systematically reward our choice of that particular group. We should not assume that once some level of compatibility or attraction is achieved, the cohesive group is "home free." On the contrary, the group must continually update and reinforce that attraction so that members will remain in the group. For example, people who join an activist group because they want to bring about some kind of social change may withdraw from the group if they find that the group spends most of the time meeting and little time actively trying to bring about change; however, members who join such an activist group because they want to make some contribution but don't know how to do so may be satisfied with the group's progress. In any case, changes in attractiveness must be communicated throughout the group so that appropriate decisions can be made concerning the group's attractiveness.

To reinforce our choices, groups must provide incentives. What incentives can the group use? We are all familiar with those used in work situations—promotions, salary increases, tenure, special privileges (such as an office with a window and carpeting). In social situations, incentives may take the form of smiles, greetings, a date, or the like. In groups such as the family, freedom and parental compliments may be incentives.

* * *

Exercise 7-2
INTERPERSONAL AND GROUP ATTRACTION

Using the groups you listed in Exercise 7-1 as references, answer the following questions:

1. In which groups was *interpersonal* attraction the primary motivation for membership? Explain.

2. In which groups was *group* attraction the primary motivation for membership? Explain.

3. Can you draw any conclusions regarding the degree of cohesiveness in certain groups and the type of attraction that led you to those groups?

SATISFACTION

One characteristic that encourages individuals to remain as members of a group is satisfaction.

The degree of *satisfaction* that members feel with being in a group depends on three elements: the requirements for membership in the group, group performance, and material rewards for membership.

On a day-to-day basis, we gain satisfaction in a number of ways from the groups to which we belong. In one group our satisfaction may come solely because we belong. Membership in Mortar Board, for example, makes one satisfied with belonging because the criteria for membership are rigid and few students are selected. Another source of satisfaction is group activity. For example, the members of a political campaign group may feel satisfaction because they believe in their candidate. Finally, we get a great deal of satisfaction when we think that we're being fairly rewarded for group activity. Such satisfaction may come about when a dorm group wins first prize in a homecoming decorating contest or when a group of accountants receives a bonus for spending extra hours on an audit project.

Satisfaction is a matter of individual perception and temperament. No amount of external pressure can make a person satisfied with membership in a particular group. Some people are satisfied in a low cohesive group because they are allowed to do their own thing. Some people are satisfied only in a group with a high level of cohesiveness. To the extent that we can work in a group that meets our needs for satisfaction and cohesiveness, we will be more effective group members.

Attraction and Satisfaction

Sometimes the higher our level of attraction to other group members or to the group, the higher our level of satisfaction. However, there are many instances in which we continue with some activity that seems attractive but is far from satisfying. For example, we may be continually attracted to an individual who provides no satisfaction for us at all. A similar thing happens when we gorge ourselves because we feel we "can't get enough of that pie."

Cohesiveness and Satisfaction

As group members experience a higher level of attraction to each other or to the group task, they become more cohesive and usually experience more satisfaction with being in the group. In general, the more cohesive a group is, the more satisfied the members are. The converse is also true: The higher the degree of satisfaction, the more cohesive the group.

Perhaps an extended example may help make our point here. Let's say that at your college or university you are attracted to a special program of study (such as a semester abroad or an intern teaching program) because of the people you know who participate in it and because the program itself is good. In other words, the group is attractive at both the interpersonal and the group levels. After you are invited to join the group and you do, what do you experience in terms of the group's cohesiveness?

First of all, as a select member of your student body for whom certain course requirements have been waived, you have a flexibility that you have been seeking ever since you first enrolled in college. In addition, you like the special attention from faculty, the emphasis on independent work, and the camaraderie you share with other group members. So according to everything that we've said about cohesiveness, your group has it. You feel that this is a collection of very close people. Are you satisfied? On all counts, the answer seems to be an emphatic yes. You are a member of this group (membership criterion), the group does what it is supposed to (performance), and you are getting credit for your work in the program (rewards). But let us see what happen when we vary the factors somewhat.

You note that not all members of the group have met the minimum grade-point requirement; that, instead, some people are in the group because of *who* they know instead of *what* they know. Another thing you notice is that a few people are doing all the work. Thus, the *group performance* is really the performance of a *few members*. Finally, you become disgusted with the number of credit hours that you are being given for the number of contact hours that you must put in. Are you satisfied? Hardly. How much longer will the group be cohesive? Not much longer.

As you can see from this example, cohesiveness and member satisfaction are closely related. It is difficult to speak of one without the other. Furthermore, satisfaction, like attraction, must be reinforced at various points in the group experience. Stated another way, the level of satisfaction varies and must be attended to continually.

✳ ✳ ✳

Exercise 7-3

SATISFACTION WITH A GROUP

Think of the groups you belong to. Rank these groups in terms of your overall satisfaction with each one.

1. Are the rankings similar to those of Exercise 7-1? How do you account for these similarities or differences?

2. In which groups are you satisfied primarily because of incentive or reinforcement?

3. What is the nature of the reinforcement? Are you consistently reinforced?

PRODUCTIVITY

At its simplest, productivity refers to what a group does, what it produces. Productivity relates directly to a group's performance, and indirectly to the rewards of group membership.

We know a group largely by its "product." Whether the group is a family, a football team, or a curriculum committee, we know what a group is supposed to do simply by hearing its title—and in spite of the variety of ways in which a group may go about performing its tasks.

Evaluating Group Productivity

A group that accomplishes what it sets out to do is not necessarily a worthwhile group. We must evaluate a group product in terms of what we expect from the group. A research and development group, for example, charged with developing a suitable rapid transit system may propose an underground subway; in Washington, D.C., such a plan would be (and was) acceptable, but in Los Angeles it would violate our expectations of what would be reasonable. Hence we may define group productivity as follows:

Group productivity is group outcome in terms of expected results.

We could evaluate group productivity by comparing completed tasks to intended tasks. We all know from experience that groups do not always get everything done that they set out to do. However, would having more time make a substantial difference in how much a group accomplishes? Our feeling is that other factors (including cohesiveness) besides time may be more important in determining how productive a group is.

Productivity, Cohesiveness, and Satisfaction

Do you believe that the group with the best product is the most cohesive? Or that the group that achieves the most has the closest working relationships? Or that the productive group is the most satisfied?

In some cases the group that produces the best outcomes is also the most cohesive and the most satisfied—but not necessarily. A group can be productive without attaining a high level of cohesiveness. In many organizations it may even be true that cohesiveness is unnecessary to productivity. The company that pays its employees "by the piece" certainly seems to have something going for it besides a feeling of "we-ness" as its output soars.

In our work with groups, we sometimes find that in the relief immediately following completion of a task, group members attribute their success to the group's closeness and perceived satisfaction but that later they have second thoughts about the reasons for the success. After all, as we have said before, dynamic changes occur as a group works on its task. Hence, the way the group's accomplishment is perceived also changes. Furthermore, in our definition of cohesiveness we noted that attraction, motivation, and common perspective are necessary in order for cohesiveness to exist in a group. But what if attraction is forced (assignment into groups by the instructor) and motivation is a matter of threat (do it or flunk). How cohesive is a group that relies on threat for success? Can such a group really point to cohesiveness as a reason for its productivity? In these cases perhaps the only real condition leading to group accomplishment is sharing a common perspective of the group's activity.

B. A. Fisher (1974) says that up to a point, cohesiveness and productivity are positively correlated. That is, as a group increases its productivity, there is an accompanying increase in cohesiveness, and vice versa. At some point, however, productivity levels off, and so extremely cohesive groups have moderate to low levels of productivity.

Apparently, viewing group productivity only as an end product limits a group's ability to develop cohesiveness. The group's product should not be viewed as some terminal behavior that ends at the group's last meeting. Rather, viewing productivity as the reason for group activity instead of as the result of it can increase a group's chances for effectiveness. Productivity can act as a motivator for group members to go on to other tasks. In turn, feeling motivated to remain in the group (that is, feeling satisfied) is likely to have a positive effect on the group's productivity.

COHESIVENESS IN RELATION TO OUR COMMUNICATION MODEL

We will now briefly discuss the ways in which cohesiveness is related to the message, communicator, climate, and control aspects of our communication model.

Messages

What verbal and nonverbal cues enhance cohesiveness? What message content? Can a group become cohesive without regard to what is said and how it is said?

As members seek to establish attraction relationships with each other, people send nonverbal messages to let others know of their attraction to them. We tend to think of such nonverbal behavior as belonging to a romantic relationship, and yet "flirting" can also lead to cohesiveness within a group.

As the group becomes closer, each member stakes out a territory that is recognized as that member's. For example, certain members sit in certain chairs, and members follow a particular order in speaking.

Messages change to affect the extent of group cohesiveness and in turn are changed by the consequent cohesive behavior. For example, in this class you have probably developed a meaningful, cohesive relationship with someone. Your level of productivity has been affected as a result, and the more you produce, the more the messages you exchange with this person need to change. As problems come up, you handle them and go on to new ones. All the while, your attraction to the group is being reinforced, and so cohesiveness is increasing.

Communicators

Communicator attitudes are particularly related to cohesiveness. As we noted in our Chapter 4 discussion of ego involvement, members who are highly involved in their positions are not likely to work harmoniously with members who espouse contrary views. For example, how much cohesiveness would you expect to find on a board of trustees composed of eight business people, two faculty members, the university president, and one student? There may be some cohesiveness on issues in which the members are all low-involved—or on issues in which they are all highly involved if their most acceptable positions all coincide. However, the student is at an initial disadvantage because he or she is perceived to be low in involvement on all issues concerning university administration and governance; it does not matter how involved the student perceives himself or herself to be. Furthermore, some members of the board may stereotype all students as malcontents and therefore value this student's opinions less.

Climate

Is cohesiveness a function of group rules, or does it lead to the establishment of new group rules? The group establishes rules for operating that dictate the level of cohesiveness. These rules help motivate people to remain in the group.

For many of us the concept of cohesiveness may call to mind very bad memories. How so? Cohesiveness may be directly related to group conflict. It's not unusual, for example, to see very close social friends who are also on the same committee seriously disagree with each other at a meeting. Often our most cohesive group—the group with a very close membership—is also the one with a great deal of conflict.

Control

As we noted in Chapter 1, this aspect of our model deals with the methods and techniques that groups can use to accomplish their tasks. A group is not likely to achieve cohesiveness unless these methods and techniques work toward member attraction and satisfaction. For example, many classroom discussion groups must select a format which will permit them to solve a problem within a limited time, usually one class period. When group members are unable to complete their task (that is, solve the problem), they may refuse to work together on a future class project. The cause of the group's failure may be the group discussion method rather than the abilities or actions of the individual group members.

SUMMARY

What are the forces that keep people together in small groups? Cohesiveness can be viewed as a process in which group members are attracted to each other, are motivated to remain together, and share a common perspective on the group's activity.

Attraction exists when people are drawn to each other initially and enjoy the relationships that follow from such attraction. Or it can exist when individuals are drawn to a group because it appears to be capable of meeting their needs and will serve as a vehicle for meeting their objectives. Attraction can be a prime determinant of group cohesiveness because it allows the group to grow from a basis of compatibility. Furthermore, attraction may exist as a result of group cohesion. As the group is allowed to operate in a highly compatible atmosphere, the level of attraction grows. In the absence of mutual reinforcement and justification for remaining in the group, however, individuals lose their feeling of attraction for the group, and commitment to the group decreases.

Like attraction, satisfaction can both result from and cause group cohesiveness. The degree of member satisfaction with a particular group depends on the requirements for membership in the group, the group's performance, and the material rewards for membership in the group. Member satisfaction with the group must be continually reinforced.

We should evaluate group productivity in terms of how well the group's achievements match expected results (which may or may not be the same as its intended objectives). As groups increase their togetherness, they tend to experience greater satisfaction and to produce more—up to a certain point. When viewed as the end-all for the group, productivity is dysfunctional and will gradually erode the members' satisfaction with the group.

In small-group settings, cohesiveness and communication are inextricably linked. Therefore, we cannot isolate cohesiveness from the other variables in our communication model: message, communicator, climate, and control. As group members become closer, nonverbal messages have more impact. Also, while the attitudes of communicators may militate against much member attraction, it can also lead to a change in member attitudes. Similarly, conflict often occurs in tandem with cohesiveness. By using certain group discussion methods and techniques, we can control the message flow and thus increase group cohesiveness, which in turn leads to increased group attraction and success.

Cohesiveness is not a state to be reached and then forgotten. It is (like the other process variables such as attraction, satisfaction, and productivity) constantly changing. Its role in group communication experiences cannot be overemphasized.

ADDITIONAL READINGS

Baird, J., and Weinberg, S. *Communication: The Essence of Group Synergy.* Dubuque, Ia.: Wm. C. Brown, 1977. The discussion on page 176 and following concerning the consequences of cohesion in groups is very helpful in understanding the forces that keep people in groups. Of particular use is their argument about the minimal level of cohesion below which people will leave a group.

Berscheid, E., and Walster, E. *Interpersonal Attraction.* Menlo Park, Calif.: Addison-Wesley, 1969. The authors' discussion of attraction as it relates to liking, anxiety, and proximity, among other variables, is easy to read and invaluable in understanding the complexities of attraction. Examples and illustrations that can be easily understood by the student enhance the readability of this book.

Cartwright, D. R. "The Nature of Group Cohesiveness," in D. R. Cartwright and A. Zander, eds., 3d ed. *Group Dynamics: Research and Theory.* New York: Harper & Row, 1968. Even though this chapter may be somewhat difficult to read the first time through, it is well worth rereading for valuable insights into the causes and consequences of group cohesiveness. Of special importance is the model (p. 92) outlining the determinants and consequences of group cohesiveness.

Davis, J. *Group Performance.* Menlo Park, Calif.: Addison-Wesley, 1969. Davis's discussion of cohesiveness as a variable affecting group performance is a must to understand the interrelation between cohesiveness and the effects of group performance. His treatment of cooperation and competition as factors related to cohesiveness deserves special attention.

Fisher, B. *Small Group Decision Making: Communication and the Group Process.* New York: McGraw-Hill, 1974. Fisher's discussion of cohesiveness (page 31 and following) as both a state and an outcome is useful to understand the interaction of all variables in the group process model. His notions of cohesiveness and productivity as social and task dimensions, respectively, bear reading and understanding.

CONFLICT

PREVIEW

* **What is conflict?**

  Intrapersonal conflict: the internal struggle an individual experiences when placed in a decision-making situation in which he or she must choose between mutually exclusive alternatives.

  Interpersonal conflict: an open difference over mutually exclusive alternatives by individuals who perceive themselves to be in disagreement.

* **How is conflict caused?**

  Conflict occurs at many levels because of differences in attitudes and in individual orientation.

* **How are power and conflict related?**

  Conflict often grows out of perceived power relationships.

* **How can conflict be resolved?**

  Understanding the individual orientations, attitudes, and power relationships can lead to conflict resolution.

* **In what ways can conflict be productive or nonproductive?**

  Conflict can be productive or nonproductive depending on how it affects the achievement of group goals.

* **How is conflict related to the group communication model?**

  As a result of group interaction, conflict is both cause and effect of other processes.

IS CONFLICT a symptom of group dysfunction or a normal outcome of group process? We believe that it is normal. Without conflict, it is difficult, if not impossible, to bring about change. Conversely, conflict appears to be a logical outcome of change. During an hour-long discussion on a topic in which group members are highly involved, for example, conflict may arise, be resolved, and lead to more conflict several times.

Conflict within the group is a subsystem of group interaction—the give and take between group members. In other words, this interaction can result in conflict. Knowledge of what conflict is, how it is caused, how it is resolved, and how it affects group communication will enable us to better manage group disagreements toward productive ends.

DEFINITION OF CONFLICT

As decision makers, we all experience conflict. Whether we are buying a car, choosing an apartment, selecting a mate, or picking a class time, we often find ourselves faced with having to choose between two or more mutually exclusive options. Choosing one of them means rejecting the other(s). Similarly, in many conflicts between people or groups, if one side attains its goal, the other side cannot. Thus, the two alternatives involved in the conflict must be incompatible. M. Deutsch (1969) has suggested that we can define conflict as simply the existence of "incompatible activities." A business group, for example, may have to choose between specializing in a few products or diversifying its line into other areas. A church group may have to decide whether to allocate money from its benevolence fund to foreign missions or to local charity projects.

Some conflicts are more stressful than others. The relative attractiveness of the alternatives involved in a conflict is one determinant of the degree of conflict. When we perceive one option as more attractive than another, there is usually little conflict; we simply choose the other option. But when both options are equally attractive or unattractive, we have trouble deciding. One option may be as appealing or unappealing as the other: we want both options, or we don't want either one, and yet we must choose between them. The more nearly equal in attractiveness two alternatives are, the greater the conflict we experience. The degree of conflict also increases with the number of alternatives available to us and with the importance of the decision we must make.

Perhaps the most common type of conflict arises when a choice entails both positive and negative consequences. For example, deciding whether to continue as a member of a group may be difficult if you dislike going to the business meetings but derive satisfaction from other aspects of your association with the group. Or a group may have trouble choosing a speaker if they want to invite someone who would reinforce their position but feel that they should present an opposition speaker; in this situation, a compromise may be possible (such as presenting a debate between the two speakers) that would offset the possible negative consequences of only presenting one view or the other.

Intrapersonal Conflict

Intrapersonal conflict takes place within us and is generally thought to be resolved when we make decisions.

The internal struggle that we experience prior to a decision between mutually exclusive options is usually referred to as *intrapersonal conflict*.

Many psychologists argue that this type of conflict precedes nearly every decision that we make. Of course, once our decision is made we usually seek to justify our choice.

We experience intrapersonal conflict daily. Take, for example, the conflict over which of two possible electives to enroll in. Choosing one means not choosing the other. A decision must be made. Your advisor gives you information, as do your friends. There are advantages and disadvantages to both classes. Finally, you choose one over the other.

Although intrapersonal conflict takes place within us, it is often reflected in our communication with group members. A group member who experiences internal conflict over the group's handling of a specific task will probably clash openly with other group members before the matter is resolved (Coser, 1956). The relationship between intrapersonal conflict and satisfaction with other group members and group tasks is very important.

Interpersonal Conflict

Assume you are a member of an executive council of a tutorial group for various ethnic students. The group has just lost its school funding and is faced with two choices: operate the program through student fees or drop the program. Obviously, something has to be done, and doing one thing means rejecting the other. Some group members say that the program is the school's responsibility and that it's unfair to make the students pay. Other members say that regardless of where the responsibility lies, the ethnic students are being harmed. The arguments go back and forth.

This situation is more complex than intrapersonal conflict because of the addition of other communicators and the communicators' perception of themselves as being in disagreement. The conflict is operating on an interpersonal level.

Interpersonal conflict occurs when there is an open difference over mutually exclusive alternatives by individuals who perceive themselves to be in disagreement.

By this definition, conflict between group members is more than the mere holding of hostile attitudes. Rather than operating on a subtle, internal level, interpersonal conflict takes place in the interaction between two or more group members (Coser, 1956). We

know that individuals are in conflict when they indicate their opposition either verbally (whether in name-calling or rational disagreement) or nonverbally (as by smirking, drumming one's fingers on the table, or furrowing one's brow). In a sense, negative feedback is a form of conflict behavior, for individuals may use words, facial expressions, or tone of voice to indicate their opposition. Because the conflict is out in the open, we are better able to describe it, resolve it, and even channel it into productive group activity.

CAUSES OF CONFLICT

There may be many levels of causes of conflict. The issue at hand, such as meeting times or member attendance, may vary greatly in importance from one conflict to another. The dynamics that underlie the precipitating cause or source, whatever it is, are of more concern to us here.

* * *

Members of the class should pair off and position themselves in different parts of the room or in different rooms. One member of the pair is identified as *A*, the other as *B*, for the duration of the following activity:

First phase: Description. Member *A* describes to *B* what *A* observes about *B*. *A* is to comment on nonverbal cues only—clothes, face, and the like. All statements are to be descriptive and nonevaluative. When *A* has finished, *B* does the same. Neither member is to react to comments made by the other at this time.

Second phase: Hypothesis. Without any comments from *B*, *A* states as many hypotheses (evaluative statements) as possible about *B's* attitudes, values, beliefs, behaviors, and so on. When *A* has finished, *B* makes evaluative statements about *A*. The following statement might be the kind that would be generated: "You would probably vote Democratic."

Third phase: Verification. Both parties react to the hypotheses generated. *B* begins by reacting to the hypotheses that *A* made. *A* does the same in terms of the hypotheses made by *B*. Each member of the pair should also comment at this time about the descriptive statements made during the first phase of the exercise.

Now answer the following questions:

1. Did you find it difficult to offer nonevaluative statements in the first phase of the exercise? Why or why not?

2. How accurate were the hypotheses about your attitudes, values, and the like?

3. Was it difficult to predict your partner's attitudes, values, and the like? Why or why not?

Individual Orientation:
Competition or Cooperation

In general, individuals bring to the group one of two orientations or perspectives: competition or cooperation. A person who has a competitive orientation perceives a situation in win-lose terms. In sports, for example, the rules specify that the person or team with the most points, best record, or fastest time will be the winner—all others will be losers. Even though runners-up may be recognized and awarded prizes also, competition basically requires that as one side approaches victory, the other side faces defeat.

A person with a cooperative orientation believes that the "reward" of the situation can be shared. This orientation does not preclude conflict: rather, it acknowledges that the most efficient means of handling a group struggle is through cooperation.

Competition can lead to conflict, but conflict does not have to be competitive. Conflict can occur in either a competitive or a cooperative orientation. These orientations are the most powerful determinant of the context in which conflict occurs.

Classroom discussion generally takes place in a cooperative environment where the goals are consensus and member satisfaction. The group members work together to accomplish some group objective that will show all the participants to be "good" group members. Conflicts that occur during the discussion are generally resolved using some agreed-upon rules. However, when a particular group assignment is being graded on the basis of individual contributions, members may try to outshine one another. Although the group's purpose is discussion for the group's good, the reward system is structured for the emergence of winners and losers.

The orientation individuals bring to the group is directly related to their personality characteristics. Past experiences with individuals familiar to us and observations of individuals unknown to us enable us to make fairly accurate guesses about how they will behave in a group. We may see some people as authoritarian, others as cocky, and others as timid. Milton Rokeach (1960) has identified individuals who demonstrate blind loyalty to a system as highly dogmatic. These individuals are closed-minded and generally resist attempts by other group members to compromise or reach consensus on issues.

Individual orientation is conveyed through messages. Members make clear very early in the group's deliberations which orientation they have, the manner in which they will resolve conflict. From messages we can also learn the amount of trust that members have in each other, the extent to which they will share their views, what their attitudes and personality characteristics are, and how powerful they perceive themselves to be.

* * *

Answer these questions in relation to the small groups to which you belong.

1. What is your orientation as you participate in the small groups to which you belong? Does it change from one group to another?
2. What is the orientation of other group members in the various groups?
3. Is a group's method of conflict resolution primarily cooperative or competitive? Is the group's activity usually within a competitive or cooperative orientation?

Relationship between Power and Conflict

Power can be manifested in a variety of ways.

Power is the perceived influence that exists between individuals or groups.

J. R. French and B. Raven (1959) identify five kinds of power, each based on a different source of power and a different relationship between the parties.

1. Reward power: The ability to present rewards to or for another, often as added incentive for a positive activity or behavior.
2. Coercive power: The ability to affect the behavior of another by punishment unless the behavior is performed.
3. Legitimate power: The assigned right—because of the organizational structure, for example—to expect another individual to conform to one's wishes.
4. Referent power: The power one person has over another person because the latter identifies with the former.
5. Expert power: The power an individual has because he or she is perceived to be knowledgeable—an expert—regarding a specific problem or field.

Characteristics relating to the amount and source of a person's ability to influence others can fit into one or more of these five categories.

Individuals are placed in power positions because they have something that the other members of the group do not. For example, the more knowledge one has in a certain area, the higher the position in the organizational structure that person is likely to occupy. The positions of power in a classroom discussion are often held by individuals who have read the assigned material; they have more information than those who did not complete the reading.

Research shows that in cohesive groups there is more of an attempt by members to influence each other and a greater likelihood that members will be influenced by each other (Cartwright and Lippitt, 1961). It seems reasonable to assume that there will be conflict in groups in which we engage in some form of behavior to influence each other.

Conflict can grow out of perceptions of power relationships. We

all strive to attain some position of power. Most of us have at one time or another engaged in open disagreement with an individual over some issue that calls any of these various types of power into question. The notion, for example, that an instructor's statement is true because he or she said it can lead to conflict. Of course, the conflict (or power struggle) may be confounded by previously held attitudes or highly dogmatic predispositions.

Communicator Attitudes

Interpersonal conflict can result from hostile feelings or attitudes (Coser, 1956). Let's use an example to see how an attitude can lead to conflict.

A group of faculty members and students are discussing the role of the undergraduate student in curriculum development. The students feel that the role ought to be a strong one; the faculty feels that the status quo is fine. Whether conflict will erupt from these hostile attitudes depends on several factors, including the involvement of the parties in the issue and their orientations. If the students are seniors in their last semester of college, the group task may not be as important to them as an upcoming job interview or their current course load. Individuals who are less involved in an issue are likely to be persuaded to change their position. Conflict may become entrenched, however, if the faculty members enter the discussion with a win-lose attitude, or if the students see this as an opportunity to "get" the establishment.

In general, attitudes can be viewed as the root of conflict, but they do not necessarily lead to conflict. Moreover, various attitude-related variables (such as the context and the other parties) may mediate the effect of the contrary attitudes.

When member satisfaction is high, conflict is likely to be minimal. Perceived similarity of interests, similarity of personalities, and a high level of group cohesiveness can provide for high

* * *

Exercise 8-3
CAUSES OF CONFLICT

Answer the following questions in relation to a group to which you belong—perhaps your favorite group, your primary social group, or a task group.

1. How much intrapersonal conflict do you experience in this group?

2. What kinds of power, if any, do you see operating in the group? Are the power relationships clearly defined?

3. Which message elements by specific members generate interpersonal conflict within the group? Do any changes in the messages result from the conflict?

4. Is the group cohesive? If so, how did it get that way? Have you found that group conflict can lead to a more cohesive group?

5. Which members (including yourself) do you perceive to be high or low in dogmatism? How do they behave when conflict arises?

member satisfaction with the group's activity along with minimum conflict. In groups with a cooperative orientation, conflict occupies very little of the group's attention. However, if group members are competitive and base their satisfaction on winning, then conflict may be more prominent.

Conflict can be an integral part of a group's purpose. For example, in an encounter group conflict is a necessary ingredient. A group that has as its primary purpose the sharing of information needs a mechanism to deal with the conflict that may occur when information presented by one group member is in opposition to that presented by another member.

CONFLICT RESOLUTION

There are many situations in which members are openly hostile to each other. Issues are brought up, conflict ensues, but resolution may or may not occur.

Conflict resolution refers to the process of solving a group conflict—whether by eliminating the conflict, reducing it to the members' satisfaction, or managing it to allow further group activity.

The way in which we deal with conflict depends on the orientation we bring to the group. Individuals who always compete in small-group discussions are unlikely to resolve their differences through cooperative strategies.

If the people have a pre-existing cooperative orientation toward one another, they are likely to resolve a conflict of interest by a cooperative process; if they have a prior competitive orientation, they are likely to resolve it by a competitive process. (Deutsch, 1967, p. 46)

For conflict resolution to occur, it is important that the orientation the individual brings to the group be consistent with the group orientation. Inconsistency between these two orientations makes the treatment of conflict very difficult. Conflict resolution also requires that the parties to the conflict have some similarity of understanding of the conflict issue itself.

Conflict behavior can result in attitude change, which constitutes some degree of conflict resolution. This change in attitudes need not be a complete reversal—this rarely happens; it may be simply a modification of the parties' positions, a reinforcement of existing attitudes, or agreement on some third position.

Highly dogmatic individuals tend to resist more conventional forms of conflict resolution such as compromise. The conflict itself may make them more convinced of their own position. Research indicates that highly dogmatic people solidify their position during negotiations with an opponent (Druckman, 1967). They are much more resistant to compromise than are less dogmatic people.

When conflict involves individuals who have reward power and who operate from a competitive orientation, the resolution of the conflict is likely to be in terms of a win or a loss and so can be harmful to the group's goal. On the other hand, if reward power is invested in group members who operate from a cooperative orientation, the results can be satisfying for all group members.

In a conflict between a professor and a student over a particular grade that has been given, the reward power position cannot change; the best that can be hoped for is a compromise, not a shifting of the responsibility to the student. In some other conflict situations the power position may be more flexible. For example, the disagreement between a prospective donor and an organization representative who is soliciting a sizable amount for his institution has many possible resolutions, one of which may be to increase the donation dramatically.

Coercive power conflicts are not likely to occur, but if they do, the resolution is usually without beneficial ends. The coercive power position is very resistant to change, and anything short of a coup will not yield the conflicting parties beneficial results.

Conflict growing out of a difference between individuals holding legitimate, referent, or expert power positions can be beneficial to all concerned. In these cases, parties to the conflict generally hold a cooperative orientation toward resolution of any disagreement, and the resolution should provide high member satisfaction. With referent power, for example, there is a strong drive on the part of the individuals to identify with each other.

Thinking of interpersonal conflict as behaviors that grow out of hostile or antagonistic attitudes facilitates conflict management. Unless the parties to the conflict actually see themselves in disagreement with each other, the issue cannot be managed. Perhaps, one of the reasons that a conflict involving dogmatic people can be very difficult to resolve is that they see only their own point of view—no other workable alternative exists besides their own.

Conflict management is much more difficult when individuals react to each other as representatives of groups rather than as opponents for the particular issue under discussion. A conflict between conservatives and liberals, for example, may be more symbolic than real if the parties do not accurately perceive themselves to be in disagreement over the same issue.

✳ ✳ ✳

Exercise 8-4
CONSENSUS/CONFLICT

Generate a list of ten to twelve topics that are very important on your campus. As individuals, rank these campus-related topics from most important to least important. (Do not combine any topics.)

Divide the class randomly into groups of five members each. As groups, rank the topics from most important to least important. (Do not combine any topics.) Do not average or vote as a means of arriving at the group consensus.

Now answer the following questions:

1. How close to your initial ranking is the final group order?

2. Which members of your group were most powerful? Why?

3. Describe the outstanding conflicts, if any, in your group.

EFFECTS OF CONFLICT

Most of us think of conflict as a negative group activity. However, it can be productive (functional).

In general, conflict is *productive* when members are satisfied and they have gained—both as individuals and as group members—from the conflict (Deutsch, 1969).

Group conflict is *nonproductive* (dysfunctional) when group members feel some dissatisfaction or loss as a result of it.

Whether conflict within the group is productive or nonproductive depends on a number of variables—including individual objectives, the group's task, initiating issues, and the location of power within the group.

Productive conflict can serve several functions. First, it can reinforce the individuality of group members. Acceptance of conflict within the group can offset the restrictions on individuality that naturally accompany group membership. Conflict can allow individual members to present their positions regardless of how much they differ from the group norm. In a sense, this principle of productive conflict underlies all other useful purposes of interpersonal disagreement.

Second, conflict can help the group accomplish its specified task by clearly defining the issues under discussion, bringing forth various solutions to a group problem, and helping the group get rid of underlying hostilities that would otherwise keep the group from reaching its goal.

Third, conflict is productive when it generates cohesiveness in the group. Conflict tends to unite some individuals who would normally refrain from making alliances (Coser, 1956). Conflict can also demonstrate that the members of the group trust each other and are comfortable taking certain risks. Conflict that arises in a cohesive group tends to be very amenable to resolution; for the most part, it is more productive than conflict in an uncohesive group.

Fourth, conflict can define the power relationships within the group. Powerholders within a group often engage in a struggle for group leadership. During this conflict, the rivals argue their case openly, and all group members have a chance to participate in the group's decision to bestow power on one or more individuals. Member satisfaction increases because of this participation. By keeping power struggles "within the family," so to speak, the group becomes a stronger collection of individuals and is more likely to create a cohesive atmosphere. As L. Coser (1956) has noted, conflict is most productive when it aids in the establishment and maintenance of a group balance of power.

Nonproductive Conflict

Conflict behavior within a group tends to be nonproductive when group goals are subverted in favor of individual objectives. People who join groups for purely individual gain and openly disagree with other members in order to further their own objectives generally use the showdown strategy. Such behavior impedes the group process and may cause the disagreement to escalate beyond the point of resolution.

Some groups have a very low tolerance for conflict arising within the group or impinging on it from outside. An authoritarian group such as the military would be an example. Conflict is usually nonproductive when it occurs in a group with a very limited capacity to handle it. The conflict between police and demonstrators at the 1968 Democratic convention in Chicago is an example of this type of nonproductive conflict.

> The rigid police system was unable to tolerate the minor disturbances of the students' crusade or the comparable rigidity of the militant leaders who were spearheading the demonstrations. Such mutual rigidities prevent the development of an equilibrium and riots result. Almost the same type of *polarized rigidity* may be found on every campus where troubles have erupted in recent years. (Keltner, 1970, p. 230)

Such conflict occurs not only between groups (intergroup conflict) but also within a group, as when group members assume an all-or-nothing attitude toward a problem under discussion. This rigidity cuts down the usefulness of conflict. Generally, interpersonal conflict within the group is nonproductive when the conflict goes beyond its initiating causes and continues long after these causes have been forgotten or become irrelevant (Deutsch, 1969).

Conflict behavior can dramatically affect the postconflict verbal and nonverbal messages. Having engaged in conflict characterized by loaded language, facial contortions, and intense gesturing, group members may modify their language and nonverbal cues.

As a result of conflict, individuals may act more openly and come to trust each other more. Of course, there is the possibility that individuals will reject each other. However, even this behavior can lead to cohesiveness within the group. Cohesiveness is perceived trust and risk-taking. These behaviors tend to give group members the feeling that their opinions and positions are worthwhile. Thus, even if their positions are rejected, they become stronger group members simply because they were recognized and their positions respected.

Directly related to the cohesiveness of a group is member satisfaction with the group activity and with the product of the group deliberations. Conflict is probably the toughest test of member satisfaction. The extent to which individual group members expend their energies resolving some disagreement takes away from the energy available to implement the group solution.

* * *

Exercise 8-5
PRODUCTIVE AND NONPRODUCTIVE CONFLICT

Answer the following questions in relation to the group that you find most fulfilling personally.

1. Is conflict in this group useful?

2. Does it lead you to trust other group members more? Are your group relationships more stable because you are not afraid to engage in conflict?

3. How many times have the ground rules under which the group operates caused you to refrain from suggesting a solution that you had thought of?

4. Does conflict in this group aid the members in making decisions?

5. How often has conflict developed because group members refused to see any value in sharing or compromising a position?

CONFLICT IN RELATION TO OUR GROUP COMMUNICATION MODEL

Conflict is the result of group interaction. It is impossible to note all the variables that operate within the group communication process. Our selection represents our best guess as to the basic factors affecting conflict in group communication. We may not have discussed factors that you consider most relevant to conflict in your particular groups. Self-esteem and source credibility, for example, are affected by interpersonal conflict within the group, but we have discussed other aspects of productive and nonproductive conflict.

You can see from our presentation that conflict can be both cause and effect of other variables in the group communication process. For example, communicator attitudes can lead to conflict behavior (open antagonism), which can in turn lead to a change in these attitudes; also, conflict affects messages and is in turn affected by them. Cohesiveness is another example of a group communication variable that interacts with conflict: After a conflict has been resolved, a group may feel more unified, but the consequent understanding and trust among members may make them feel freer to engage in conflict. This, in its simplest form, is the system in action: One factor affects another, which affects another. Similarly, variables such as attitude and dogmatism are inextricably bound together, for it is difficult to imagine an individual with a strong personality characteristic such as dogmatism without seeing that person as also holding highly involved attitudes on a variety of issues.

SUMMARY

Conflict behavior is a complex subsystem operating within the larger communication system. Conflict generally arises when a choice must be made between two or more mutually exclusive alternatives. The more nearly equal the alternatives are in attractiveness or unattractiveness, the more intense the conflict is likely to be. Decision making is also very difficult when both positive and negative outcomes will result from our choice. Interpersonal conflict occurs as an open difference between individuals who perceive themselves to be in disagreement, whereas intrapersonal conflict occurs only within the individual. Each type of conflict, however, often feeds the other.

Interpersonal conflict within the group (intragroup conflict) may come about as a result of hostile attitudes. As conflict develops, it involves communicator evaluations not only of the issue at hand but also of the context and the other parties to the conflict. Conflict can also grow out of differences in perceptions of the power positions. It influences power relationships by opening up new power positions and maintaining a group balance of power. If we know the roles that attitudes, dogmatism, and power play in conflict situations, we can better recognize emerging conflicts, especially power-based ones, and deal with them as they arise.

Verbal and nonverbal messages can act as the vehicle for both conflict and its resolution. The quality of the resolution to a conflict depends almost entirely on the individual orientation to the situation. If it is competitive, then win-lose criteria will be applied, and member satisfaction and group productivity will be minimal. If the orientation is cooperative, conflict may still occur, but the processes used to resolve it will lead to high member satisfaction and, presumably, greater group cohesiveness.

Finally, interpersonal conflict within the group can be productive or nonproductive. It should not necessarily be avoided in group decision making. Productive conflict can reinforce the individuality of group members, help the group accomplish its specified task, generate cohesiveness in the group, or define the power relationships in the group. Nonproductive conflict occurs when the group goals are subordinated to individual goals.

Whether conflict is productive or nonproductive, it is still both cause and effect of changes in the group communication system. The constant potential for conflict requires that we be in a position to propose methods for resolving conflict as it arises. In a general sense, the recognition of conflict behavior is a method of resolution.

ADDITIONAL READINGS

Coser, Lewis A. *The Functions of Social Conflict.* New York: Free Press, 1956. Probably the single most influential treatment of social conflict, this is not an easy book to read and understand; it deals with a "number of basic propositions which have been distilled from theories of social conflict."

Jacobson, Wally D. *Power and Interpersonal Relations.* Belmont, Calif.: Wadsworth, 1972. This is a very sophisticated and scholarly treatment of the power variable and its operation in a variety of circumstances. This work contains virtually all relevant research in the area. It may be somewhat difficult for the student to read, but worth the time required.

Keltner, John W. *Interpersonal Speech Communication: Elements and Structures.* Belmont, Calif.: Wadsworth, 1970. A comprehensive and easy-to-read treatment of conflict and its relationship to communication behavior. The presentation of the dimensions and systems of controversy-conflict (p. 231) is particularly useful for the small-group member.

V

CONTROL

---

* * *

CHAPTER 9
PROBLEM SOLVING

We begin the chapter by offering our definition of problem-solving behavior—recognition and attempted alleviation of some relevant difficulty. We discuss two problem-solving patterns that focus on member interaction and thought processes: (1) Bales's interaction process analysis, a method of analysing interaction in group problem solving and (2) reflective thinking, a thought-process-oriented approach to problem solving.

CHAPTER 10
METHODS OF DISCUSSION

This chapter examines methods or procedures for presenting a group discussion, which is defined as the face-to-face interaction of two or more people engaged in information sharing, problem solving, and self-maintenance. Six methods of discussion are examined: (1) round table, (2) dialogue, (3) panel, (4) colloquy, (5) symposium-forum, and (6) lecture-forum. We conclude by considering three problem-solving procedures: the reflective thinking pattern, the ideal solution pattern, and the single question pattern.

CHAPTER 11
SMALL-GROUP TECHNIQUES

We examine four discussion techniques developed either to assist group interaction or to promote an understanding of roles within the group. These techniques are brainstorming, buzz sessions and Phillips 66, posting, and role playing. Consideration is then given to the nominal group technique. We close with an examination of the Delphi technique.

* * *

9

PROBLEM
SOLVING

PREVIEW

✳ **What is problem solving?**

Problem solving is recognition and attempted alleviation of some relevant difficulty.

✳ **What are the key phases leading to an interactive group atmosphere?**

One is orientation; another is deliberation.

✳ **What are two basic problem-solving viewpoints or perspectives?**

Group interaction is one problem-solving viewpoint; another is thought processes.

✳ **What is the interaction process analysis?**

Interaction process analysis is a means of classifying member interaction. It describes both task and social-emotional dimensions of the group.

✳ **What is the reflective thinking process?**

The reflective thinking process is a procedure or set of stages for training the mind to respond to problems. Through it group members can identify the scope, specificity, limits, and alternate solutions to a problem.

THE LOCAL board of education meets to decide the best way to approach the voters for a bond issue to build a new high school.

A fraternity committee gets together to discuss plans for a weekend party.

Members of the student government and representatives of the university administration convene to create a new governance system.

The United Nations General Assembly meets to agree on the best way to collect delinquent dues from member nations.

These four examples of group deliberations have at least one thing in common: a problem in need of solution.

Problem solving is a small-group task that involves the recognition and attempted alleviation of some relevant difficulty.

The key term in this definition of problem solving is *relevant*. Group members must perceive that the problem and their attempts to solve it are important to them.

Every day we face situations that call for decision making—what food to eat, which class to take, what people to meet, which groups to join. Generally, we go about this day-to-day decision making without consulting other people. However, there are many circumstances in which we must make decisions as a group. Recall that group communication is the verbal and non-verbal give and take of the group members. At no other time is this exchange more crucial than during problem-solving deliberations.

TWO STAGES IN GROUP INTERACTION

Imagine a collection of people who do not interact. You might think of a group of sullen commuters, or perhaps an audience of people not speaking to each other, or even the people in your most boring lecture class.

G. Phillips and E. Erickson (1970) define interaction as "an exchange of meanings or communications." It is the group's activity—its business. This interactive behavior serves as the vehicle for every task that the group faces, and it is affected by the strength of relationships within the group.

Achieving this interactive relationship is not easy. Think of a group that you joined when it was first being formed and in which the members were all initially strangers. By now there is probably a healthy interaction in the group, but if you look back on the early stages of that group's life, you probably find that there were some trying times. There are generally two stages leading to the establishment of an acceptable interactive atmosphere: orientation and deliberation.

Orientation

The orientation stage is typified by unsure communication—a kind of "chicken dancing" in which participants identify members' attitudes and feelings toward certain objects or events.

Think of your first few days in this class. You might have known a few of your classmates but, for the most part, your peers and the instructor were probably strangers to you. What was your reaction? What was the nature of your communication? Guarded? Innocuous? Safe? You made tentative judgments about classmates and the instructor—judgments that by now you have confirmed or rejected. You entered this group and existed in it for some time at a very low level of interaction.

Think for a moment about your group's ability to solve problems at this orientation stage. Limited? Sure it was, because member give and take was restricted. Much of your behavior was random—without pattern or system.

Have you ever joined a group during its organizational meeting and elected officers? What happened? The individuals who talked the most were elected. Why? Because the group was merely a collection and not an interactive or dynamic body. Thus, the individuals' ability to carry out meaningful elections was severely limited.

At the *orientation* stage of group life members are disoriented and lack the ability to meaningfully solve problems.

They may be interacting, but their communications are not substantive enough to allow them to address complex issues.

Deliberation

After the members have become oriented toward the group and its goals, they enter a phase of interaction that we can refer to as the *deliberation* stage. In this stage of the group's life *trust* emerges among the members. You take chances, you know the others, you identify with the group's functions. The sharing, the interaction, is more complete and represents a more honest exchange of communications among group members.

Often, members can enter this stage simply because they have spent considerable time with each other on some common task. They are able to take communication risks that were impossible at the earlier stage of group life.

At the *deliberation* stage interaction is at its fullest and problem-solving behavior is most productive.

* * *

Exercise 9-1
INTERACTION AND PROBLEM SOLVING

List the difficulties that you have encountered during the past 24 hours. No matter how trivial the issues may be, list them. Now ask yourself the following questions:

1. Do my problems generally involve the same individual(s)?

2. Do my difficulties come about as a result of interaction with others? Do they lead to interaction with others?

3. What is my most common method of problem solving when I interact with others? Do I withdraw? Do I work it out at the time? Do I postpone the problem?

GROUP INTERACTION AND PROBLEM SOLVING

Group interaction is important in problem solving.

A group's ability to develop a dynamic interaction is directly related to its problem-solving behavior. Conversely, a group's problem-solving ability is directly related to its ability to develop a dynamic interaction.

As a small group goes about solving its problems, making decisions, and committing itself to action, its success depends directly on the quality of its interaction.

Analyzing Group Interaction

In order to analyze group interaction in problem-solving deliberations, we need a way to categorize member behavior. R. Bales (1950) devised such a method, which he called interaction process analysis (IPA). Bales's model (Figure 9-1) is based on the notion that group members have two types of orientation: task (the job that they have to do) and social-emotional (the personal relationships with the other group members).

The task area of group interaction shows up in the group members' questions and attempted answers, both of which generally

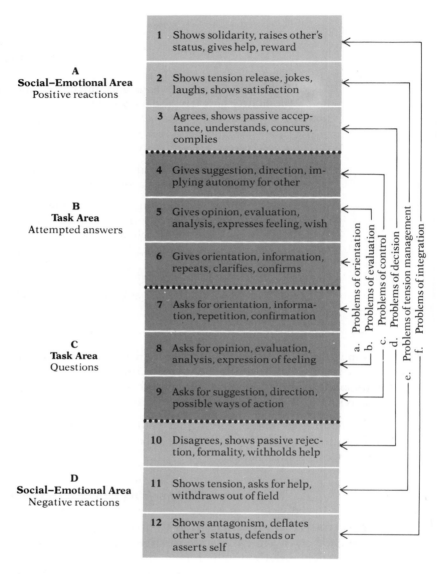

FIGURE 9-1. Interaction process analysis: categories and major problems. (Bales, 1951, p. 258)

contain information rather than emotion. If we are preoccupied with the task dimension of our group, we spend most of our time asking and answering questions. Even the eloquent speeches we may make are generally in response to questions by other group members. In contrast, the social-emotional area encompasses the

positive and negative reactions that group members express. When we are more concerned with this dimension, we spend most of our time evaluating information or people.

As shown in Figure 9-1, Bales proposed six types of problems that are logically applicable to any interaction system: orientation, evaluation, control, decision, tension management, and integration. We can think of these problems as stages through which the problem-solving group moves. Thus, at its earliest meetings a group interacts about orientation matters. Later, the group focuses on matters of evaluation, control, decision, and tension management, and finally on integration.

For each of the four kinds of communication acts or behaviors Bales specified three behaviors; each of these is noted in Figure 9-1. Of course, there are more interactive behaviors than just the twelve recognized in this model. Joining these behaviors are lines (labeled *a*, *b*, *c*, *d*, *e*, and *f* in the figure) that indicate the problem classification. For example, if a person asks for information (behavior 7) and another group member answers (behavior 6), the interaction is identified as a problem of orientation.

Results of Analyzing Group Interaction

Using the IPA, Bales obtained some significant findings on the occurrence of the behaviors being analyzed. As shown in Figure

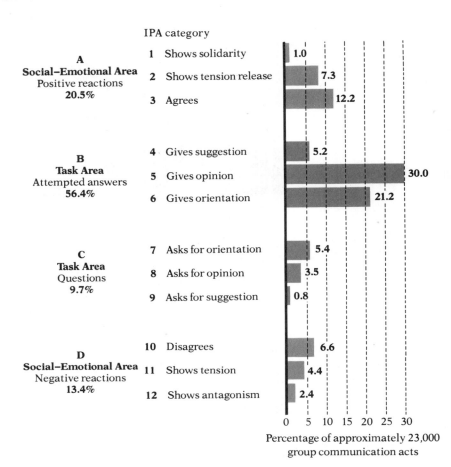

FIGURE 9-2. IPA categories and percentages. (Data from Bales, 1951, p. 262)

9-2, he found that more behaviors were classified as "gives opinion" (category 5) than any other classification and that the fewest behaviors were classified as "asks for suggestion." These data imply that group members spend the most time giving opinions and the least time asking for suggestions or, to put it another way, that group members are most likely to give opinions and least likely to ask for suggestions.

Why are group members reluctant to ask for direction or for possible ways of acting in a certain situation? Could it be that we become so involved in our own approaches to the problem that we think others have little to offer? You will note, however, that although giving suggestions does not occur very often either, there are six or seven times as many instances of it. Similar discrepancies occur among the other pairs of behaviors.

The interaction among members of a mature group has been analyzed as follows (Bales, 1953):

Social-emotional area: positive reactions	25%
Task area: attempted answers	56%
Task area: questions	7%
Social-emotional area: negative reactions	12%

A group whose behaviors can be classified approximately according to these percentages is doing well. However, if, for example, 56 percent of a group's communicative acts are questions and only 7 percent are answers, the group is not functioning well; the task may be so unclear that members must spend most of their time seeking clarification, only to find that not many answers are available. Similarly, major deviations from the percentages for the social-emotional areas may indicate difficulties. For example, a group in which 40 percent of all communicative acts are devoted to negative reactions and only 8 percent to positive reactions would have far too much disagreement, tension, and antagonism. Using the percentages for a mature group as a norm can help us find the causes of breakdowns in the various groups to which we belong.

* * *

Exercise 9-2
USING INTERACTION PROCESS ANALYSIS (IPA)

Observe a permanent small group over several days. Using the twelve IPA categories developed by Bales, answer the following questions:

1. What is the relationship between task-oriented and social-emotional-oriented behaviors? Specify.

2. Can you identify leadership on the basis of the behaviors?

3. Can you identify cohesiveness within the group? What behaviors have you observed that lead you to your conclusion that cohesiveness does or does not exist?

4. Can you identify obstructionists within the group? Which of the categories that you have observed led you to your conclusion?

THOUGHT PROCESSES AND PROBLEM SOLVING

John Dewey's (1910) reflective thinking process is a rather elegant set of procedures for "training the mind" to respond to problems. In essence, his argument is that in our attempts to support some belief, our minds examine the belief (problem), analyze it, and select a meaningful solution. The reflective thinking process is probably the most popular pattern for problem-solving discussions.

Many people think of the reflective thinking process as a procedure or as an organizing model for small-group discussion. However, it is naive to conceive of the Dewey model as merely a set of procedures for organizing a problem. Although the process is a method, it is also a theory that is especially useful in predicting and describing group problem-solving behavior.

Reflective thinking involves the recognition of the following "logically distinct steps" (Dewey's language) in the resolution of a problem:

1. A felt difficulty
2. Its location and definition
3. Suggestion of possible solutions
4. Development of the suggested solutions
5. Further observation and experimentation leading to acceptance or rejection of a solution

Ordering the phases in the reflective thinking approach should not be taken as a contradiction to a process orientation. Having moved through one phase, or step, does not mean that we no longer experience or employ it. These steps interact with each other in a very systematic way. The phases are dynamic, and our interpretation constantly changes, depending on the material under discussion.

A Felt Difficulty

Recognizing a felt difficulty is crucial to the problem-solving group's existence. There must be recognition of some difficulty or important issue before the group begins deliberations. Thus, the first step in the reflective thinking process involves some degree of group consensus about the problem facing the group.

Of course, we can easily recognize a problem that hits us squarely in the face: our group is broke, or we are under attack, or some people are seeking admission to the group. These situations contain definite elements for a group to deliberate on. A more difficult kind of problem for a group to come to grips with is a problem that may be felt by some members and not by others: the Jewish student who feels some discrimination by other members, the woman who feels that male chauvinistic attitudes where she works are keeping her from being promoted, the faculty member who feels that his department is deteriorating but cannot convince others of the problem. These problems are not easy to identify, but they are still problems. Perhaps the most difficult problem for a group to deal with takes the form of vague feelings that something is wrong. Dewey called such feelings "undefined uneasiness."

The group must come to some agreement on the nature of the problem facing it, and this must be done before the group members can settle down to the task of problem solving.

Location and Definition

Having identified the problem, the group is faced with the task of defining the problem—its scope, specificity, and limits. This step calls for a clear definition of terms in order to locate the problem. How did the problem start? How did it develop? Many other questions that probe the complexity of the felt difficulty must be asked and answered.

Sometimes this second step coincides with the first step. For example, in bringing outside speakers to campus, a student group in charge of the "Great Issues" series has usually invited establishment speakers but now desires more diversity in the views presented. In this situation the felt difficulty (lack of diversity) and the definition of the problem (too many establishment speakers) are virtually inseparable.

Ask yourself the following question: When I am faced with a problem, do I pay more attention to finding out what the problem is or to finding out how to solve it? Failure to define the problem before moving on to looking for alternatives hampers the process. Problem solving is hard enough without making it more difficult by failure to know as much as you can about the problem that you are trying to solve.

We cannot overemphasize the importance of the definition stage of the reflective thinking process. This is the area in which most groups fall far short of the demands of the Dewey model.

Although many group members seek to move right past the definition stage and into the solution stage, the location and specific delimitation of the problem can be the most crucial step in the entire problem-solving sequence. If the group cannot logically define and delimit its problem, later discussions will be random at best.

Suggestion of Possible Solutions

Now we must consider what to do. At this stage, we offer as many alternative solutions as we can. We deal with ideas or guesses for the solution, without evaluating them. The group's primary task is to get some courses of action out on the table for later evaluation and examination.

For most groups, suggesting possible solutions is probably the first thing they do when trying to solve a problem. How many times do we jump right into what ought to be done? Probably more than we care to admit. Using the reflective thinking process, however, by the time we arrive at this step we have analyzed and explored the problem so that we know its nature and limits.

Development of Suggested Solutions

Step 4 in the reflective thinking process calls for a thorough examination of the proposed solutions and analysis of those solutions according to criteria resulting from the group's previous deliberations. These criteria might include cost, feasibility, practicality, and time. For example, if the group decided during the second stage that the solution—whatever it is—is to be enacted that year, then a solution that calls for long-range implementation would be inappropriate. Groups tend to forget that they have developed such criteria, but they are essential to logical decision making.

Dewey argued that it is at this step, when the implications of the solutions are tested, that the reasoning capability of the group comes into play. This stage also involves a great deal of member activity. If the group is large enough, subgroups may be formed to handle the various investigations.

Some groups cease to exist at this stage. These groups are special committees, task forces, and others whose sole purpose is to gather information and propose several feasible alternatives.

Usually, however, groups are expected to come up with a specific solution to a problem. Members are faced with committing themselves to some action.

Further Observation and Experimentation

In the final step of the reflective thinking process the group seeks some verification of the suitability of the suggested solution. Up to this point, the group's conclusions have been hypothetical; they need some kind of testing such as a pilot program. In a way, we are observing, as we did in steps 1 and 2. We are seeing whether our solution works.

In the example of the speakers committee, the test might be to interview the person whom the students have selected. But it is not always easy to test solutions. In some cases it might be wise to make our judgments tentative, for a designated period of time. We do such things with elections and with membership on certain committees; a person is elected or appointed for an definite term of office. Whatever the observation or verification procedure, it is necessary that the suggested solution be tested.

An Example of the Reflective Thinking Process

Now that we have examined each of the phases in the reflective thinking process as Dewey outlined them, we can apply these steps to a particular problem. Our example is simplified—perhaps oversimplified—so that we can take a detailed look at the process.

At a particular university, undergraduate students have over the years complained about the two-year foreign language requirement but have offered no unified resistance to it. Now, however, some students have presented to the university's scholarship-standards committee, which is composed of both faculty and students, petitions to have the requirement abolished. The committee meets to discuss proper disposition of the complaint.

What is the felt difficulty—the problem? Members of the committee perceive the problem differently. One view is: "What can we do to justify the requirement?" Another is: "How can we best handle these troublemakers?" The committee members agree that the problem facing them is multifaceted, for it includes justifying the requirement, handling the discontented students, and examining the reasons for continuing the requirement. The committee agrees on the problem for discussion: "What ought to be the university's policy toward the two-year language requirement?"

The committee decides that it must define the terms of the problem. What is the current requirement? What does the university catalogue say about it? What is the university policy as now enforced? Why was the requirement originally enacted? How long has it been in force? These and many more questions must be answered before the group can have more than surface knowledge of the problem. However, the group does not consider whether the problem can or will be solved. At this stage, the group is concerned only with knowing what the problem is. Furthermore, discussion of the issue does not mean rejecting the status quo. The group is analyzing and exploring the problem without the distraction of suggested solutions.

After several days or months of discussion, the members agree to entertain some thoughts about the future course of action. They meet and express their ideas, neither accepting nor rejecting any proposed solution. Three specific solutions are advanced: (1) drop the requirement, (2) reduce the requirement to one year, or (3) retain the requirement as is.

The group members evaluate the proposed solutions in terms of the criteria, advantages, and disadvantages. After lengthy discussion, solution 1 is rejected because it would mean that several graduate teaching assistants would have no work. Moreover, the requirement has been in existence for forty years, and the objection to it has just recently been proposed; thus, to capitulate to the dissidents would be a very harmful precedent. Solution 3 is rejected because most committee members cannot justify requiring two years of a language when there are other subjects that deserve as much attention. In addition, a committee would hardly be credible if it met for an extended time and only reaffirmed the status quo. (Don't laugh. By such logic some committees are formed and maintained.) Solution 2, a compromise, is the chosen alternative. It has all the benefits of the other two solutions, and committee members really see the advantage of that required year.

The committee is ready to test and verify its chosen solution. The decision is made to try this system for a limited time and to charge a group with monitoring the new requirement. This new group will report to the main committee regularly over the next two years.

Through using the reflective thinking process, the committee systematically and logically formulated and resolved a problem. They spoke about the scope and nature of the problem only after they agreed on what the problem was. They proposed solutions to the problem only after they had defined its scope. Finally, they did not simply choose a solution and hope that it would work. They tested the adequacy of the solution to their problem.

❉ ❉ ❉

Exercise 9-3
USING THE REFLECTIVE THINKING PROCESS

Divide into groups of five to eight members. Select a campus problem for which group members have a high level of involvement. Discuss the issue using Dewey's method of reflective thinking. The exercise should run over several days so that each step of the process is adequately examined. At the end of each stage of the process conduct a group evaluation of the deliberations. The following questions should be used as guides for these evaluations:

1. Did one individual "take charge" of the group?

2. Which member(s) was most task-oriented; which was most social-emotional oriented?

3. Was the problem well formulated?

4. Were assertions supported?

SUMMARY

Group interaction is important in problem-solving communication. By our definition, communication is a process in which messages act as a linkage between people. Interaction process analysis (IPA) affords us the opportunity to examine the nature of the linkage messages—their characteristics, their origins, and the types of feedback they elicit. This method of interaction analysis provides some specific categories of communicative messages that we can use in analyzing group problem solving. It also provides a profile of how a good, effective, mature group ought to behave. Researchers have found that groups that work harmoniously are usually characterized by a preponderance of information-giving messages. In other words, when the group commits itself to the task, much of the communicative activity consists of supplying data rather than asking questions.

Whereas the IPA identifies specific categories of communicative behavior, the reflective thinking process allows us to view these interaction behaviors in a broad context. The Dewey model gives us some idea of the overall process involved in problem solving. According to this model, the group first determines that it has a difficulty, then locates the problem through complex analysis and exploration, proposes various solutions, evaluates the solutions and selects one, and tests the solution. In Chapter 10 we will consider different procedures that can be used by groups to solve particular problems.

ADDITIONAL READINGS

Davis, James H. *Group Performance*. Menlo Park, Calif.: Addison-Wesley, 1969. While many of the research studies cited may seem complex and very difficult to read, Davis's treatment of person, environment, and task variables provides an excellent analysis of problem-solving circumstances. Of particular interest is his discussion of interactive effects in groups.

Mortensen, C. David. *Communication: The Study of Human Interaction*. New York: McGraw-Hill, 1972. Mortensen's treatment of communication networks (Chapter 9) describes the way in which messages flow within a group. These interactive channels provide insight into means of analyzing problem-solving behavior. Of particular interest is his discussion of information transmission in a variety of network settings.

Psychology Today: An Introduction. Del Mar, Calif.: CRM, 1970. Chapter 32 ("Small Groups") is an easy-to-read overview of several facets of small-group behavior. Of particular interest to our discussion of problem-solving activity is the treatment of various issues beginning on page 603. You will find the discussion of Bales's model, for example, to be clear and graphically impressive.

10

METHODS
OF DISCUSSION

PREVIEW

* **What is group discussion?**

The most common form of group communication, group discussion is defined as two or more individuals in face-to-face
interaction for the purpose of information sharing, problem
solving, and/or self-maintenance.

* **What are methods of discussion?**

A discussion method is a preselected procedure for conduct-
ing a group discussion. Six methods of discussion are:
Round table
Dialogue
Panel
Colloquy
Symposium-forum
Lecture-forum

* **What are three problem-solving procedures?**

Reflective thinking pattern
Ideal solution pattern
Single question pattern

WHAT IS group discussion? How is group discussion different
from group communication? Are they the same? Imagine the following situations:

1. The student senate proposes that students be given more representation on faculty committees. The president of the senate contacts the
   dean of students to inform him of the proposal. The dean of students
   asks for an informal meeting with three student representatives. The
   four meet in the student union and over coffee discuss how to present
   the students' ideas on committees at a meeting of the faculty committee. One student suggests that each present a separate area of the proposal. The other students and the dean agree.

2. A meeting is held that afternoon by the faculty. Several faculty members are present when the students arrive. With faculty sitting in front and facing the students, a student takes the floor and explains the overall proposal. The other two students follow with separate reports on the desirability and implementation of the proposal. Following the presentation, the students are questioned by the faculty committee. The committee chairman takes the floor, summarizes the comments of students and faculty members, and appoints a subcommittee to study the students' proposal.

3. The following day the student senate reconvenes. The senate representatives at the faculty committee discuss the events of the previous day. Several senators pose questions and offer comments concerning the next step to be taken.

All three situations are examples of group discussion. Notice the similarities in each situation. First, all three situations had two or more individuals talking on a specific topic. Second, group members in each situation were involved in face-to-face interaction. Third, the primary modes of communication were verbal and nonverbal communication. And, fourth, each discussion situation had a specific purpose or goal.

Group discussion is a process involving two or more individuals in face-to-face interaction for the purpose of information sharing, problem solving, or self-maintenance.

From this definition we can see that group discussion is a form of group communication. Some speech communication teachers suggest that only serious and systematic talk about a clearly specified topic can be considered group discussion; the term connotes something more than mere group conversation. However, by our definition, only a relatively small percentage of group communication could not be termed group discussion—for example, people talking on the telephone. Group discussion is the most common form of group communication.

Discussion involves face-to-face interaction. Each group member must see and hear the other. The members modify their behavior in response to each other's behavior. This interaction can be informal and conversational, as is common at parties when friends stand around talking, or it can be very formal and follow a specifically designed format, as in the case of the television program "Meet the Press."

In a discussion the major modes of interaction are verbal and nonverbal messages. We interact principally by talking with other group members; but our facial expressions, posture, gestures, and tone of voice also affect the discussion process. These nonverbal messages are very important.

Group discussion has a specific purpose or goal: information sharing, problem solving, or self-maintenance. These goals are not mutually exclusive. In fact, no problem-solving discussion can be carried on without the sharing of information by group members. A group discussion concerning self-maintenance must entail gathering information about individual and group problems and solving problems created by personality differences in the group. This purpose or goal must be apparent to all members. A committee may meet to solve a concrete problem, such as how to raise money for charity; a study group, which uses discussion for information sharing, may come together to prepare for a final exam.

Ideally, each member makes contributions that help the group reach its goal. Cooperation between group members is crucial. We are not suggesting that conflict be eliminated from a group discussion. The differences and disagreements that arise during a discussion are valuable to the group process. However, all members must work toward producing a product that will meet the needs of the group.

* * *

Communication Diary   10-1

Answer the following questions in relation to your communication diary entries.

1. Do all your group situations conform to our definition of group discussion?

2. What percentage of your communication in groups can be considered group discussion?

3. Compare your diary entries and percentage estimates with those of your classmates.

COMMUNICATOR RESPONSIBILITIES

Some people are excellent communicators in a group discussion. They ask good questions, are excellent leaders, are able to analyze and synthesize information, make important contributions to the discussion, and develop solutions from the materials presented. Yet, when they deliver a speech, they are not as effective. Their speech is poorly organized, and their delivery is stilted or boring.

Differences in successful performance can be attributed to the fact that each type of oral communication requires a different set of skills. The skill of organizing a large amount of information for a speech is not necessary for short give-and-take conversational remarks commonly found in most group discussions. In addition, persuasive strategies can be a detriment to the group process. Indeed, a forceful delivery, desirable in many public speaking situations, may be neither helpful nor acceptable within a group context. Appropriate, effective communicator behavior depends on understanding and adapting to the specific communication situation.

Group discussion requires that each communicator have a specific responsibility for speaking and listening during the discussion. Senders and receivers of communication constantly change. Each group member is a listener, then a speaker, then a listener, and so on. However, we send important cues even when listening. We are always simultaneously sending and receiving. The close proximity of group members makes us sensitive to others' mannerisms. Their facial expressions, posture, and tonal responses all affect the communicator.

Discussion participants are accountable for what they have said or heard. Dishonesty, faulty reasoning, and lack of evidence can lead to a challenge by other group members. The responsibility for validating another member's comments may rest with all members of the group, a group leader, or a recognized expert in the group. The group situation determines what individual or individuals are to assume this responsibility.

Before arriving at a final conclusion, discussants *ideally* investigate, explore, and evaluate information or the solution, in terms of the group goal rather than their personal goals. The discussants attempt to find the best evidence, the most reasonable solution.

* * *

Exercise 10-1
RESPONSIBILITIES OF COMMUNICATORS

Ten students at your college gather at your home to consider new rules for student discipline—two students from the student senate, the rest from various other campus organizations. During the first part of the meeting, the two senate members discuss the relationship between the senate and the administration. One student asks about the types of discipline that are considered appropriate by both the administration and senate. The same two students discuss the issue for an hour. One student suggests that they all ask the administration for its recommendations regarding student discipline. The other group members do not respond. One student suggests they go out and have a pizza. The group disperses.

1. Was this a group discussion situation?

2. What could have been done to encourage members to meet their responsibilities more fully?

3. Was any value derived from the group meeting?

4. What could have been done to improve this group meeting?

DEFINITION OF DISCUSSION METHOD

The basic elements of communication do not change from one group situation to another, but the communicative procedures used during discussions vary with the group's purpose, the subject being discussed, and the people to whom the discussion is directed.

A *discussion method* is a preselected procedure for conducting a group discussion.

A group discussion can be informal or formal, private or public. Of course, there are various degrees and combinations of both these characteristics. The more informal a group discussion, the fewer the restrictions placed on the method of interacting. As the method of discussion becomes more formal, it controls or restricts the group interaction to a greater degree.

Informal discussion, such as usually occurs between friends, is the most common form of group discussion. When we talk with friends at a party, we exchange ideas, rambling from one topic to another. There is no specific format or set of procedures that we have agreed on beforehand. This kind of informal discussion is also called a private discussion. It is carried on only for the benefit of those taking part in it. A discussion for the benefit of an audience is called a public discussion. Classroom discussions are public, and nonparticipating classmates constitute the audience. A public discussion is more formal in its planning and execution than a private discussion.

All discussion methods, formal or informal, private or public, make use of a chairperson. This person facilitates the efficient operation of the group discussion. Although the exact functions depend on the specific discussion method used by the group, the overriding function is to assist the group in reaching its ultimate goal. The importance of the discussion person varies with the discussion method as well as the situation. In formal, public discussions the chairperson's responsibilities are usually more important than in informal, private discussions. However, even in the latter type of discussion the chairperson would have a major role if he or she had to mediate internal conflicts inhibiting the exchange of ideas between discussion participants.

A group member may be made chairperson because he or she is recognized as the leader, is appointed by some external authority, or best fulfills the requirements for chairing a particular discussion. Do not confuse the terms *chairperson* and *leader*, however. They are not necessarily synonymous. As often happens in classroom discussions, the actual leader of a group might emerge during the discussion and yet remain a discussion participant rather than becoming the chairperson; his or her ability to handle group members may serve better outside the position of discussion chairperson.

SIX DISCUSSION METHODS

Traditionally, discussion methods have been classified into six major categories: round table, dialogue, panel, colloquy, symposium-forum, and lecture-forum. These methods vary in the degree of control that each involves (Figure 10-1). Only the round table can be considered solely an informal method of discussion

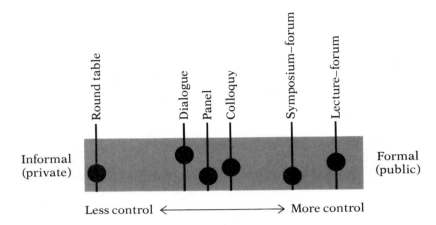

FIGURE 10-1. The six methods for presenting group discussions can be viewed on a continuum from informal to formal, private to public, and less control to more control.

in that the messages are issued strictly for the benefit of the immediate group. This method places the fewest restrictions on the discussion process. The dialogue can be either private or public. The remaining four methods always have an audience.

The various types of public discussion may be followed by a period in which the audience is allowed to ask questions. This is called the *forum* period. It gives audience members a chance to raise questions about the ideas presented, bring to the attention of the discussants ideas that they may have overlooked, and suggest additional interpretations of the materials.

The Round Table

A get-together among friends to study for an exam or a meeting of a fund-raising committee are examples of a round-table discussion.

> A *round-table* discussion is a group discussion held without an audience and with all group members entering into a free exchange of ideas.

This method is used extensively in small decision-making groups and small learning groups. It is said to have originated with King Arthur and the Knights of the Round Table. (Whether this is fact or legend is not certain.) The king would present problems to his knights seated around his table, who would in turn discuss the problem in a climate of equality.

The round table consists of a chairperson and at least two additional members. The chairperson's primary function is to encourage participants to engage in a free interchange of opinions and ideas.

The procedure for a round-table discussion is as follows:

1. The chairperson opens the meeting.
2. The chairperson introduces the members and the question for discussion.
3. The chairperson throws the topic open for discussion.
4. Members discuss the topic; the chairperson summarizes throughout the discussion and provides transitional remarks when the discussion shifts from one phase of the problem to another.
5. At the completion of the discussion, the chairperson summarizes the discussion and closes the meeting.

During a round-table discussion, the chairperson and group members may be seated around a table or in a circle. If a rectangular table is used, the chairperson may assume a central position by sitting at the head of the table. The important feature of the seating arrangement is that all discussants be able to see and communicate with each other.

ADVANTAGES AND DISADVANTAGES. Ideally, the round table provides all group members with an opportunity to express their opinions and attitudes. This group interaction, it is hoped, will stimulate group members to refine their thinking, adjust their views of other members' ideas, and allow members to achieve some balance of opinions on an issue.

The round table rarely functions as we would like it to. The discussants may not have all the information they need. Imagine five white students discussing the effect of racial prejudice on an individual's self-esteem. Their lack of first-hand knowledge about the topic could lead to an inadequate conclusion.

Although the actual number of participants is flexible, too many participants make the group unmanageable. The larger the group, the less opportunity an individual may have to participate and the greater the chance that one or two members will dominate the others. As the size of the group increases, the members may not be able to maintain an intimate relationship with one another, and the individual's attraction to the group (cohesiveness) may decrease.

Another disadvantage of the round-table method is lack of organization. Members may ramble from topic to topic. The chairperson must control the discussion and direct it toward its ultimate goal. The larger the group, however, the more difficult it is to exercise control.

The Dialogue

Imagine two television commentators analyzing a speech delivered by the president of the United States. This is a public dialogue. If you were ever interviewed for a job, you have participated in a private dialogue.

A conversation between two people in front of an audience or in private is a *dialogue*.

The procedure for a dialogue is as follows:

1. One participant introduces himself or herself and the other participant.
2. One participant presents the area to be covered and begins to question the other.
3. If an audience is present, the dialogue may be followed by a forum period conducted by one participant.
4. One participant completes the discussion by summarizing the material covered.

The physical arrangement of the dialogue is flexible. It may consist of two persons seated across a desk from each other as in a job interview, or two people seated on a stage, one questioning the other. In the public dialogue, the participants and audience should be able to see each other easily. A dialogue held before a listening audience is usually followed by a forum period. Radio and television dialogues may or may not have an audience or forum. The "Tonight Show" has an audience but no forum. A dialogue between a newscaster and a potential candidate for public office rarely has an audience.

PARTICIPANT ROLES. During the discussion, one of the two participants must act as the leader, guiding the conversation, questioning, providing transitions, and so on. The leader may also conduct the forum period, if there is one. That person guides a public dialogue in such a way that it will be most intelligible and in the best interests of the audience. With one individual in control, it is easy to keep the dialogue within the established time limits.

Often one of the discussants is an expert on the topic, and the other acts as an interviewer. When interviewing political candidates or officeholders, many journalists assume a devil's advocate role. Although the format of the dialogue is preplanned, the participants do not rehearse or prepare speeches. Interviewers may, however, be prepared with a list of questions they wish to ask. This method is somewhat less formal than the symposium and provides many of the same opportunities for conversational exchange as the panel and round-table methods of discussion do.

ADVANTAGES AND DISADVANTAGES.   This method may be the most advantageous in imparting ideas if an expert does not have time to prepare a lecture or is ineffective as a lecturer.

Care must be taken, however, to ensure that the topic of discussion is interesting to the audience as well as to the participants. Experts who tend to make their talks too technical for their listeners must be careful to discuss their subject at a level that can be understood by the audience. If the topic is presented in technical terms, one participant must use questions to clarify and define the material. Television newscasters are usually very adept at simplifying technical material. The dialogue participants should not become so involved with each other that they forget the audience. Finally, like the panel, this method induces a tendency to digress and to become disorganized at times.

The Panel

If you asked your friends what discussion method they see most often, they would probably answer "the panel." The label *panel* has been used at times to describe the format in which a group of newspaper columnists interview a political candidate, a host converses with a number of guest celebrities on a television show, a committee of experts meet privately to develop organizational policy, and a specially appointed committee presents pertinent information to its club membership. Actually, only the committee reporting its findings to the larger group is truly following the panel method of discussion.

A *panel* is a discussion held before an audience, with all group members entering into a free interchange of ideas.

Panelists, as those group communicators are called, speak for the benefit of the audience as well as to fellow discussion members. The function of the panel is to solve problems, arrive at a consensus, or illuminate ideas for the advantage of the audience.

A panel consists of a chairperson and the group members. There is no set number of discussants, but it usually ranges from four to six. A television news program may use only three group members, thus giving each panelist more time to express a viewpoint. The more panelists, the more unwieldy and difficult to operate the discussion effectively.

The panel procedure is as follows:

1. The chairperson opens the discussion with a question or statement of the topic.
2. The chairperson introduces the panel members to the audience.
3. The chairperson draws the panel members into informal conversation on the topic.
4. The panel members discuss the topic; the chairperson clarifies, summarizes, and provides transitions as needed during the discussion.
5. Questions are solicited from the audience (optional forum).
6. The chairperson summarizes the discussion.

The panel members enter into a free interchange of ideas; that is, there is no preset order in which the panel members offer their contributions. To encourage this freedom of interaction, the group members must be seated so that communication between them can flow easily. Since a panel is presented before an audience, the semicircle seating arrangement is recommended to enable the audience to see and hear group members without difficulty.

ROLES OF PANELISTS AND CHAIRPERSONS. Panel members do not bring prepared speeches to the discussion, but this does not mean they are not properly prepared. Careful preparation in anticipation of likely topics and the need for facts is vital in a panel discussion. Panelists are usually chosen because they can supply facts needed for well-informed discussion or because they represent views held by members of a larger group.

The chairpersons, who are panel members, do not have the same responsibilities as regular panel members. They do not enter into the discussion as participants. Their primary responsibility is to allow the panelists to discuss freely and openly. They present the problems or topics to the panelists for discussion but remain in the background. Chairpersons are instruments for an effective presentation. They are concerned with the procedures of the meeting that help bring forth appropriate content.

At the beginning of the panel, chairpersons introduce the problem for discussion by giving brief information, the reason for the discussion, and an explanation of the way the panel will be conducted. In introducing the panel members to the audience, they may make note of the group members' background and experience with the discussion topic. During the discussion, they may provide transitional statements between group member statements. These comments serve mainly to clarify statements, summarize ideas, and keep the discussion focused on the topic. At the conclusion of the panel discussion, chairpersons summarize the results, briefly pointing out areas of agreement and conflict.

ADVANTAGES AND DISADVANTAGES.   The panel is an excellent vehicle for group discussion. Its conversational informality generally makes it more interesting than other public methods of discussion. The informality creates a relaxed atmosphere, which in turn reduces the tensions and anxiety most communicators feel when speaking before an audience. Because all group members have a responsibility to the discussion, a feeling of teamwork and cooperation can develop. Group-member cooperation is desirable but may not necessarily develop.

The panel method can entail some problems. The informal conversational format can hinder a group by making it difficult to follow specific organizational patterns. Many panel members digress and discuss tangential issues. Some may monopolize the conversation and prevent other group members from expressing their ideas, causing some group members to withdraw from the discussion. On the other hand, some group members may fail to contribute their share to the discussion. This behavior is likely to persist as long as the other panelists cover the inadequacies with their participation.

The Colloquy

The colloquy is unique among discussion methods, and it is the least known or used method. It was created in order to work out problems and devise new methods in the field of adult education. Originally, the colloquy consisted of questioning and reporting of information by a group of experts. Unfortunately, the questioning during the discussion period tended to slow down the proceedings, and to turn the discussion into a question-and-answer session between the experts and the audience. Since then, two different formats for the colloquy have been developed.

SINGLE-PANEL FORMAT. In the single-panel format there is a chairperson and a panel of experts. The procedure is as follows:

1. The chairperson introduces the expert panel and topic.
2. The discussion follows the panel discussion format except that the audience is allowed to question or comment when an important issue arises.

If the chairperson or a member of the panel feels that a solution is being neglected, that a disagreement exists, or that the material is unclear, then the audience is asked to comment or ask questions. Once the issue is resolved, the panel continues its regular discussion until another need for the audience arises. The physical arrangements of this method are identical with those of the panel discussion.

TWO-PANEL FORMAT. The second format (two panels) uses much the same format as the original colloquy. A lay panel is chosen in advance to prepare the discussion. An expert panel is selected consisting of individuals with special knowledge of the subject. The procedure for the discussion is as follows:

1. The chairperson introduces the lay panel, expert panel, and discussion topic.
2. The discussion topic is open to comments by the lay panel.
3. The lay panel and chairperson ask questions of the experts when information is needed; experts add information that the lay panel has overlooked.
4. A forum period follows the regular discussion; questions can be directed to both lay and expert panels.
5. The chairperson closes the discussion by summarizing the proceedings.

The lay panel, with the assistance of a chairperson, proceeds as in the regular panel discussion. When special information is needed, the lay panel and chairperson may ask questions of the experts. The experts do not take an active part in the regular discussion, but may introduce information that is being overlooked by the lay panel. Immediately following the discussion, the audience may react to the comments made by both panels.

The physical arrangements are identical with those of the panel, except that there are two panels. The chairperson is seated at the center of the stage and is flanked by both panels. This allows the two panels both to see each other and to be seen and heard by the audience.

ADVANTAGES AND DISADVANTAGES. The first colloquy procedure is probably the most efficient method for using experts and meeting audience needs. The second procedure has the advantage of making use of both lay people and experts. Because the major part of the discussion is conducted by the lay panel, the communication is more likely to be understood by the audience. At the same time, expert advice is immediately available. If the experts use technical language, the lay panel can clarify the information for the audience.

In the first colloquy format, intermittent questioning can consume too much time. The experts may also use too much technical jargon for their audience. In the second colloquy format, the experts may not be needed or may be used very little. This is a waste of experts' time, talent, and effort. Sometimes this format turns into a question-and-answer period between the lay and expert panels, or the expert panel dominates the discussion and usurps the responsibilities of the lay panel. Despite these disadvantages the colloquy is an effective, though not the most efficient, method of discussion.

The Symposium-Forum

Imagine you are seated in an auditorium with 250 other students. Seated on the stage are three representatives of your ethnic studies program. Each member gives a five-minute talk. One speaks about black studies, the second on Chicano studies, and the third on Far Eastern studies. Following their presentations, you are permitted to question the three group members.

A *symposium* is a public discussion in which each group member gives a talk on one area or phase of the discussion topic.

This method of presentation is a relatively formal one and comparatively easy to organize.

The symposium consists of a chairperson and a number of group members, as determined by the topic and time available for discussion. The topic is divided into preselected components, and each part is assigned to a specific group member. Division of the topic may be chronological, spatial, or by any order suitable for presenting the material to the audience.

The procedure for a symposium-forum is as follows:

1. The chairperson introduces the question for discussion and the areas to be covered by the speakers.

2. The chairperson introduces each speaker and his or her specific area.
3. The speaker discusses an area of the topic.
4. The chairperson provides transitions between the speakers.
5. The chairperson conducts the forum period. If a panel discussion follows the symposium, the chairperson and speakers follow the procedures listed in our discussion of the panel.
6. At the completion of the discussion, the chairperson summarizes the material presented.

Because group members do not interact freely during a symposium, they are usually seated in a straight line, with the chairperson near the center of the group. As in a public speaking situation, a speaker's stand, or podium, is generally provided.

PARTICIPANT ROLES. Group members are usually chosen because they represent particular positions on a problem or have special competence, expertise, or information in an area of the discussion topic. On a college campus, participants in an information-sharing symposium conducted on the role of student government might consist of the student body president, a student senator, the dean of students, and the president of the college. Each discusses the student government from his or her own perspective.

Symposium chairpersons do not give speeches on an area of the discussion topic. Their primary responsibility is to introduce each speaker and the area of the presentation. After each speech, chairpersons relate the forthcoming speech to the preceding one. If a forum period follows the speeches, chairpersons direct the questions and comments submitted by the audience.

Unlike either the panel or the round table, symposium members do not interact freely. A symposium participant does not have an opportunity to respond to ideas presented by speakers that follow.

A FORM OF DISCUSSION? It has been argued that, because no direct interaction between speakers exists, the symposium cannot be classified as a form of group discussion; we agree. The standard symposium format does not conform to our definition of group discussion; group members do not communicate in a reciprocal fashion and therefore are not truly interacting. Speakers can adapt their comments to what other speakers have already said, but they cannot question or communicate with the previous speaker. To be a true form of group discussion, a symposium must be followed by a forum and/or panel period in which the group members interact with each other or with the audience.

PURPOSE. The symposium is used for much the same purposes as is the panel. Whether we select the panel or symposium depends partly on the discussion topic. If the problem can be easily divided into areas, it may be better to use the symposium. Since each speaker is assigned a specific area, a symposium presentation requires more preparation than a panel.

ADVANTAGES AND DISADVANTAGES. Because the problem is divided into specific areas, the symposium presentation tends to be better organized and follows a predetermined pattern. This also helps to remedy the narrowness of having one individual deliver a speech covering the entire topic. A number of speakers can provide a number of approaches to a single topic, and this variety can help to hold audience interest.

Since a symposium is organized beforehand, it is less adaptable than the round table or the panel. But the symposium does remain somewhat flexible in that the topic can be divided to anticipate the situation and audience demands.

The symposium presupposes competent speakers, and—unlike the panel—one mediocre or poorly prepared discussant may cause the symposium to fail. Yet, not all group members may be effective communicators in both formal and informal communication situations. In the panel, topics assigned to ill-prepared members can be covered by the other speakers, because all group members have a responsibility to know the total topic in general. In the symposium this is difficult, if not impossible. Group members have the responsibility for only certain topic areas and may not be familiar with the area for which the discussant is responsible.

A long-winded speaker may use up time needed by the other speakers to present their materials. In addition, if the division of areas overlaps, it is not unusual for one speaker to cover another speaker's topic, leaving that speaker with little or nothing to say. Chairpersons must control the time used by speakers. They can remind the discussants of this time limit at the start of the symposium, or stop discussants who exceed the time limit, and ask them to summarize their remaining talk briefly.

The Lecture-Forum

Throughout the semester your instructor presents a number of lectures dealing with group communication. You are permitted to question and comment on your instructor's remarks. This method of discussion is called the lecture-forum.

The *lecture-forum* is the form of group discussion in which the audience listening to the speaker is given an opportunity to make comments and ask questions regarding the presentation.

The lecture-forum is always public. It is the most formal method of discussion.

The lecture-forum has two purposes. First, it supplies new information and motivation about a topic or problem. Second, it allows the audience to participate in the discussion—to clarify obscure points, obtain additional information, and express opinions.

The physical arrangements for this method are simple. A speaker sits or stands either at floor level or on a stage in front of an audience. Another individual often introduces the speaker to the audience.

A FORM OF DISCUSSION? Some people argue that the lecture-forum is not a form of discussion, but a type of public speaking because there is no group interaction during the lecture—communication is one way from speaker to audience. However, during the lecture the audience interacts continually with the speaker on a nonverbal level. At times audience members may interrupt or are permitted to question the speaker, and during the forum period audience and speaker interact. Thus, the lecture-forum is in fact a two-way process and is a form of discussion.

ADVANTAGES AND DISADVANTAGES. The lecture-forum can easily be arranged. With only one speaker, it is usually better organized, and the use of an expert speaker can guarantee a complete and detailed presentation. Since the audience cannot comment or question until after the lecture, information can be conveyed quickly without distractions or interruptions.

There are, however, some problems associated with this method. The speaker who is recognized as an authority is rarely questioned. How often have you seriously questioned your instructor's lectures? An irresponsible speaker may distort facts, use emotional appeals, or selectively bias the materials. (Listen to a white supremacist discuss the validity of using IQ tests in schools consisting predominately of black or Chicano students.) It also may be difficult to keep a speaker from exceeding the time limit. If a speech is too long, the speaker may leave little or no time for audience participation. When this occurs, group discussion does not exist. The speaker who is an expert may use language too specialized for the audience to comprehend. Poor speakers can ruin an entire program.

* * *

Exercise 10-2
SELECTING A DISCUSSION METHOD

What discussion method would you choose for the following situations?

A. A group of thirty students, all in the same social club, are having a meeting at which the topic for discussion is "How can group membership be increased?"

B. A group of students must plan how to present the topic "What should be done about prison reform?" to your class.

C. At a meeting open to all students, the student senate must deal with alternative methods for funding the Economic Opportunities Program on campus.

D. Ralph Nader is coming to campus to speak on the latest safety devices in nuclear power plants.

E. Your ecology club, composed of interested college students and ecology experts from the biology department, usually has thirty members in attendance at its meetings. The club will discuss "How can we prevent oil pollution of our waterways?"

In selecting the discussion method, ask yourself the following questions:

1. Is the method private or public?

2. What is the goal of the group discussion?

3. Can the information be presented in more than one way? If your answer is yes, why did you select one method over another?

---

* * *

Exercise 10-3
PRESENTING A GROUP DISCUSSION

1. The class should be divided into small groups (six members maximum).

2. Each group selects a topic for discussion and a method for presenting that discussion. Since this public discussion may be your first, a topic that involves presenting information to the class rather than attempting to solve a problem would probably be a better choice.

3. Present a thirty-minute discussion.

PROCEDURES FOR PROBLEM SOLVING

The methods of discussion examined in the previous section are often used when groups are solving problems. Each method establishes certain patterns that control the interaction of group members. However, the methods do not provide an organizational plan for solving problems. Many groups do not solve their problems systematically. Members become frustrated, dissatisfied, and bored when their group's approach to problem solving is unsystematic and even irrational. However, groups can follow preselected plans for solving problems. Their problem-solving activities need not be unsystematic or confusing.

In order to provide an organizational framework, procedures have been developed for solving problems. In this section, we will examine three patterns of problem solving: the reflective thinking pattern, the ideal solution pattern, and the single question pattern. These procedures are to be used within the interaction pattern established by the discussion method. Brainstorming is sometimes included as a pattern for problem solving; however, that section will appear in Chapter 11 as a discussion technique.

* * *

Communication Diary   10-2

Answer the following questions in relation to your communication diary entries.

1. How many times do you ask others to help solve your problems?

2. How many times do you ask others for information pertaining to:

school _____

friends _____

work _____

family _____

3. How many times do friends ask your assistance in solving a problem or in gathering information for some specific task?

4. Can you identify any consistent pattern of communication occurring when you talk with a group of friends?

A Problem-Solving Situation

In order to illustrate how each pattern operates in a problem-solving discussion, we will use the following problem-solving situation.

THE CAMPUS PARKING CRISIS

While eating lunch with some students from your group discussion class, you mention that you were late for the mid-term.

"Why were you late?" one friend asks, "Did your car break down?"

"No, I just couldn't find a damn parking place!"

"You're kidding," another friend adds, "I couldn't find one yesterday."

"Neither could I," a third friend points out, "In fact, I haven't been able to park on campus the last three days."

Each group member recalls being unable to find a place to park at least once during the last week. Realizing that your failure to find a parking spot is not unique, you suggest that your friends meet later that day to discuss ways to solve the parking problem. All agree to form a committee. Someone suggests that more students be added to the committee to make it more representative. The students meet that afternoon in the student union. Interest is high. You have a worthy goal: How can we guarantee parking places for students on campus?

Notice that the problem—failure to find parking space on campus—has been put into the form of a question.

Questions of Fact, Value, and Policy

Three kinds of problem questions are used in problem-solving patterns: questions of fact, questions of value, and questions of policy. Many discussions deal only with questions of fact. These include such questions as: "Does a college degree mean more income for individuals over a lifetime?" "Is discrimination still prevalent in our society?" Educational groups are usually concerned with problems of fact. Group and individual research in the library or laboratory are best for providing the answers to questions of fact. Spontaneous discussion groups whose purpose is to solve a question of fact may be at a disadvantage. Such groups may lack the necessary first-hand information to provide an adequate solution to the problem. In our parking problem, the students may have to gather information from fellow students, faculty, and staff prior to any intelligent discussion of the problem.

Questions of value require the group to assess the worth of some object, idea, concept, or person; for example, "Is a college degree worthwhile?" "Is discrimination bad?" Questions of value

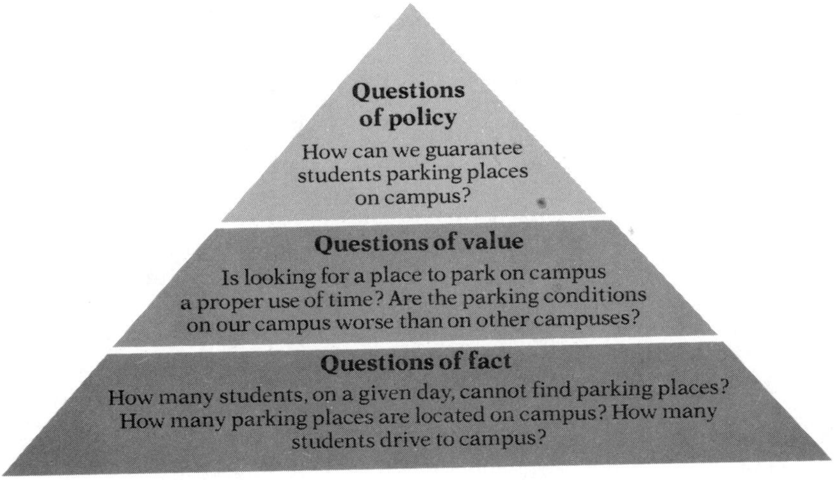

FIGURE 10-2. Questions of fact and value must be considered before satisfactory answers to questions of policy can be found.

require evaluating a problem against certain practical or ideal standards. If the standards are unclear, it will be difficult to resolve the problem. Questions of fact must be answered prior to solving a question of value. For example, before we can decide on the value of a college degree, we might want to find out whether college graduates earn more than do noncollege graduates and what proportion of business executives have college degrees.

A question of policy requires that the group arrive at a specific course of action in order to solve the problem. "What can students do to clean up the environment?" "How can we guarantee peace in the world?" A discussion involving a question of policy must first consider questions of fact and value. Figure 10-2 illustrates this point.

✳ ✳ ✳

Exercise 10-4

QUESTIONS OF FACT, VALUE, AND POLICY

Select four of the subject areas listed below and construct three problem-solving questions for each area. Make one a question of fact, one a question of value, and one a question of policy.

Women's Rights	Military Aid
School Busing	College Costs
Nuclear Power	Marriage
Income Tax	Drugs
Air Pollution	Athletic Scholarships

Reflective Thinking Pattern

This form of problem solving is based on Dewey's reflective thinking sequence, which we presented in Chapter 9. Now, however, we will modify the original reflective thinking process to illustrate how it can be used to structure a discussion that involves solving a problem. This problem-solving pattern consists of six steps:

1. Recognize the problem.
2. Locate and define the problem.
3. Analyze the problem.
4. Establish criteria for evaluation of solutions.
5. Suggest solutions to the problem.
6. Select and test the final solution.

RECOGNITION OF THE PROBLEM. The fact that individuals are members of a discussion group does not guarantee that they will recognize the problem confronting the group. In our campus parking problem, the group members did not recognize the problem until they all shared their experience of not being able to find a parking place; until their initial discussion, they thought that their frustration was unique.

In this stage of problem solving, group members consider the significance and urgency of the problem, its effect upon the group and individuals. For any student who often cannot find a parking place within a reasonable distance from class, the problem of parking becomes significant and urgent.

Once the group becomes aware of the problem, a goal emerges. Our group of students will look for a way to guarantee each student a parking place on campus.

DEFINITION OF THE PROBLEM. After recognizing that a problem exists, group members must determine the exact nature of the problem. They must define and clarify terms, recognize possible limitations, and establish the extent of the problem. Before group members propose solutions to any problem, they should clarify the meaning of words and ideas in the problem question. It may be necessary to rephrase the problem question, so that it can be understood.

The question "How can we guarantee each student easy access to classes?" can be interpreted in terms of parking problems, location of buildings on campus, congestion of students on campus walks, and so on. Obviously, a question so worded could present difficulties, if the group's only intent is to study campus parking problems. "How can all students be guaranteed parking places on campus?" is more specific and restrictive in meaning. Its intent clearly identifies the group's purpose.

The group must recognize any limitations inherent in a discussion of the problem. If a problem is too broad to be discussed at one meeting, it may be divided into subproblems to be handled at several meetings. If the group can meet only one time, it must limit the scope of its problem. Class periods, for instance, offer a relatively short time to work with a problem, and so the discussion problem should be limited to fit the time available.

Groups, particularly classroom groups, attempt to solve problems that are outside their span of control. As a classroom exercise this is acceptable; however, in real life, group members must work on problems that they can control. The problem "How can all students be guaranteed parking places on campus?" is one that group members have some power to solve; they can work with other legitimate campus groups to implement proposals. We have all seen a number of problems on our campuses settled in this manner.

The group must be able to gather the materials needed to solve the problem. For example, little in the way of factual materials can be gathered for the problem "What does God look like?" However, if we change the problem to "What characteristics do individuals ascribe to God" then we may be able to gather data that can be applied and used in solving the problem-question.

ANALYZING THE PROBLEM. At this stage the group seeks to gather enough information to evaluate the problem. Group members must find the information that will indicate how serious the problem is, who is being affected, where the problem is occurring, why the problem exists. Fact finding consists of pooling the information resources of all group members. If group members do not have the needed information, the problem-solving session will be relatively unprofitable.

In our parking problem, we might ask: How many students can't find parking? 10 percent? 75 percent? Are students affected only after 9:00 A.M.? Is parking difficult all over campus or in specific locations? These questions attempt to answer the most important question of all: Why can't students find parking places on campus? We are attempting to locate the cause(s) of the problem.

Locating the exact cause of a problem is sometimes difficult. Ask yourself the question "Is increased abortion the cause or ef-

fect of legalizing abortion?" This question is not easy to answer. The number of abortions can increase when laws against abortion are relaxed; however, because of the danger involved in illegal abortions, an increasing number of abortions can spur legislators to enact less strict abortion laws.

Groups are often so superficial in their analysis of problems that they fail to differentiate between causes and symptoms. In the early 1970s a group of students on one campus became involved in campus protests. The college administration dealt with the protesters by placing them on probation. No longer protesting, the group began to have weekly drug parties. After being arrested by the campus police, most of the group members were expelled. The campus authorities were treating the symptoms of the problem but not resolving or eliminating the causes, feelings of loneliness and alienation.

Analyzing a problem involves not only gathering information (particularly about the problem's causes) but also testing the information. Here is a set of standards for testing factual material in a problem-solving discussion (Phillips, 1973, pp. 103–105):

1. Is the information factual, inferential, or evaluative?
2. Are the facts current?
3. Are the facts drawn from acceptable authorities?
4. Are the statistical statements biased?
5. Are eyewitness statements confirmed?

An inference is a statement about the past or future based on present information. For example, the statement "Parking places will become scarcer as student population increases" is an inferential statement based on present facts. The evaluative statement "The present campus parking situation is poor" could be derived from a factual statement such as "50 percent of the student population can't find campus parking" or "Students must arrive on campus by 8:00 A.M. to be assured a parking place close to their classes." Evaluative statements ask a group member only to agree or disagree with them. Inferences and evaluations should not be treated as factual information in problem solving.

People sometimes fail to obtain the most recent information bearing on a problem. The number of students driving to campus in 1970 would probably be of little help in attempting to find the present need for parking; the number might have changed drastically since that time. Using facts that are outdated can lead to erroneous conclusions and affect the quality of the group's decision or solution to a problem.

An authority is a qualified person in a specific field. A person may be an authority in one field but not in another. Jane Fonda is well qualified to speak on acting, but is she an expert on domestic policy? Whether an authority is qualified is sometimes difficult to ascertain. In our original problem, we might ask the advice of campus police who control the selection of parking areas on campus; their suggestions on the extent of the parking problem could be viewed as authority-based information.

Statistics provide a concise form in which to present large amounts of data. However, statistical data can be manipulated to provide a specific interpretation, and people do not always know how to interpret statistics. The group may have to call on an expert for assistance.

Each person views the same experience differently. Ask any three people in your class to describe the same event, and you will find three different views of it. We are all different psychologically and physiologically. If facts needed by the group are based on personal experience, it might be best to search for individuals who have had similar experiences to verify the observation.

* * *

Exercise 10-5

FINDING AND TESTING INFORMATION

If you were to participate in a problem-solving discussion dealing with the following three areas, where would you go for facts? What specific references would you use?

National health plan
Energy crisis
Innovations in education

Is your information current? Is it drawn from authoritative sources?

ESTABLISHING CRITERIA FOR EVALUATING SOLUTIONS. In this step the group establishes certain standards for judging each problem solution. The ultimate question each group must ask is "What standards or criteria must be met before a solution can be acceptable to us?" In attempting to solve our parking problem the group might ask: Is the solution practical? Will it cost too much? Will the people who have the power to implement the solution do so? The criteria established by the group limit the range of acceptable solutions to be considered later.

SUGGESTING SOLUTIONS TO THE PROBLEM. Once the facts have been accumulated and tested and the criteria established for evaluating the solutions, the group can begin to suggest possible solutions to the problem. Sometimes groups use the brainstorming technique to draw out many possible solutions. The solutions proposed should be realistic and based on the factual information provided by group members.

SELECTING AND TESTING THE FINAL SOLUTION. After determining the advantages and disadvantages of each solution, the group selects the one that provides the most advantages and the fewest disadvantages. This step involves examining each solution against the criteria established earlier and comparing the most acceptable solutions.

In classroom discussions, the group rarely has time to test its selected solutions. However, if a group puts a final solution into effect and finds that it is unworkable or impractical, the group may go back to the previous step to examine new solutions.

Ideal Solution Pattern

This problem-solving pattern, which consists of four steps, emerged from practical experience with managerial groups (Kepner and Tregoe, 1965). Let's see how this pattern can be used with our problem-solving example—the campus parking crisis.

1. Is there agreement on the nature of the problem?

    In their initial discussion, the students discovered that they were unable to find parking spaces on campus. The intent of their meeting in the student union was clear—to search for a means to improve student parking. They all agreed on the nature of the problem.
2. What would be the ideal solution from the point of view of all parties involved in the problem?

    At the meeting the group would state the ideal solution: Every college student driving to campus can find a parking space at the place and time desired.
3. What conditions affecting the problem can be changed so that the ideal solution can be achieved?

    The group collects the facts needed for determining not only what is occurring but also what can be done to resolve the dilemma. Suppose the students found that (1) the campus has 3,000 parking places, (2) during peak hours, 3,500 students attempt to park on campus, and (3) an average of 10,000 students drive cars to campus each week. From these facts the students learn that the campus needs 500 more parking places to meet student demand. However, the college does not have the space needed for 500 additional parking places (and no money for converting the land even if it were available). The group then examines alternative solutions to the problem: (1) providing tram service from off-campus parking areas or (2) asking students to share rides to campus, thus reducing the total number of cars driven to campus.
4. Of the solutions available, which one best approximates the ideal solution?

The first alternative does not solve the basic problem of not being able to find a parking place on campus. The second alternative does provide a means for alleviating the campus traffic congestion while providing each student with a parking place on campus. Furthermore, no new parking places will have to be found on campus, and there will be no cost to the college. The second alternative comes closer to the ideal solution and so would be adopted by the group as the solution to the problem.

Single Question Pattern

This pattern, which consists of five steps, was developed by Carl E. Larson (1969) from descriptions of the reasoning process used by successful and unsuccessful problem solvers. Again we will illustrate this pattern with our parking problem example.

1. What single question provides the answer that is needed to accomplish the group's purpose?

   The student group states the problem question as "How can we guarantee every student driver a parking place on campus?"

2. What subquestions must be answered before the group can answer the single question they have formulated?

   Questions such as "How many students drive to campus?" and "How many parking places are there on campus?" need to be answered before making an intelligent answer to the problem question.

3. Does the group have sufficient information to answer confidently the subquestions?

   To answer the subquestions, the students must do some research.

4. What are the most reasonable answers to the subquestions?

   The students find that of the 10,000 students who drive to campus weekly, 3,500 drive to campus at peak hours, but there are only 3,000 parking places on campus. If the students could not find all the information they need to answer their subquestions, they would have to use whatever information is available in order to arrive at the most reasonable answers.

5. Assuming that the answers to the subquestions are correct, what is the best solution to the problem?

   From the limited information the students have on the problem, it appears that increasing the number of parking places would be the best solution to the problem.

* * *

Exercise 10-6
COMPARING PROBLEM-SOLVING PATTERNS

Divide the class into three groups. Each group is given the same problem and asked to arrive at a solution to it using the problem-solving pattern assigned to them: either reflective thinking, ideal solution, or single question. After the groups have solved the problem, ask each other the following questions:

1. Which pattern produced the best solution?
2. Which pattern was easiest to operate within the group?
3. Which pattern produced the greatest group-member satisfaction?

Is One Problem-Solving Pattern More Effective Than Another?

J. K. Brilhart and L. M. Jochem (1964) compared three different problem-solving patterns (brainstorming, a form of reflective thinking, and a pattern based on Bales's stages) and found the value of the reflective thinking pattern to be "dubious at best, and harmful at worst." Noting that this study failed to examine the final solution, O. Bayless (1967) attempted to find which pattern produced the best final product. He examined three patterns of problem solving and found that neither the pattern nor the quantity of ideas affect the quality of the final solution, but that the nature of the problem the group deals with does influence the effectiveness of the discussion.

Familiarity with a problem appears to provide a more secure group environment. Insufficient information on a particular problem tends to make group members feel inadequate to their task; in turn, this feeling of inadequacy may cause frustration, inhibit the group's ability to communicate, and leave group members unsatisfied with the group's decisions. For example, a group of students would probably fare much better when selecting the best method for teaching college courses than when formulating U.S. foreign policy. Students who are required to present a number of problem-solving discussions are sometimes forced to select problems in areas in which they have little expertise or information. Lack of information and familiarity with a problem does not necessarily stop a group from attempting to solve the problem, but it can affect the quality of the solution that is finally selected.

C. E. Larson (1969) investigated the ability of groups to solve a problem accurately using the three problem-solving patterns we have presented. As with the earlier studies, the reflective thinking pattern was found to be the least productive. The single question and ideal solution patterns did not differ significantly from each other in their accuracy in solving problems.

It would appear that successful group problem solving can be facilitated by the selection of the proper method for the particular problem with specific group members. We should not assume that the reflective thinking pattern, taught in most group-discussion classes and used most frequently by groups, is the most appropriate and desirable method for successful problem solving. If a problem-solving pattern fits, we should use it. We should not be forced into an inflexible pattern for solving all problems that confront us.

SUMMARY

Group discussion is the face-to-face interaction of two or more persons engaged in information sharing, problem solving, or self-maintenance. As such, group discussion is the main type of group communication. The participants in a group discussion must assume responsibility for both speaking and listening during the discussion as appropriate.

The methods for presenting group discussion vary in degree of formality, publicness, and control. Formal, public group discussions exercise greater control over messages, the interaction of group members, and the structure of the situation than do informal, private group discussions.

There are six basic discussion methods: round table, panel, symposium-forum, dialogue, colloquy, and lecture-forum. The purpose, basic procedure, and format of each involves the participants in different ways. These methods establish patterns for controlling the interaction of group members. The methods do not, however, control what is said or the order in which a discussion deals with a particular problem or topic. In order to structure a problem-solving discussion, procedures can be followed to provide organization for the process. Three commonly used procedures are reflective thinking, ideal solution, and single question. The group must select the set of procedures that fits its problem. No one format operates effectively with every problem.

ADDITIONAL READINGS

Applbaum, Ronald L. *Fundamentals of Group Discussion.* Palo Alto: Science Research Associates, 1976. This instructional module provides a simple, clear explanation of how one prepares and presents a group discussion.

Beal, George M.; Bohlen, Joe M.; and Randabaugh, J. Neil. *Leadership and Dynamic Group Action.* Ames: Iowa State University Press, 1962. The authors give a how-to approach for using group discussion methods. Each method is examined by answering why, when, and how.

Potter, David, and Anderson, Martin P. *Discussion: A Guide to Effective Practice.* 3d ed. Belmont, Calif.: Wadsworth, 1976. This readable book, full of exercises, emphasizes the application of discussion principles to practice.

11

SMALL-GROUP
TECHNIQUES

PREVIEW

✳ What are discussion techniques?

Four discussion techniques that developed either to assist
group interaction or to promote an understanding of roles
within the group are:
  Brainstorming
  Buzz sessions and Phillips 66
  Posting
  Role playing

✳ What is the nominal group technique?

The nominal group technique is a highly structured group
discussion used to generate ideas and solutions in order to
reach a group decision by mathematically pooling group
member judgments.

✳ What is the Delphi technique?

The Delphi technique is a method for systematically gathering individual judgments on a particular topic by using a set
of sequential questionnaires interspersed with feedback based
on the results of previous questionnaires.

IN CHAPTER 1 we stressed the critical effect communication has
on social interaction in the small group. No matter what the nature of the group or its purpose, it uses communication to establish social interaction and to achieve its goals. In Chapter 10,
we examined six methods of discussion; however, use of these
methods does not guarantee successful group interaction. Discussion methods merely provide a format for information sharing or
problem solving. They do not provide the information or solutions. Only through interaction can group members provide the
ideas needed.

Individuals sometimes do not express their solutions to a problem because they fear being criticized. To prevent such occur-
rences and facilitate communication by group members, a
number of discussion techniques can be used in conjunction with
group methods. We shall examine three of these techniques: (1)

brainstorming; (2) buzz sessions and Phillips 66: and (3) posting.

As we learned in Chapter 6, group members' roles are crucial in the group process. Discrepancies between perceived roles and role expectations of group members can result in conflict, inhibiting the group efforts as well as the group members' adaptation and integration. So it becomes important that each group member understand his or her role and the role of others in the group. We will discuss role playing as a means of coming to this understanding.

Lastly, we shall explore two program planning techniques—nominal group technique and Delphi technique—which might be used by groups concerned with developing new programs or changing existing programs.

DISCUSSION TECHNIQUES

The discussion techniques developed in this chapter serve the purpose of improving the group communication process by assisting group interaction or promoting an understanding of role behavior.

Brainstorming

In many group discussions, some members lack self-confidence, are discouraged from contributing, or are not given the opportunity to be creative. The purpose of brainstorming is to remove these inhibiting factors in order to promote group interaction.

Brainstorming is a small-group discussion technique designed to encourage the free exchange of ideas and solutions between group members.

The brainstorming procedure is simple.

1. Decide on the area or issue with which the group must cope; state the problem clearly.
2. Appoint a secretary to write down all ideas. The role of secretary may rotate, so that each member has a chance to contribute fully to the brainstorming session.
3. Set a time limit for the session.
4. Appoint a chairperson to enforce brainstorming rules.
5. Set up an informal physical arrangement.
6. Ask the group to discuss the selected area or issue freely.
7. Bring the session to a halt when the time limit is reached.

There are four basic rules for conducting a brainstorming session:

- Think of both ideas and solutions.
- Strive for quantity rather than quality.
- Welcome all contributions.
- Do not evaluate or criticize any idea or solution offered.

As A. F. Osborn (1957), p. 84) has stated, "The wilder the idea, the better; it is easier to tame down than to think up." Participants are encouraged to add to, subtract from, combine, and modify others' solutions. This process is called *piggybacking*. The results of the brainstorming can be compared and evaluated afterwards.

Results of research on the usefulness of brainstorming have been inconsistent (Shaw, 1976). However, one study (Brilhart and Jochem, 1964) found that brainstorming tended to produce more and better solutions than did the other two problem-solving patterns being evaluated. Also, there is some evidence that, with longer work periods, groups produce more ideas from brainstorming than do individuals working alone. The problem is that group members must first have the ideas that are drawn out in a brainstorming session; if they do not, the session is not very productive. It is also difficult for group members not to evaluate or criticize others' ideas. Group members who do not refrain from criticizing may be asked to remain quiet or to leave the group; but this maneuver can change the climate from one fostering the free exchange of ideas to one with rather prominent restrictions.

* * *

Exercise 11-1
BRAINSTORMING

Divide the class into groups of five or six. Each group is given the same problem to brainstorm about, perhaps one of the following four:

How can we create equality among races in America?
What should be done about water pollution?
How can the United States achieve energy independence?
How can we control political campaign spending?

Each group brainstorms about the problem for ten minutes. After the groups share the results of the brainstorming, answer the following questions—the first six in relation to your own brainstorming group, and the last three in relation to all the groups.

1. Did you want to evaluate the contributions of other group members?

2. Did one individual or leader dominate the session?

3. Did members piggyback ideas or solutions?

4. Did you feel free to communicate as the session progressed? If your answer is no, why not?

5. Did some group members contribute more than other members?

6. Did all group members have an opportunity to participate?

7. Did certain groups arrive at more solutions?

8. Did some groups have a higher quality of solutions?

9. Why does a particular group arrive at more solutions or have a higher quality of solutions?

Buzz Groups and Phillips 66

Two techniques often used to encourage audience participation in a discussion are buzz groups and Phillips 66.

A *buzz group* is a small group (sometimes as few as two people) drawn from a listening audience that converses briefly on a specific question dealing with a discussion topic.

Of course, the smaller the buzz group, the more opportunity each member has to participate. However, in any buzz group all members are given the chance to express their reactions to the question. The buzz group procedure is as follows:

1. The audience is divided into groups of four (sometimes two) to ten.
2. A chairperson is appointed for each group.
3. Each group discusses one aspect of the problem or topic presented to the entire audience. The topic should not take more than one hour to discuss.
4. The chairperson presents the group's opinions to the entire audience.

Because their opinions are forwarded through a chairperson, group members take active roles and yet remain anonymous. The chairperson's presentation allows the entire audience to benefit from the group's findings.

Imagine that as part of an audience of forty students, you have just heard a panel discussion on what can be done to clean up the environment. The chairperson divides the audience into eight groups of five and asks your group to discuss the question "How can we rid our air of smog?" The group makes you the chairperson and then discusses the problem in a round-table format. After the discussion you present the group's conclusions to the panel and the other audience groups. This is one example of how a buzz group works.

Phillips 66 is somewhat different from the buzz group.

Phillips 66 refers to a small group whose function is to briefly discuss an area of a topic or problem and to develop questions about it.

Phillips refers to the creator's name, and *66* stands for six persons discussing for six minutes. However, group size and time are more flexible than the title suggests. The procedure is as follows:

1. The audience is divided into groups of three to eight.

2. A chairperson is appointed for each group.

3. A time limit of six to ten minutes is usually established for the group discussion.

4. The group develops questions concerning the discussion topic for the primary discussion group.

5. The chairperson presents the group's questions to the primary discussion group. Alternatively, the chairperson for the primary discussion group collects the questions from the small groups and presents them to the primary discussion group. In either case, the primary discussion group answers the questions in the presence of the audience.

When the alternative procedure is used in step 5, the small group members may feel less a part of the discussion.

The success of either the buzz group technique or the Phillips 66 technique rests on five principles.

• The participants must feel qualified to discuss or question the topic under discussion; it must be of interest and relevance to them.

• The groups must know what is expected of them. Asking for a decision is more specific than just asking for comments on a problem. Also, a summary of each member's opinions on the problem would not accomplish the group's goal of reaching a specific decision.

• The group must be small enough that the members can interact easily. The larger the group, the harder it is to achieve that interaction. In a large group that is later divided into many small groups, only brief reporting of conclusions is feasible.

• The time allotted for the discussion should suit the topic and the size of the groups. If the topic would take more than an hour to discuss, then buzz groups or the Phillips 66 technique should not be used.

• The prime goal of a smaller group is to encourage participation; thus the group must be careful to maintain a free and informal climate.

These techniques do not require the planning and careful preparation that many small-group discussions do; we should not expect the results to be comparable. Besides, the time allotted is too short to go through the entire problem-solving process. These techniques are most useful in situations calling for quick reactions to simple assignments. They are much better in pointing up problems than in solving them.

* * *

Exercise 11-2
PHILLIPS 66

After the first formal discussion in your class, divide the class audience into groups of five or six students. Each group will formulate two questions dealing with the discussion topic. The primary discussion group will then respond to the questions generated by the small groups. After the forum period, answer the following questions:

1. Did every group member have an opportunity to participate?
2. Was there a duplication of questions and, if so, how was it handled by the primary discussion group?
3. Did you feel as if you were involved in the discussion?

Posting

During a discussion, group or audience members sometimes ask questions prematurely or out of context. Such questions can put the group on the defensive or embarrass the questioner. The group may not be able to answer the question because members do not have the needed information. Posting can help handle this problem.

Posting is a technique for listing questions or ideas that the group or audience members have regarding the discussion topic; depending on when they are gathered, these questions or ideas can then be dealt with in various ways.

The procedure for posting is as follows:

1. The chairperson states when posting will be conducted: prior to the discussion, during the discussion, or immediately after the discussion.
2. The chairperson records all questions or ideas.
3. If the questions or ideas are gathered before the formal discussion, they can be used as a basis for organizing the discussion. This procedure ensures that the information desired will be discussed.
4. If the questions or ideas are gathered during a formal discussion, the extent to which they are used will depend on the time available. If time is limited and the questions are significant, more discussions may be needed, or the group may select the most important questions for immediate consideration.

5. If the questions or ideas are gathered after a formal discussion, a skilled group may develop a supplementary presentation around the questions, which are then subjected to open discussion.

Posting serves several functions. First, it can raise the level of interest among group members and audience. Group members may find that they have common questions or problems. By selecting the most important questions, the group can address itself to problems that are familiar and capable of competent, adequate analysis. This procedure reduces the fear of having to discuss unknown problems.

Second, posting can help clarify problems, particularly those that have emotional overtones. By exposing individual orientations (attitudes, biases) toward a problem, posting can alleviate possible confusion or even hostility over personal interpretations. For example, some members of a group meeting to consider racism in America might see racism as a moral issue while others might see it as an economic problem; posting would help everyone recognize the different viewpoints.

Third, posting can help a group agree on a specific problem for discussion. For example, a group discussion on U.S. China policy may falter because group members are discussing two different areas—social and cultural. If each group member is asked to state his or her view of the problem and all ideas are posted, then the group can decide which area would be the most fruitful for discussion. Handling each area separately would increase the group's chances for agreement on solutions.

As in brainstorming, the recorder accepts all contributions during posting. This can be a spur to member participation. In posting problems, recorders must try to understand the meaning intended and translate the contributions into understandable form. A chairperson may ask group members to help interpret the questions and thus give them more opportunity to interact. If an attempt is made to clarify and resolve differences, posting can result in more cohesiveness and improved communication in the group.

Posting has at least two potential drawbacks. First, it is time-consuming. When posting is used during a discussion, time is spent listing and selecting questions for future discussion. Second, the success of the technique depends on the discussion leader, who must record and sometimes evaluate the questions and ideas. The leader who is perceived as a critic and judge, rather than as an aid to the discussion, may cause group members and audience participants to hold back from contributing their questions and ideas.

ROLE PLAYING

We learn a way of behaving that is acceptable to other group members, and that behavior is the role we are expected to play in the group. Our roles are, in part, a consequence of our communication with other group members. Roles are affected by the group environment and the group members' perceptions of it. Frequently, our perceptions are not realistic. We may not have prior experience with each other or with the problem under discussion, and so we have difficulty evaluating each other's behavior in the group setting. Group members must be able to clarify their expected roles. One technique that can provide group members with an understanding of their roles within the group is called role playing.

> *Role playing* is an individual dramatization of a problem or situation.

During role playing group members put themselves into specific roles in specific situations; they can try on various roles. Afterward they can evaluate their performances and so come to understand group roles and processes better.

Although role playing is like acting on stage, the participants are not asked to perfect their roles. The situation is fictional; it only approximates reality. Role players are to behave as they normally would except for the specific requirements of the role they have been given. In other words, they are to do the best job of communicating in a group that they can unless their role specifically requires ineffective communication behavior.

Playing Oneself and Others

Three types of roles are enacted in role playing. The first is just playing oneself. Groups members attempt to learn more about how they themselves act rather than how others in the group feel or act. Since role playing can be more informal, flexible, and permissive than real life, it releases the inhibitions that normally cloak group members' interactions. The more freedom of expression that group members feel, the greater the communication of true feelings, attitudes, and beliefs.

In the other two types of roles, called *role switching* and *role reversal*, players take different roles than they would under normal conditions. In many U.S. cities, one day a year is set aside for high school students to switch roles with officials in the community. This role switching helps students understand the role of city officials, although it does not provide a base from which the students can judge their own roles in group situations. Role reversal occurs, for example, when management assumes the role of labor, and labor the role of management. By playing the role of the other, each party can gain insight into the other's behavior and become more sensitive to the other's position on an issue. When the parties resume their real-life roles, more realistic bargaining may result.

Role playing was first used in psychological therapy and has since been applied to a wide range of human activities from education to business. In group discussion, role playing is often used as a tool for demonstration. For example, a group concerned with increasing its productivity (defined in this case as formulating as many solutions to a problem as possible) creates a problem-solving situation and attempts to view how it arrives at solutions to the problem. The role-playing situation provides a concrete example for subsequent analysis. This evaluation is crucial. The group's primary concern is not how much group members learn while participating, but how much knowledge they gain from evaluating the situation.

Role playing is also used for practicing discussion skills. For example, a group may want to develop members' ability to solve problems. An imaginary problem-solving situation is developed. Participants are then asked to go through the problem-solving process. From the role playing the group members learn how they should behave in the group and ways to modify their behavior. During the subsequent evaluation the group members refine their observations and suggest ways to improve group behavior. The emphasis, however, is on the role playing rather than on the evaluation.

Role playing can help individuals in the group as well as the group as a whole. On the individual level, role playing can provide insight into the effectiveness of individual roles in the group. When others take our role, we have a unique opportunity to see ourselves as others see us. Although this may be embarrassing, it can show us where our behavior needs adjusting. It can point out more effective behaviors that we can learn to use in place of ineffective behaviors. For example, a person who tends to monopolize a group discussion may learn ways to draw out the opinions of other group members.

Role playing can help the group to function more effectively as a unit. It can help eliminate problems of communication that arise from failure to understand how the group should operate. Ideally, all members of the group are part of the role playing either as role players or as observers and evaluators. This allows each member to play a part in the group's development. It provides not only a vehicle for learning discussion skills but also more group satisfaction.

Role playing should start with simple situations. It is important that the objectives be clear and well defined. However, there are many procedural variations for implementing role playing. A procedure can be selected for its ability either to provide the group with the greatest understanding of its problem or to develop the skill necessary for dealing with group or individual problems. In the suggested readings for this chapter, several texts have been listed that explain the different types of role-playing procedures.

Problems and Limitations of Role Playing

Many people lose their sense of reality when involved in role playing. They have difficulty assuming roles because they do not perceive the situation as resembling real life. Many participants tend to embellish their roles; this embellishment does not produce a realistic context in which to study either an issue or an interpersonal problem.

Role playing cannot solve all problems related to understanding individual and group needs. Its success depends heavily on the group members' abilities to be creative. If the group members do not use their imaginations, it can be a waste of time. If the group members are receptive, creative, and cooperative, role playing can be an effective tool for improving group interaction and communication.

* * *

Exercise 11-3
ROLE PLAYING

Ameriville, a town of 20,000 in the West, has some industry and a heterogeneous population of various religious, racial, and ethnic groups. There are four grade schools, one junior high school, and one high school.

Mr. White has been the superintendent of schools in Ameriville for three years. This spring, his contract is up for renewal. For several weeks the board of education has been discussing whether to renew the contract. A decision must be made at the next board meeting to allow Mr. White adequate notice if he is released. The debate centers around three major issues:

Progressive education. Some people in the community feel that Mr. White has gone much too far in bringing so-called progressive methods of education into the schools. It is asserted that not

Exercise 11-3 continued

enough attention is given to reading, writing, and arithmetic and that a lot of time is devoted to "social adjustment" and controversial social and political issues that children are not adequately prepared to talk about. Other people feel that the most up-to-date knowledge about the psychology of learning is being employed, and that children should be informed on matters concerning racial prejudice, sex education, and so on.

Administrative abilities. Some teachers (mainly the older, more conservative ones) have complained about extra time they are expected to devote to various faculty committees; they feel that teachers who try to maintain high standards and discipline are passed over for promotions, favorable teaching assignments, and the like. Other teachers feel that Mr. White is a dynamic administrator who is simply trying to inject more democracy into the running of the schools.

Off-the-job activities. Mr. White is an active member of the local chapters of the Americans for Democratic Action and the American Civil Liberties Union. When asked to give speeches before the Rotary Club and other service organizations, he often delves into controversial political and social issues, such as advocating the elimination of racial and religious barriers in the community and the elimination of censorship. Many people feel that a superintendent of schools should be more impartial. Others feel that it is not only his right but his duty as a private citizen to engage in whatever activities off the job he sees fit.

Procedure:

1. Ask for six volunteers from the class.
2. Assign the following roles:
   Mr. White
   Chairperson, board of education
   Four board of education members, two who support and two who oppose renewing Mr. White's contract
3. Situation: The six role players are in the board of education conference room, and their task is to decide whether to renew Mr. White's contract.

Immediately after the role-playing situation, answer the following questions:

1. Were the role players realistic?
2. What communication problems did the role players confront and/or create?

Examine the role-playing group in terms of the following questions:

1. Did group norms develop?
2. What communicator variables influenced the discussion?
3. Was conflict present? How was it resolved?
4. Was the group cohesive?
5. Was group conformity an important variable?
6. What styles and functions of leadership were manifest in the situation?
7. What types of messages were communicated? Which messages had the greatest impact on the role-playing situation?

PROGRAM PLANNING TECHNIQUES

Many groups use techniques to increase participation and creativity during problem-solving meetings associated with group planning. When groups attempt to increase participation and pool judgments of group members, special group techniques are required. We shall explore two such techniques: nominal group technique and Delphi technique.

Nominal Group Technique (NGT)

Although group interaction plays a crucial role in idea clarification and evaluation, it may be of less value during the fact-finding phase of problem solving. The nominal group technique (NGT) calls for a separate process for each phase of problem solving and yet encourages group member participation. It also incorporates mathematical voting techniques to reach a group judgment, thus reducing the chances for errors in group decision making.

> The *nominal group technique* is both a problem-solving and an idea-generating strategy; it maximizes face-to-face participation among group members and pools the judgments of individuals to reach decisions.

NGT, developed by Andre L. Delbecq and Andrew H. Van de Ven in 1968, has been used by organizations in health, social service, education, industry, and government.

Nominal group technique consists primarily of four steps (steps 4-7 below), but it can also entail three preliminary steps and two later ones:

1. The group selects a leader-recorder.
2. The leader-recorder selects and prepares the meeting room and provides necessary supplies.

3. At the start of the meeting the leader-recorder clarifies group objectives and member roles.
4. Group members write down their ideas (individually and silently) for solving a problem.
5. On a flip chart the leader records the ideas (one at a time from each group member) generated during the writing period.
6. The leader monitors a discussion of each recorded idea for purposes of clarification and evaluation.
7. The members vote individually on the priority of ideas; the group decision is derived through the ranking of group member votes.
8. Repeat step 6 if the vote is inconclusive.
9. Repeat step 7 to arrive at a final group vote.

We will illustrate NGT by examining a hypothetical meeting of 18 individuals to find ways to raise money for the local chapter of the American Cancer Society. The group begins by selecting a leader (who will also serve as group recorder). The leader selects and prepares the meeting room—a room large enough to accommodate three groups of six individuals seated around rectangular tables (large enough to provide a writing space for each person) set far enough apart that the groups do not interfere with each other. Before the meeting the leader also acquires (1) a flip chart for each table, (2) a roll of masking tape, (3) a supply of 3 x 5 cards for each table, and (4) pens, pencils, and paper for each participant.

Once the members are in the meeting room and seated in their small groups, the leader clarifies the group objective (to suggest methods for raising the most money for the local American Cancer Society chapter) and member roles (to share ideas and work together for the next hour). The leader then provides each participant with a question to answer on a worksheet, specifying that the members not talk during the brief time allotted for this activity.

In the next NGT step the leader writes the participants' ideas on a flip chart visible to the entire group. The leader proceeds around each table until all the ideas generated during the silent period are listed:

1. auction	7. door-to-door canvassing
2. telethon (radio/television)	8. mail solicitation
3. bake sale	9. telephone solicitation
4. house parties	10. Las Vegas night
5. dinner-dance	11. educational clinic
6. car washing	12. lottery

The next step, discussion of each idea, serves to clarify the ideas; it is not for debating ideas or winning arguments, however. Clarification entails discussion of the logic and relative importance of an idea. For example, method 11 on the chart is not self-explanatory; the group member who suggested it might explain that this method involves charging people for educational programs provided by the local chapter.

After the group has clarified the meaning of each idea and given arguments for and against them, the members must determine the relative importance of the ideas. They rank the items by listing the five most important ones on the 3 x 5 cards. The six members in one small group rank the methods as follows:

Method	Rank
1	1, 4
2	1, 1, 2, 2, 2, 3, 4
5	1, 4, 4, 5, 5
7	1, 2, 2, 3, 3, 3, 5
8	1, 2, 3, 4, 5
9	3, 5
12	4, 5

By observing the ratings, the group has located the ideas that are the most important and should be acted on—telethon, door-to-door canvassing, dinner-dance, and mail solitication. However, if the group could not easily select the ideas from observing the preliminary vote, the participants would discuss the preliminary vote in order to further clarify the ideas. For example, method 8 received a wide range of rankings (1–5). The group would explore why the ratings varied so greatly. Several members may have misunderstood the process. Others may be misinformed about the amount of funds that can be raised using this method. Provided with the proper meaning and information, members might change their ranking of the method.

For the final group vote, the group follows the same voting procedures used for the preliminary vote. Our group might finally select two methods for use in the next fiscal year—telethon and door-to-door canvassing.

The leader is vital to the NGT process. This person must be sure that the behaviors proper to each step are observed. For example, during the writing period the leader must discourage any group member from talking or looking at the worksheets of others. Later, when ideas are being listed on the flip chart, the leader must discourage members from engaging in private conversations or from discussing the ideas rather than merely listing them. In the clarification phase it is the leader's job to keep the members from getting into arguments.

NGT is a useful program planning technique. However, for routine meetings, in which the focus is on information exchange and coordination, other leader-centered meeting formats are more appropriate. When the purpose of the meeting is to bring together a group for negotiation or compromise, bargaining techniques are useful. Finally, for policy setting in a representative body, parliamentary procedure and its variants are appropriate (Delbecq, Van de Ven, and Gustafson, 1975).

* * *

Exercise 11-4
NOMINAL GROUP TECHNIQUE (NGT)

Here is a list of topics suitable for conducting the NGT in your classroom.

What should be included in a general education program?

How can humanities programs be made more practical?

What type of communication program should be developed for college students?

Divide the class into groups of five or six members. Each group will discuss the same topic and arrive at a group decision using the NGT. After the NGT session, answer the following questions:

1. Did you find it difficult to generate solutions?

2. Did the leader provide clear instructions as you proceeded through the NGT process?

3. Did the leader prevent group members from disrupting the NGT process?

4. Did group members attempt to evaluate solutions during the clarification stage?

5. Did the group have difficulty selecting the final solution(s)?

6. Did all group members have an opportunity to participate in the clarification stage?

7. Did you have to discuss the preliminary vote? If your group had a preliminary vote discussion, did group members restrict their participation to clarifying their decisions?

Delphi Technique

The Delphi process was developed by Norman Dalkey and his associates at the Rand Corporation. It was originally used to predict technological developments. Presently, the technique is used extensively in program planning for (1) determining possible program alternatives, (2) exploring assumptions or information used to reach group judgments, (3) seeking information that can lead to group consensus, (4) relating individual judgments on a topic from a variety of disciplines, and (5) educating group participants about a range of issues related to the discussion topic.

The *Delphi technique* is a method for systematically gathering individual judgments on a particular topic through sequential questionnaires interspersed with feedback based on the previous questionnaires.

Unlike the NGT, the Delphi technique does not require the participants to be in close physical proximity. Thus, it can be used by managers, administrators, scholars, and others who cannot come together for face-to-face interaction.

Participants are asked initially to respond to a broad question regarding problems, solutions, forecasts, and/or information exchange. Subsequently, they respond to new questions developed from their responses to the preceding questions. The process is completed when a decision has been reached or when sufficient information has been exchanged among participants.

Although the NGT takes a relatively short time—60 to 90 minutes—the minimum time for conducting the Delphi method is about 45 days. Thus, if a group has only a short time, it may be unwise to use this technique. Since the information used in Delphi comes from written responses to questions, a group should not use the technique with individuals who have difficulty reading or writing.

Three types of participants are involved in Delphi situations. First, individuals who will use the results of the Delphi study. Normally, this work group is composed of five to nine staff and decision makers. The group develops and analyzes the question, evaluates the responses, and revises the questionnaires. The second type of participant is a professional staff worker who guides the work group through the Delphi process. Finally, there are individuals who answer the questions. A successful Delphi study depends on the selection of qualified respondents in the problem area.

Table 11-1 illustrates a ten-step Delphi process and schedule

TABLE 11-1 PROCEDURES FOR THE DELPHI TECHNIQUE

Activities	Estimated Minimum Time for Accomplishment (days)
1. Develop the Delphi question	0.5
2. Select and contact respondents	2.0
3. Select sample size	0.5
4. Develop Questionnaire 1 and test	1.0
a. Type and send out	1.0
b. Response time	5.0
c. Dunning time (if used)	3.0
5. Analyze Questionnaire 1	0.5
6. Develop Questionnaire 2 and test	2.0
a. Type and send out	1.0
b. Response time	5.0
c. Dunning time (if used)	3.0
7. Analyze Questionnaire 2	1.0
8. Develop Questionnaire 3 and test	2.0
a. Type and send out	1.0
b. Response time	5.0
c. Dunning time (if used)	3.0
9. Analyze Questionnaire 3	1.0
10. Prepare a final report	4.0
a. Type report and send out	1.0
b. Prepare respondents' report	1.0
c. Type report and send out	1.0
Total estimated minimum time	44.5

developed by Delbecq, Van de Ven, and Gustafson (1975). It begins with the formulation of the Delphi question. The question must be clearly understood by all the respondents in order to ensure proper responses. For example, let's imagine a Delphi study in which the decision makers and staff are involved in exploring methods for raising money for the American Cancer Society. We begin by asking: What methods can be used to raise funds? Which methods raise the most funds? Which methods are practical and which are impractical for the American Cancer Society?

We then select and contact our respondents. We must select individuals who want to participate, who have relevant information and time to devote to the study, and who will generate results that can be justified. The number of respondents used varies, but thirty has been suggested as a good size. Let's assume that our work group draws up a list of 200 possible respondents (we want one respondent from each state, and individuals must have experience in raising funds at the state or local level). The participants are contacted by the work group, and told what will be

---

QUESTIONNAIRE 1

Please list all the methods that one might use to raise funds for the American Cancer Society. Please be clear and concise.

Methods   *Comments*

Signature _____
(optional)

FIGURE 11-1.   Typical first questionnaire, as used in the Delphi technique.

required of them and how the results will be disseminated to all chapters of the American Cancer Society.

The work group is now ready to develop the first questionnaire (Figure 11-1) and test. It is more general than subsequent questionnaires. The questionnaire is sent with a cover letter (Figure 11-2) telling respondents how to fill out the questionnaire,—when

---

Dear   :

Thank you for participating in our efforts to list methods for acquiring funds for the American Cancer Society. Your responses will be used by the national office to develop programs for local chapters.

Please list the various types of funding methods that can be used by local chapters in our organization. I have attached a questionnaire on which you are to list the funding methods. Please complete the questionnaire and return (in the envelope provided) to my office for analysis by _____.

At the conclusion of our study you will receive a copy of the results.

Thank you for your assistance.

Sincerely,

FIGURE 11-2.   Sample cover letter to accompany the first questionnaire, as used in the Delphi technique.

to return it, the purpose of the study, and how results will be used.

Once the participants have returned the questionnaire, the work group develops a composite list of methods suggested by the respondents. On the basis of this list, the work group develops a second questionnaire (Figure 11-3), which provides respondents with information obtained from the first questionnaire. In general, the second questionnaire provides three benefits:

1. It indicates the positions of the respondents. The participants can clearly see the areas of agreement and disagreement. Perhaps, all of our participants might list a lottery as a viable fund-raising method.
2. It identifies areas in which a respondent's meaning was unclear. For example, the type of lottery may need to be specified.
3. It provides a basis for understanding. All participants are provided with an understanding of each other's position.

QUESTIONNAIRE 2

Please examine each of the items identified in Questionnaire 1 as a possible method for raising funds for the American Cancer Society. If you wish to comment (that is, to agree, disagree, or clarify), please do so in the space provided. Also, feel free to add new funding methods. Finally, please rank the five most important methods as you perceive them at this time.

Priority Vote	Items from Questionnaire 1	Comments
ـــــــ	1. lottery	
ـــــــ	2. telethon	
ـــــــ	3. home parties	
ـــــــ	4. raffle	
ـــــــ	5. dance	
ـــــــ	6. concert	
ـــــــ	7. door-to-door canvassing	
ـــــــ	8. bake sale	
ـــــــ	9. car wash	
ـــــــ	10. dinner dance	

FIGURE 11-3. Typical second questionnaire, as used in the Delphi technique.

QUESTIONNAIRE 3

Final Vote Requested	Preliminary Vote Results	Item	Summary of Earlier Comments
		1. Lottery	Respondents generally felt that a
_____	_200_	[and so on for each item]	lottery could be handled by a small number of workers. . . .

FIGURE 11-4. Sample format for third questionnaire, as used in the Delphi technique.

This questionnaire asks participants to (1) review the items listed and make comments, (2) add new methods if desired, and (3) vote for the five most important items. Again, a cover letter asks for the return of the questionnaire by a certain date.

After receiving the second questionnaire back, the work group tallies the votes for each item and summarizes comments made about the items. The third and final questionnaire (Figure 11-4) provides a vehicle for respondents to review their prior responses and express evaluations of each item. Analysis of the third questionnaire follows the same procedure as for the previous questionnaires.

The work group is now prepared to write the final report summarizing the goals, process, and results of the study. This report should serve as a basis for action by the decision makers. In our example, the fund-raising methods that receive the highest final vote might be recommended as fund-raising tools for the local chapters of the American Cancer Society. All respondents must be given a summary of the third questionnaire to complete the Delphi process.

SUMMARY

We have examined a number of techniques for either promoting group interaction or teaching individuals how to function more effectively in groups. The group discussion techniques examined in this chapter are used because members of the group or audience are often hesitant about participating in the group process. Unless the group can establish an environment in which members of the group or audience feel free to interact, the success of the group is in jeopardy. Increased participation by the group or audience members may lead to increased group involvement, increased group and audience satisfaction with group product, and increased group cohesiveness.

Role-playing techniques with group discussion methods or other group laboratory techniques can provide increased awareness of group, clarifying and possibly solving problems developed during group interaction. If group members have a greater understanding of their own roles and the roles of others in the group, it may facilitate social interaction, thereby enhancing the group's potential for success. Finally, the program planning techniques, nominal group and Delphi, facilitate the development and modification of programs.

ADDITIONAL READINGS

Beal, George M.; Bohlen, Joe M.; and Randabaugh, J. Neil. *Leadership and Dynamic Group Action.* Ames: Iowa State University Press, 1962. Pages 197–99 and 246–60 of this text provide an excellent outline of brainstorming, buzz groups, and role-playing techniques—including procedures, advantages, and disadvantages of the group techniques.

Coon, Arthur M. "Brainstorming: A Creative Problem-Solving Technique." *Journal of Communication* 7 (Autumn 1957), 111–18. This article provides a good overview of the brainstorming process.

Delbecq, Andre L.; Van de Ven, Andrew H.; and Gustafson, David H. *Group Techniques for Program Planning.* Glenview, Ill.: Scott, Foresman, 1975. This text is an excellent, easy-to-read guide on nominal group and Delphi techniques. It explores the rationale behind the techniques and illustrates how to use them in program planning.

Maier, Norman R. F. *Problem-Solving Discussion and Conferences.* New York: McGraw-Hill, 1963. The text (pp. 161–71) provides an excellent overview of the posting technique and its application to management situations.

THE LEARNING THRU DISCUSSION METHOD

The use of discussion groups in educational environments to assist in the learning of course materials is common. Seminars and performance courses are well-established in college curriculums. Students frequently prepare for exams together. However, the value of using discussion groups for learning cognitive materials is open to question. While educators agree that groups are successful for formulating attitudes, sharing opinions, or producing an emotional effect, instructors question whether groups are effective in producing student mastery of subject matter assigned in a particular course.

Can a discussion group method assist you in learning materials in your college courses? Yes, it can. However, the group must channel member interaction toward the group goal—learning the assigned materials in a particular course. The key to a successful learning group is the ability of group members to structure and control their interactions.

In 1969 Ida S. Hill and William Fawcett Hill developed a group discussion method called *learning thru discussion*. The purpose of this discussion method was to provide a structural model by which students in a discussion group can control their learning of assigned materials. The structural format developed by Hill (1977) is called the group cognitive map—a term derived from work on the programming of a logical sequence of steps for problem-solving groups. Like a discussion outline, the group cognitive map provides an orderly sequence for specific group interaction:

1. Define terms and concepts.
2. State author's message in general.
3. Identify major themes and subtopics.
4. Allocate time.
5. Discuss major themes and subtopics.
6. Integrate material with other knowledge.
7. Apply the material.
8. Evaluate author's presentation.
9. Evaluate group and individual performance.

Note that the first four steps are not intended to deal specifically with an instructional assignment. The actual discussion of the assignment occurs after the time allotments are made in step 4. Table A-1 provides a checklist to follow during your use of the group cognitive map and a means for evaluating group performance as required in step 9. Let's examine each step in the discussion process.

STEP 1

When students get together to study for an exam, they generally spend considerable time discussing issues unrelated to the group goal or arguing about the materials under study. The group can avoid these pitfalls by first defining key terms and concepts in the assigned materials. In a beginning course—whether biology, management, philosophy, or whatever—mastering the language of the discipline plays a significant role. Most objective tests are designed to evaluate one's knowledge of these terms. Thus, defining terms and concepts will help you prepare for course evaluations and provide a basis for exploring the content in assigned readings.

How does this step operate in practice? Suppose you and four classmates have formed a group to study for an examination on Chapter 2 of this text. Together you would begin to construct a group cognitive map by defining such terms as verbal messages, language, and communicator styles. If the group stops at this stage of the discussion, however, group members will probably not truly understand the chapter content or be able to relate the material and apply the terms and concepts to practical situations. Beware the tendency to devote the entire discussion to defining terms.

TABLE A-1 Learning Thru Discussion

Steps in the Cognitive Map	Ratings				
	1 Excellent	2 Very Good	3 Adequate	4 Not Entirely Adequate	5 Poor
1. Define terms and concepts.					
2. State author's message.					
3. Identify major themes and subtopics.					
4. Allocate time.					
5. Discuss major themes and subtopics.					
6. Integrate materials.					
7. Apply materials.					
8. Evaluate assignment.					

STEP 2

In this step the group delineates the purpose of the assigned material. When a text includes general statements about content such as previews and summaries, this step is easier for a group and need not take much time. For example, Chapter 2 of this text states at the outset that it will examine (1) how verbal messages facilitate and impede group interaction in performing group tasks, (2) how these messages reflect varying communicator styles, (3) various barriers to communication within a small group, and (4) language skills that help make group interaction more effective. Some written material, such as a philosophical treatise, is not as straightforward and requires considerable intellectual effort on the part of group members to formulate the author's purpose.

STEP 3

Having agreed on the author's message, the group should be ready to identify the major themes or subtopics in the assigned materials. Most textbooks are organized into identifiable sections or subsections. In our text, for instance, Chapter 2 is divided into several major sections: the nature of language, the functions of verbal messages, communication styles and their effects, barriers to communication, and pathways to effective message sharing in small groups. Several sections are further subdivided. The section on barriers to communication is broken down into message meaning, individual experience and message meaning, and defense-arousing communication. However, many essays and articles are not as highly structured and require the group to sort out the major themes and subtopics.

STEP 4

The study group must now determine how to allocate its time during the remaining stages of the discussion. This step is important because group members may otherwise spend too much unnecessary effort on one or more later steps. Since the group sets its own time limits, it can adjust the time to be devoted to the activities involved in steps 5 through 9.

Which steps are required for learning the assignment? Is the group preparing for a test that will assess general comprehension of the text material, or does the instructor expect students to integrate the material with previous lessons or to apply it to practical situations. It's not uncommon for a speech instructor to establish as a goal that students apply text contents to real communication situations; your instructor might require you to read Chapter 10, for example, and then solve a problem using the ideal solution pattern. Applying assigned materials may take considerably more time than discussing major themes.

Accurately allocating specific blocks of time for group discussion activities can be quite difficult. Inexperienced groups rarely estimate accurately how much time will be needed to complete future steps. Nevertheless, group members must make their best estimates.

Group members are frequently frustrated when unable to execute the discussion steps in the allotted time. The timing of any discussion process cannot be completely controlled. Deviations from the time schedule are permitted, but must be handled in a manner that doesn't prevent the group from achieving its assigned goal.

STEP 5

Having made some initial time decisions, the group can proceed to discuss the major themes and subtopics developed in steps 2 and 3. It's important that the study group concentrate on the author's message and not on the participants' opinions regarding assigned materials. For instance, most students in an introductory speech class have opinions on the impact of language on communicator styles but have read little about the subject; they may want to discuss these personal opinions, which are based on common sense, rather than the author's positions. Remember, pooled ignorance does not produce wisdom. The study group should first become acquainted with what the authorities in the field say about the major themes or subtopics.

The purpose of this strategy is not to forbid personal opinions or interpretations, but to avoid unnecessary disagreements, arguments, conflicts, or diversions at this stage of the discussion. When group participants disagree on a particular theme, they tend to take sides and avoid discussing the content of the author's message. Group members who have difficulty stifling their personal opinions should be reminded that these opinions can be aired during step 8.

If the assigned readings that are being discussed cover a large number of major themes or subtopics, the group may need to save time by eliminating the assignments that are already understood or those that can be readily learned without group assistance.

STEP 6

Students often complain that instructors fail to integrate class materials, that assignments are too fragmentary, and that teachers are too concerned with isolated bits of information. This accusation is often justified. In addition, we know from learning theory that isolated facts are the first to be forgotten. In order to avoid fragmented learning, group discussion participants need to relate assigned materials to ideas, terms, and concepts presented in previous classes or courses. For example, when students discuss role behavior (Chapter 6), they can integrate the information on roles with the ideas presented on verbal messages (Chapter 2) by discussing the types of communicator styles used in specific roles.

In beginning courses students may not have much information to integrate early in the course. However, as the course proceeds or in advanced courses this step can be extremely important for student learning and should be allocated considerably more time.

STEP 7

Materials that appear unrelated or personally meaningless to students are usually easily forgotten. Group discussion members should therefore attempt to assess the application value of the content being learned. The material presented in Chapter 11, for instance, has direct personal application. Brainstorming can be used in many private and public discussions to obtain solutions and ideas or to stimulate participant interaction. Most speech communication courses, even beginning ones, have the advantage that students generally have little trouble seeing how the material relates to their own lives. Discussion group members can easily provide examples of language bias or of conformity behaviors in the family, at work, or in campus organizations, for example.

STEP 8

In this step group members are encouraged to evaluate the assignment—the author's presentation. Criticizing or interpreting the materials can be a constructive process. The group uses this step as a goal-directed outlet for personal opinions. In addition, this step can facilitate the development of critical thinking abilities. In fact, developing these abilities may be more important to future learning situations than any materials assigned in a specific college course.

In some beginning courses the assignments may not arouse much personal reaction, and so the time needed to complete this step may not be very long. However, as one acquires more knowledge of a field or deals with controversial material (for example, assignments on intercultural communication breakdowns), the group may need to allot a considerable amount of time for this step.

STEP 9

Hill (1977) suggests that the last ten minutes of the discussion be devoted to diagnosing and evaluating group and individual effectiveness. While some groups prefer to handle group problems as they occur, such action has several disadvantages. First, the group will have great difficulty staying within its allotted time and thus will find it extremely hard to follow the group cognitive map. Second, group members may become overly sensitized to their own problems and thus become defensive and frustrated. Third, the goal of this discussion method is to assist learning and not to analyze individual roles or group process problems. The group goal may be unattainable if members enter into an endless discussion of group or individual problems earlier in the discussion.

A FEW LAST WORDS

The discussion method is not a panacea for learning. It is only one possible device for assisting you in future learning situations. Like any discussion entailing information sharing or problem

solving, it requires preparation on the part of discussion participants. You should read the assigned materials at least once before
the discussion.

We suggest that before you use the learning thru discussion
method you read *Learning Thru Discussion* (1977), which provides
a detailed explanation of the discussion method. The text investi-
gates the group cognitive map and required group roles and
member skills, and lists criteria for a good study group discussion.
We have presented this discussion method in the belief that it can
assist you in future courses and learning situations as well as in
your present educational situation.

REFERENCES

Adorno, T. W.; Frenkel-Brunswik, E.; Levinson, D. J.; and Sanford, R. N. *The Authoritarian Personality.* New York: Harper, 1950.

Argyle, M. *The Psychology of Interpersonal Behavior.* Baltimore: Penguin, 1967.

Argyle, M., and Dean, J. "Eye contact, distance, and affiliation." *Sociometry* 28 (1965): 289–304.

Argyle, M., and Kendon, A. "The experimental analysis of social performance." In *Advances in Experimental Psychology,* edited by L. Berkowitz, vol. 3, pp. 55–98. New York: Academic Press, 1967.

Asch, S. E. "Effects of group pressure upon the modification and distortion of judgments." In *Groups, Leadership and Men,* edited by H. Guetzkow. Pittsburgh: Carnegie Press, 1951.

Baird, J. E., Jr. "Sex differences in group communication: A review of relevant research." *Quarterly Journal of Speech* 62 (1976): 179–92.

Baird, J. E., Jr., and Weinberg, S. B. *Communication: The Essence of Group Synergy.* Dubuque, Iowa: Wm. C. Brown, 1977.

Bales, R. "A set of categories for the analysis of small group interaction." *American Sociological Reveiw* 15, 2 (1948): 255–265.

Bales, R. *Interaction Process Analysis: A Method for the Study of Small Groups.* Cambridge, Mass.: Addison-Wesley, 1950.

Bales, R. "A theoretical framework for interaction process analysis." In *Group Dynamics: Research and Theory,* edited by D. Cartwright and A. Zander, 3d ed. New York: Harper & Row, 1968. First ed., 1953.

Barch, A. M.; Trumbo, D.; and Nangle, J. "Social setting and conformity to a legal requirement." *Journal of Abnormal and Social Psychology* 55 (1957): 396–98.

Barnlund, D. C. *Interpersonal Communication.* Boston: Houghton Mifflin, 1968.

Bass, B. M.; McGehee, C. R.; Hawkins, W. C.; Young, P. C.; and Gebel, A. S. "Personality variables related to leaderless group discussion." *Journal of Abnormal and Social Psychology* 49 (1953): 120–28.

Baxter, J.; Winter, E.; and Hammer, R. "Gestural behavior during a brief interview as a function of cognitive variables." *Journal of Personality and Social Psychology* 8 (1968): 303–7.

Bayless, O. L. "An alternate pattern for problem-solving discussion." *Journal of Communication* 17 (1967): 188–97.

Beck, D. "Communication through confrontation: A case study in intergroup conflict reduction." Paper presented to the International Communication Association Convention, Atlanta, 1971.

Bell, G. B., and Hall, H. E. "The relationship between leadership and empathy." *Journal of Abnormal and Social Psychology* 49 (1954): 156–57.

Beloff, H. "Two forms of social conformity: Acquiescence and conventionality." *Journal of Abnormal and Social Psychology* 56 (1958): 99–104.

Benne, K. D., and Sheats, P. "Functional roles of group members." *Journal of Social Issues* 4 (1948): 41–49.

Berg, I. A., and Bass, B. M. *Conformity and Deviation.* New York: Harper & Row, 1961.

Berlo, D. *The Process of Communication.* New York: Holt, 1960.

Bernard, J. *The Sex Game: Communication between the Sexes.* New York: Atheneum, 1973.

Birdwhistell, R. *Kinesics and Context: Essays on Body Motion Communication.* Philadelphia: University of Pennsylvania Press, 1970.

Blake, R., and Mouton, J. *The Managerial Grid.* Houston: Gulf Publishing, 1964.

Blake, R., and Mouton, J. *The New Managerial Grid.* Houston: Gulf Publishing, 1978.

Borg, W. R. "Prediction of small group role behavior from personality variables." *Journal of Abnormal and Social Psychology* 60 (1960): 112–16.

Bormann, E. G. *Discussion and Group Methods: Theory and Practice,* 2d ed. New York: Harper & Row, 1975. First ed., 1969.

Brilhart, J. D., and Jochem, L. M. "Effects of different patterns on outcomes of problem-solving discussion." *Journal of Applied Psychology* 48 (1964): 175–79.

Burgoon, M.; Heston, J. K.; and McCroskey, J. *Small Group Communication: A Functional Approach.* New York: Holt, Rinehart and Winston, 1974.

Burke, P. "Authority relations and behavior in small discussion groups." *Sociometry* 29 (1966): 273–349.

Cartwright, D. "The nature of group cohesiveness," In *Group Dynamics: Research and Theory* edited by D. Cartwright and A. Zander, 3d ed. New York: Harper & Row, 1968.

Cartwright, D., and Lippitt, R. "Group dynamics and the individual." *International Journal of Group Psychotherapy* 7 (1957): 86–102.

Cartwright, D., and Zander, A., eds. *Group Dynamics: Research and Theory,* 3d ed. New York: Harper & Row, 1968. 2d ed., 1960.

Cattell, R. B., and Stice, G. F. "The dimensions of groups and their relation to the behavior of members." Champaign, Ill.: Institute for Personality and Ability Testing, 1960.

Cohen, A. *Attitude Change and Social Influence.* New York: Basic Books, 1964.

Coser, L. *The Functions of Social Conflict.* New York: Free Press, 1956.

Crutchfield, R. S. "Conformity and character." *American Psychologist* 10 (1955) : 191–98.

Cushman, D. P., and Craig, R. T. "Communication systems: Interpersonal implications." In *Explorations in Interpersonal Communication,* edited by G. Milles. Beverly Hills, Calif.: Sage Publications, 1976.

Delbecq, A. L.; Van de Ven, A. H.; and Gustafson, D. H. *Group Techniques for Program Planning.* Glenview, Ill.: Scott, Foresman, 1975.

Deutsch, M. "Conflict and its resolution." Paper prepared for the Interdisciplinary Colloquium sponsored by the Speech Association of America and U.S. Office of Education, Racine, Wis., 1967.

Deutsch, M. "Conflicts: Productive and destructive." *Journal of Social Issues* 25 (1969): 7–41.

Deutsch, M. "Toward an understanding of conflict." *International Journal of Group Tension* 1 (1971): 42–54.

Deutsch, M., and Krauss, R. *Theories in Social Psychology.* New York: Basic Books, 1965.

Dewey, J. *How We Think.* Chicago: D. C. Heath, 1910.

Dittman, A. T. "The relationship between body movements and moods in interviews." *Journal of Consulting Psychology* 26 (1962): 480.

Drucker, P. *Technology, Management and Society.* New York: Harper & Row, 1970.

Druckman, D. "Dogmatism, prenegotiation experience and simulated group representation as determinants of dyadic behavior in a bargaining situation." *Journal of Personality and Social Psychology* 6 (1967): 279–90.

Efran, J., and Broughton, A. "Effect of expectancies for social approval on visual behavior." *Journal of Personality and Social Psychology* 4 (1966): 103–7.

Ekman, P., and Friesen, W. "The repertoire of nonverbal behavior: Categories, origins, usage, and coding." *Semiotica* 1 (1969), 49–98.

Exline, R., and Winters, L. "Affective relations and mutual glances in dyads." In *Affect, Cognition and Personality,* edited by S. Tomkins and C. Izard, pp. 319–30. New York: Springer, 1965.

Fearing, F. "Toward a psychological theory of human communication." *Journal of Personality* 22 (1953–54); 73–76.

Festinger, L. A. *Theory of Cognitive Dissonance.* Evanston, Ill.: Row, Peterson, 1957.

Festinger, L. A.; Schachter, S.; and Beck, K. *Social Pressures in Informal Groups.* Stanford, Calif.: Stanford University Press, 1950.

Fiedler, F. E. *A Theory of Leadership Effectiveness.* New York: McGraw-Hill, 1967.

Fisher, B. A. "Decision emergence: Phases in group decision-making." *Speech Monographs* 37 (1970): 53–66.

Fisher, B. A. *Small Group Decision Making: Communication and the Group Process.* New York: McGraw-Hill, 1974.

Freed, A. M.; Chandler, P. J.; Mouton, J. S.; and Blake, R. R. "Stimulus background factors in sign violation." *Journal of Personality* 23 (1955): 499.

French, J. R. and Raven, B. "The bases of social power." In *Studies in Social Power*, edited by D. Cartwright. Ann Arbor: University of Michigan Press, 1959.

Gergen, K. *Social Psychology: Explorations in Understanding*. Del Mar, Calif.: CRM Books, 1974.

Gergen, K., and Taylor, M. G. "Social expectancy and self-presentation in a status hierarchy." *Journal of Experimental Social Psychology* 5 (1969): 79–92.

Gibb, C. A. "Leadership." In *The Handbook of Social Psychology*, edited by G. Lindzey and E. Aronson, 2d ed., vol. 5. Reading, Mass.: Addison-Wesley, 1969.

Goldberg, A. A., and Larson, C. E. *Group Discussion*. Englewood Cliffs, N.J.: Prentice-Hall, 1975.

Gouron, D. S. *Discussion: The Process of Group Decision-Making*. New York: Harper & Row, 1974.

Greer, F. L. "Small group effectiveness." Institute Report No. 6, Contract Hour-1229 (00), Institute for Research in Human Relations, Philadelphia, 1955.

Guetzkow, H. "Differentiation of roles in task-oriented groups." In *Group Dynamics: Research and Theory*, edited by D. Cartwright and A. Zander, 3d ed. New York: Harper & Row, 1968.

Gulley, H. E., and Leathers, D. G. *Communication and Group Process*. New York: Holt, Rinehart and Winston, 1977.

Hall, E. *The Silent Language*. Garden City, N.Y.: Doubleday, 1959.

Halpin, A. *Theory and Research in Administration*. New York: Macmillan, 1966.

Haney, W. *Communication and Organizational Behavior: Text and Cases*. Homewood, Ill.: Richard D. Irwin, 1973.

Hare, A. *Handbook of Small Group Research*. New York: Free Press, 1962.

Hare, A., and Bales, R. "Seating position and small group interaction." *Sociometry* 26 (1963): 480–86.

Harnock, R. V.; Fest, T. B.; and Jones, R. S. *Group Discussion*, 2d ed. Englewood Cliffs, N.J.: Prentice-Hall, 1977.

Harvey, O. J., and Consalvi, C. "Status and conformity to pressures in informal groups." *Journal of Abnormal and Social Psychology* 60 (1960): 182–87.

Hayakawa, S. *Language in Thought and Action*. New York: Harcourt Brace Jovanovich, 1949.

Haythorn, W. "The influence of individual members on the characteristics of small groups." *Journal of Abnormal and Social Psychology* 48 (1953): 276–84.

Hersey, P., and Blanchard, K. "Life cycle theory of leadership." *Training and Development Journal*, May 1969.

Hersey, P., and Blanchard, K. *Management of Organizational Behavior*. Englewood Cliffs, N.J.: Prentice-Hall, 1972.

Hill, W. *Learning Thru Discussion.* Beverly Hills, Calif.: Sage Publications, 1977.

Hollander, E. "Conformity status and idiosyncracy credit." *Psychological Review* 65 (1958): 117–27.

Homans, G. C. *Social Behavior: Its Elementary Forms,* revised ed. New York: Harcourt Brace Jovanovich, 1974. First ed., 1950.

Hovland, C. I., and Janis, I. R. *Personality and Persuasibility.* New Haven: Yale University Press, 1959.

Huenergardt, D., and Finanda, S. "Micromomentary facial expressions as perceivable signs of deception." Paper presented to the Speech Association of America, New York, 1969.

Jennings, E. "The anatomy of leadership." *Management of Personnel Quarterly,* No. 1 (Autumn 1961).

Jones, E.; Davis, K.; and Gergen, L. "Role playing variations and their informational value for person perception." *Journal of Abnormal and Social Psychology* 63 (1961), 302–10.

Kay, E.; French, J.; and Meyer, H. *A Study of the Performance Appraisal Interview.* New York: Behavioral Research Service, General Electric Co., 1962.

Keltner, J. *Interpersonal Speech Communication.* Belmont, Calif.: Wadsworth, 1970.

Kepner, C., and Tregoe, B. *The Rational Manager: A Systematic Approach to Problem Solving and Decision Making.* New York: McGraw-Hill, 1965.

Knapp, M. *Nonverbal Communication in Human Interaction.* New York: Holt, Rinehart and Winston, 1972.

Koontz, H., and O'Donnell, C. *Principles of Management: An Analysis of Managerial Functions.* New York: McGraw-Hill, 1972.

Larson, C. E. "Forms of analysis and small group problem-solving." *Speech Monographs* 36 (1969): 452–55.

Lefkowitz, M.; Blake, R. R.; and Mouton, J. S. "Status factors in pedestrian violation of traffic signals." *Journal of Abnormal and Social Psychology* 51 (1955): 704–6.

McClelland, D. *The Achieving Society.* Princeton, N.J.: D. Van Nostrand, 1961.

McCroskey, J. C. "Oral communication apprehension." *Human Communication Research* 4 (1977): 78–96.

Mack, R., and Snyder, R. "The analysis of social conflict—toward an overview and synthesis." *Journal of Conflict Resolution* 1 (1957): 212–48.

Mann, R. D. "A review of the relationships between personality and performance in small groups." *Psychological Bulletin* 56 (1959): 241–70.

Maslow, A. H. *Motivation and Personality.* New York: Harper & Row, 1954.

Mehrabian, A. *Silent Messages.* Belmont, Calif.: Wadsworth, 1971.

Milgram, S. "Group pressure and action against a person." *Journal of Abnormal and Social Psychology* 69 (1964): 137–43.

Miller, G. R., and Burgoon, M. *New Techniques of Persuasion.* New York: Harper & Row, 1973.

Miller, G. R., and Steinberg, M. *Between People: A New Analysis of Interpersonal Communication.* Chicago: Science Research Associates, 1975.

Mintz, N. "Effects of esthetic surroundings: II. Prolonged and repeated experience in 'beautiful' and 'ugly' room." *Journal of Psychology* 41 (1956): 459–66.

Mortensen, C. D. *Communication: The Study of Human Interaction.* New York: McGraw-Hill, 1972.

Nadler, E. B. "Yielding, authoritarianism, and authoritarian ideology regarding groups." *Journal of Abnormal and Social Psychology* 58 (1959): 408–10.

Nakamura, C. Y. "Conformity and problem solving." *Journal of Abnormal and Social Psychology* 56 (1958): 315–20.

Newcomb, T. M. *Personality and Social Change: Attitude Formation in a Student Community.* New York: Holt, Rinehart and Winston, 1943.

Osborn, A. F. *Applied Imagination.* New York: Scribner's, 1957.

Pearce, W. B. "The coordinated management of meaning: A rules-based theory of interpersonal communication." In *Explorations in Interpersonal Communication,* edited by G. R. Miller. Beverly Hills, Calif.: Sage Publications, 1976.

Phillips, G. *Communication in the Small Group.* 2d ed. Indianapolis: Bobbs-Merrill, 1973. First ed., 1966.

Phillips, G., and Erickson, E. *Interpersonal Dynamics in the Small Group.* New York: Random House, 1970.

Pigors, P., and Myers, C. *Personnel Administration,* 6th ed. New York: McGraw-Hill, 1969.

Pittenger, R., and Smith, H., Jr. "A basis for some contributions of linguistics to psychiatry." *Psychiatry* 20 (1967): 61–70.

Reddin, W. *Managerial Effectiveness.* New York: McGraw-Hill, 1970.

Rokeach, M. *The Open and Closed Mind.* New York: Basic Books, 1960.

Rosenbaum, M. E., and Blake, R. R. "Volunteering as a function of field structure." *Journal of Abnormal and Social Psychology* 50 (1955): 193–96.

Rosenfeld, L., and Civikly, J. *With Words Unspoken: The Nonverbal Experience.* New York: Holt, Rinehart and Winston, 1976.

Russo, N. "Connotation of seating arrangements." *Cornell Journal of Social Relations* 2 (1967): 37–44.

Sainsbury, R. "Gestural movements during psychiatric interviews." *Psychosomatic Medicine* 17 (1955): 458–69.

Schachter, S. "Deviation, rejection, and communication." *Journal of Abnormal and Social Psychology* 46 (1951): 190–207.

Seghers, C. "Color in the office." *The Management Review,* 1948.

Sereno, K. K. "Ego-involvement: A neglected variable in speech communication research." *Quarterly Journal of Speech* 55 (1969): 69–77.

Sereno, K. K., and Bodaken, E. M. *Trans Per: Understanding Human Communication.* Boston: Houghton Mifflin, 1975.

Sereno, K. K., and Mortensen, C. D. "The effects of ego-involved attitude on conflict negotiation in dyads." *Speech Monographs* 36 (1969): 8–12.

Shaw, M. E. *Group Dynamics: The Psychology of Small Group Behavior.* 2d ed. New York: McGraw-Hill, 1976.

Sherif, C. W.; Sherif, M.; and Nebergall, R. E. *Attitude and Attitude Change: The Social Judgment–Involvement Approach.* Philadelphia: W. B. Saunders, 1965.

Sherif, M., and Sherif, C. W. *An Outline of Social Psychology.* New York: Harper & Row, 1956.

Simmel, G. *Conflict.* Translated by K. H. Wolff. Glencoe, Ill: Free Press, 1955.

Simons, H. W. "Introduction: Interpersonal perception, similarity and credibility." In *Advances in Communication Research,* edited by C. D. Mortensen and K. K. Sereno. New York: Harper & Row, 1973.

Sommer, R. *Personal Space: The Behavior Basis of Design.* Englewood Cliffs, N.J.: Prentice-Hall, 1969.

Steinzor, B. "The spatial factor in face-to-face discussion groups." *Journal of Abnormal and Social Psychology* 45 (1950): 552–55.

Stogdill, R. M. "Personal factors associated with leadership." *Journal of Psychology* 25 (1948): 35–71.

Stogdill, R., and Coons, A., eds. *Leader Behavior: Its Description and Measurement.* Research Monograph No. 88. Columbus, Ohio: Bureau of Business Research, Ohio State University, 1957.

Swensen, C. H. *Introduction to Interpersonal Relations.* Glenview, Ill.: Scott, Foresman, 1973.

Tannenbaum, R., and Schmidt, W. "How to choose a leadership pattern." *Harvard Business Review* (March–April 1958): 95–101.

Tannenbaum, R.; Weschler, I.; and Massarik, F. *Leadership and Organization: A Behavioral Science Approach.* New York: McGraw-Hill, 1959.

Tomkins, S. S., and McCarter, R. "What and where are the primary effects? Some evidence for a theory." *Perceptual and Motor Skills* 18 (1964): 119–58.

Trager, G. "Paralanguage: A first approximation." *Studies in Linguistics* 13 (1958), 1–12.

Tuddenham, R. D.; MacBride, P.; and Zahn, V. "The influence of the sex composition of the group upon yielding to a distorted norm." *Journal of Psychology* 46 (1958): 243–51.

Uesugi, T. T., and Vinacke, W. E. "Strategy in a feminine game." *Sociometry* 26 (1963): 75–88.

Vroom, V., and Mann, F. "Leader authoritarianism and employee attitudes." *Personnel Psychology* 13 (1960): 125–40.

Warr, P., and Knapper, C. *The Perception of People and Events.* New York: Wiley, 1968.

Weisbrod, R. "Looking behavior in a discussion group." Unpublished report cited by M. Argyle and A. Kendon in "The experimental analysis of social performance." In *Advances in Experimental Social Psychology,* edited by L. Berkowitz, vol. 3, pp. 55–98. New York: Academic Press, 1967.

Whyte, W. H., Jr. *The Organization Man.* Garden City, N.Y.: Doubleday, 1957.

Williams, J. "Personal space and its relation to extraversion-introversion." Unpublished master's thesis, University of Alberta, 1963.

Wofford, J. "Managerial behavior, situational factors, productivity, and morale." *Administrative Science Quarterly* 16, No. 1 (1971): 10–17.

Wofford, J.; Gerloff, E.; and Cummins, R. *Organizational Communication: The Keystone to Managerial Effectiveness.* New York: McGraw-Hill, 1977.

Wyer, R. S., Jr. "Behavioral correlates of academic achievement: Conformity under achievement- and affiliation-incentive conditions." *Journal of Personality and Social Psychology* 6 (1967): 255–63.

Zajonc, R. "The process of cognitive tuning in communication." *Journal of Abnormal and Social Psychology* 61 (1960): 159–67.

Zimbardo, P., and Ebbesen, E. *Influencing Attitudes and Changing Behavior.* Reading, Mass.: Addison-Wesley, 1969.

Zimmerman, D. H., and West, C. "Sex roles, interruptions, and silences in communication." In *Language and Sex: Difference and Dominance,* edited by B. Thorne and N. Henley. Rowley, Mass.: Newbury House, 1975.

AUTHOR INDEX

SUBJECT INDEX

ABOUT
THE AUTHORS

Ronald L. Applbaum (Ph.D., Penn State University, 1969) is Dean of the School of Humanities at California State University, Long Beach, and Professor of Speech Communication. He is co-author of *Public Communication: Behavioral Perspectives, Organizational Communication: Behavioral Perspectives,* and *Strategies of Persuasive Communication and Fundamental Concepts of Human Communication.* He is co-editor of *Modules in Speech Communication* and author of the module *Fundamentals of Group Discussion.* He also has written articles appearing in *Speech Monographs, Communication Quarterly, Central States Speech Journal, Communication Education, Western Speech,* and *Journal of Communication.*

Karl W. E. Anatol (Ph.D., University of Southern California, 1974) is Associate Dean of Humanities and Associate Professor of Speech Communication at California State University, Long Beach. He is co-author of *Public Communication: Behavioral Perspectives, Organizational Communication: Behavioral Perspectives,* and *Strategies of Persuasive Communication and Fundamental Concepts of Human Communication.* He also is the author of articles appearing in *Speech Monographs, Central States Speech Journal, Communication Quarterly, General Semantics,* and *Journal of Communication.*

Kenneth K. Sereno (Ph.D., University of Washington, 1964) is Associate Professor of Speech Communication at the University of Southern California. He is co-author of *Trans-Per: Understanding Human Communication, Foundations of Communication Theory,* and *Advances in Communication Research.* He has published articles in *Speech Monographs, Quarterly Journal of Speech, Human Communication Research,* and *Western Speech Communication Journal.*

Edward M. Bodaken (Ph.D., Michigan State University, 1970) is Associate Professor and Vice-Chair of Speech Communication at the University of Southern California. He is co-author of *Trans-Per: Understanding Human Communication.* He has published articles in *Human Communication Research, Journal of Communication, Communication Monographs, Western Speech Communication Journal,* and *Computer Studies.*